THE GLOBAL HISTORY SERIES

Leften Stavrianos, *Northwestern University*
General Editor

This series aims to present history in global perspective, going beyond national or regional limitations and dealing with overriding trends and forces. The various collections of original materials span the globe, ranging from prehistoric times to the present, and include anthropology, economics, political science, and religion, as well as history.

Donald F. Lach, co-editor of this volume, is Professor of Modern History at the University of Chicago. He is the author of numerous articles in American, German, and Chinese periodicals, and the co-author of *Modern Far Eastern International Relations* (with H. F. MacNair) and *Europe and the Modern World* (with L. Gottschalk). The recent appearance of the first volume of his comprehensive study, *Asia in the Making of Europe* (Books 1 and 2) has received wide critical acclaim.

Carol Flaumenhaft is Instructor of History at Kent State University, Kent, Ohio. She holds her A.M. degree from the University of Chicago, and was a Research Associate in the Department of History there for five years.

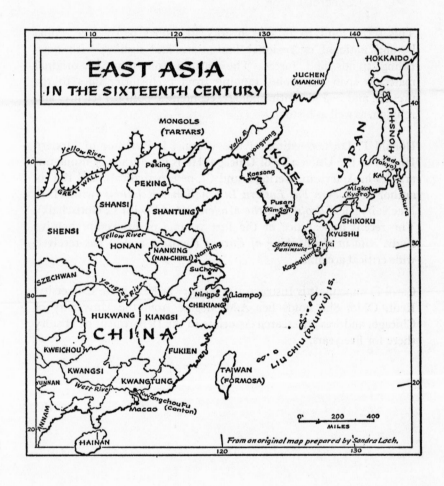

EAST ASIA
IN THE SIXTEENTH CENTURY

From an original map prepared by Sandra Lach.

ASIA ON THE EVE
OF EUROPE'S EXPANSION

EDITED BY DONALD F. LACH
AND CAROL FLAUMENHAFT

Prentice-Hall, Inc. / *Englewood Cliffs, N.J.*

A SPECTRUM BOOK

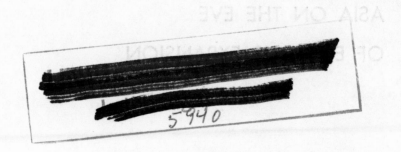

Library of Congress Catalog Card No.: 65-23294
Printed in the United States of America—C

P 04936
C 04938

ACKNOWLEDGMENTS

The editors wish to acknowledge gratefully the aid of Linda Eichmeier and Sandy Lach of the University of Chicago and Pauline Franks of the University of Akron Library. We are likewise much indebted to our respective spouses, Alma Lach and Eugene Flaumenhaft.

CONTENTS

ASIA ON THE EVE

OF EUROPE'S EXPANSION

INTRODUCTION

How would Portugal and Europe have reacted in 1498 if they had been "discovered" by Asians? Suppose several strange ships manned by odd-looking foreigners had dropped anchor at Lisbon, and, after a friendly reception by the king, had suddenly bombarded some ships in Lisbon harbor before sailing off with a trio of hostages to some unknown destination. Reversing the roles, such a series of events occurred when Vasco da Gama first visited Calicut in south India. And within the following century, shock waves set in motion by these and subsequent activities of the Europeans in Eastern waters reached to the farthest outposts of Asian civilization.

The Portuguese fleets sought initially to control Asia's maritime trade by capturing a number of strategic points, such as Goa, Ormuz, and Aden. In 1511 they seized the city of Malacca situated at the point where the Indian Ocean connects with the China and Java Seas. Shortly thereafter they reconnoitered the lands bordering the Bay of Bengal and began to survey the Indonesian archipelago. Continuing their inroads into Asia, Portuguese emissaries from Malacca first visited Canton in 1513, and by 1557 the Portuguese had permanently established themselves at Macao off the south China coast. European sailors, probably engaged in illicit coastal trade, were blown off course to Japan in 1543.

Meanwhile, in 1521, the Spaniards under Magellan crossed the Pacific, appeared in the Philippines and the Moluccas, and investigated the surrounding seas. But the Spaniards, who were occupied with empire-building in America, did not follow up their claims in Asia until after 1565. By the last generation of the sixteenth century, Jesuit missionaries had penetrated to some of the great interior political and cultural centers of India, Japan, and China, and one

1

dauntless priest had ventured into Korea as a chaplain to the Japanese Christians fighting there.

The very fact that Europeans determinedly sailed eastward, instead of Asians making their way to Europe, is suggestive of the strong sense of purpose that impelled the Europeans and testifies eloquently to the high level of their technical competence. Little more than drops in an Oriental sea of humanity, the Europeans extended their activities and retained their identity in the face of heavy odds. Thanks to sturdy war vessels, superior fire power, and rugged determination, they successfully maintained the precarious toeholds they had so arduously won. The supreme irony in the story of Europe's penetration of Asia is that the instruments that gave the Westerners their edge—the compass, astrolabe, and cannon —may all have been used in China before they were even known in Europe.

At first, European activity in Asia was confined to the southern and eastern shores of the Eurasiatic continent—today called the "Asiatic Crescent." For purposes of discussion and description, this crescent is ordinarily divided into three great regional areas: South Asia, Southeast Asia, and East Asia. Itself, a quadrilateral of continental proportions, South Asia is bounded on the north by the majestic Himalayas and on its other three sides by the Arabian Sea, the Indian Ocean, and the Bay of Bengal. Divided almost equally in area between continental and insular territories, Southeast Asia's east-west extension from Burma to the tip of Indochina is approximately the same distance as that between New York and California. The many thousand islands of Southeast Asia are dominated by the two major archipelagos of Indonesia and the Philippines. East Asia, which includes China, Japan, and Korea, is usually defined geographically as the area to the east of the great mountain and desert barrier that bisects the Eurasiatic continent.

In the days of sailing ships, the rhythms of commerce and agriculture in the "Asiatic Crescent" were regulated by a monsoonal climate. A monsoon, the Arabic word for "season," is a wind that changes direction with the changes in season. The dry monsoon of winter originates with air that has been cooled and dried from hovering over the continent's interior and flows outward in spiral fashion from the northeast to the southwest. This movement reaches its peak in constancy and force in January. The complementary wet monsoon of summer reaches its height in July when moist ocean winds, originating over the Arabian Sea, the Bay of Bengal, and the China Sea, sweep northeastward over the Asiatic landmass. Southeast Asia, which straddles the equator and lies at the center of monsoonal activity, is much hotter than temperate China and Japan and appreciably wetter than most of India.

The intense heat and abundant moisture of the monsoonal summers are as necessary as fertile soil and human industry to the production of rice, Asia's most precious food. Dry climate and rugged terrain have prevented rice cultivation from being extended to northern and western China and to northern India. But in many rice-growing areas, production was maximized, even in the sixteenth century, by maintaining water conservation systems and by planting and harvesting two or more crops each year. In south China, for example, double-cropping began in the eleventh century when early-ripening strains of rice were introduced from southern Indochina. Since rice yields more calories per unit of land than either wheat or maize, neither these cereals nor others grown there have ever replaced rice as Asia's leading crop.

Throughout history the survival, rise, and decline of Asia's population has been absolutely dependent on food production. Crop failures, because of drought or flood, have usually brought famine and decimation to Asian countries. Nonetheless, the first Europeans to write in detail about life in Asia were startled by its masses and its crowded cities. Although precise figures for the sixteenth century are not available, estimates indicate that China's population numbered about 140 million in 1600, when the combined population of Spain and Portugal was no more than 8 million. Canton, Kyoto, and Vijayanagar were judged by Europeans who had been in both areas to be more populous than the greatest of Europe's cities.

High civilizations of great antiquity, as well as isolated groups of primitive and savage peoples, flourished in Asia when the Europeans first arrived. China and India, whose civilizations were old when Rome was young, had extended their influence over many centuries to their less advanced neighbors. Indian and Chinese civilizations met and mingled most fully in Southeast Asia where they both left deep and lasting impressions on the indigenous cultures. Through Buddhism, India deeply influenced the life and history of China. And although China made no comparable contribution to India, Japan and Korea received great cultural gifts from China.

India's traditional influence in other parts of Asia was primarily religious and cultural. By the sixth century A.D., or roughly a thousand years after the Buddha's apostolate in India, Mahayana Buddhism had become one of China's leading religions. Not long thereafter it spread to Korea and Japan. When the Europeans arrived in the East, Buddhism in China, while still powerful, was experiencing intense competition from resurgent Confucianism and Taoism, China's two native faiths. In the sixteenth century, Japan and Annam were two of the world's most flourishing Buddhist communities. The Hinayana form of Buddhism was solidly entrenched in Ceylon, Burma, Siam, and Cambodia. In Java, where it had once flourished, Buddhism was on the wane. Lamaism, a less sophisticated form of Buddhism, continued to dominate the religious life of Mongolia and Tibet. As the only native faith of Asia to spread throughout the region, Buddhism in its greatest age (fourth to eighth centuries A.D.) was the most widely professed faith in the world. It was still powerful everywhere, except in India itself, when the Europeans arrived in the East.

Islam, after steadily expanding over India through several centuries (1100-1500), was transmitted to insular Southeast Asia by traders and teachers from Persia and India. Marco Polo reported that he found Muslim converts in northern Sumatra in 1292. Two hundred years later, when the Europeans arrived in Asia, Islam had made converts as far east as Brunei in Borneo, in the Moluccas, and in the southern Philippines. The Portuguese and the Jesuits, as they followed eastward in the wake of the Muslims, fought unceasingly but unsuccessfully against Islam's hold in the East Indies. Today Indonesia has one of the largest Muslim communities in the world, outnumbering for example that of Pakistan.

When the Europeans arrived in the East, they were looking for Christian allies and were only vaguely aware of how widespread were the great native religions of Asia and Islam. Their first thought was to enlist the support of the St. Thomas Christians of India's Malabar region, the Nestorian Christians of "Cathay," and Prester John's legendary Christian host in their drive to oust Islam from the East. The Muslims (known as Moors in Portugal and Spain) were old enemies of the Europeans, and something of the crusading spirit of Europe was carried into the war against Islam in the East. Only gradually reconciling themselves to the impossibility of annihilating Islam in Asia, the Portuguese sought to ruin the Muslims commercially by arrogating to themselves the profits from the far-flung network of outposts in the spice trade.

When the Portuguese arrived in India, the subcontinent was sharply divided politically, religiously, and culturally. Topography accounts in part for India's historical divisions. In total area almost the size of Europe (excluding Russia), India is divided into clearly defined geographical regions. From the Himalayas in the north to the Vindhyan hills of central India, the lowlands are watered in the west by the Indus and its tributaries and in the east by the Ganges and its tributaries. These two great river basins and centers of civilization are separated almost completely by the highlands and deserts of Rajputana. South of Vindhya to the Krishna River lies the Deccan plateau, a rough and forbidding region, difficult of access and broken into sections by valleys covered with tropical jungles. The southern tip of India, south of the Krishna, which is divided into distinct Tamil and Malayalam sectors, is more hospitable to man. Malabar, the low-lying land on the west coast where Malayalam is spoken, is the locale of the Calicut and Cochin markets where the Portuguese first invaded the spice trade.

To 1500 these three great geographical divisions had never been united under a single ruler. Throughout its early history India was divided into a great many warring states. Traditional differences were deepened after the tenth century by mighty Muslim invasions from central and western Asia. While the Islamic invaders sometimes established a degree of political unity in north India, their rule never extended south of the Krishna and their empires centering on Delhi rarely lasted for long. After capturing the island of Goa in 1510, the Portuguese were able to hold this strategic port on India's west coast because of constant internal wars. The Muslim state of Bijapur and the Hindu empire of Vijayanagar had long fought over jurisdiction of Goa. After taking Goa from Bijapur, Albuquerque, Governor of Portuguese India (1509-1515), immediately sought the support of Vijayanagar by promising not to interfere with the trade between Goa and Vijayanagar, which was vital to the military survival of the Hindu empire. The Portuguese and the Hindus, Albuquerque knew, had a common foe in the Muslims.

The Muslims were on the defensive throughout India during the fifteenth century and the first half of the sixteenth century, a period when Vijayanagar reached its height as the greatest center of Hindu culture. In 1336, a group of Hindu refugees from the raids of the Muslims began to construct the city of Vijayanagar (Sanskrit for "City of Victory") on the southern bank of the Tungabhadra River. Starting as a small Hindu center of resistance to Islam, Vijayanagar rapidly became an imperial center which exercised jurisdiction at the height of its power over most of south India. The rulers of Vijayanagar ardently patronized distinguished Hindu scholars and poets who came from all over India to the court.

Literature in the Telegu language favored by the court flowered in these years. Hinduism, particularly the worship of Shiva and Vishnu, received new impetus from the founding of Vijayanagar. The rulers of the "City of Victory" were religiously tolerant and treated the devout of all sects with understanding and sympathy. Even after it was ravaged in 1565 by an alliance of Deccan states, the memory of the glories of Vijayanagar remained enshrined in the hearts of all Hindus.

After 1526, political leadership in northern India passed gradually into the hands of the Mughuls (variant of Mongol), a Turkish family which traced its descent from Genghis Khan and Tamerlane, the great Mongol conquerors. Akbar, who ruled the Mughul empire from 1556 to 1605, consolidated the conquests of his predecessors with his own into a great state that stretched from coast to coast and as far south as the Vindhyan hills. Jurisdiction over south India was divided among Akbar's Muslim vassals, the swiftly declining empire of Vijayanagar, and the states of Malabar. After Akbar's conquest of Gujarat in 1572 and Bengal in 1576, he learned something about the maritime activities of the Europeans, and he soon invited learned Jesuits to visit his polynational court.

Akbar himself was unwilling to accept conversion to Christianity and was bitterly hostile to Islam. The great Mughul ruler, the majority of whose subjects were Hindus, permitted the customary practices of Indian religious and secular life to be followed throughout his empire. At his court he was particularly friendly to the devotees of Jainism, an ancient Indian religion that was inspired by a contemporary of the Buddha. Sikhism, a religion confined almost entirely to the Punjab, was founded at just about the time the Portuguese arrived in India. Born of a reaction against orthodox Hinduism, it stressed the fundamental identity of all religions, an idea which appealed to the eclectic Akbar. Hinduism itself, so unknown to the early Portuguese captains that they mistook it for a primitive form of Christianity, underwent rejuvenation and revival within Akbar's empire.

Centers of unity in the history of Southeast Asia are hard to locate and to isolate. The continental states, as they appeared in the sixteenth century, were constantly engaged in wars with one another: Annamese against Cambodians, Cambodians against Siamese, Siamese against Burmese. Within the various mainland countries, despite deep cultural differences, Buddhism's teachings helped to preserve a unity of belief that transcended violent political differences and insulated the continental states from the aggressive blandishments of Islamic teachers and Christian missionaries. In the insular regions, where the commercial stakes were highest and the native governments weakest, Muslims and Christians alike were able to grasp a share of economic and political control and to propagate their faiths.

In all historical periods, the major centers of population in continental Southeast Asia have been located in the fertile alluvial plains of the great river valleys and deltas. The Irrawaddy, Menam, and Mekong rivers, relatively isolated from one another, have provided the sites for the modern states of Burma, Siam (Thailand), and Cambodia. The narrow Malay Peninsula, whose hardwood forests defied primitive implements, was only thinly populated in the sixteenth century and its inhabitants were forced to live from seafaring, commerce, and small-scale tin mining. Malacca, which had superseded Singapore in the fifteenth century, was the nexus of Asia's international commerce when the Europeans arrived in the East. Siam, probably then the most populous and powerful state of Southeast Asia, still claimed suzerainty over Malacca when Albuquerque conquered the Malay port in 1511.

Malacca's rise to commercial supremacy in the fifteenth century coincided with naval expeditions sent into southern waters by the Ming rulers of China and with the expansion of Islam into Southeast Asia. Politically, the Malay sultans of Malacca acknowledged the suzerainty of China and paid tribute to the Ming court; religiously, they accepted the teachings of the Prophet and aided in the propagation of Islam into the archipelago. Because of Malacca's prominence in international commerce, the Malay language was the *lingua franca* of foreign trade. Most of the languages now spoken in the archipelago are related to commercial Malay.

The numberless islands of the archipelago lie scattered over a great triangle, with Sumatra, New Guinea, and the Philippines at the vertices. It was not the largest islands of the archipelago (Sumatra, Borneo, and New Guinea), however, that most attracted the Europeans. Albuquerque and Magellan were lured to the East by what they had learned about the Moluccas or the Spiceries, mere flecks of land sprinkled across the equator southeast of the Philippines. The survivors of the Magellan expedition, who completed the first circumnavigation of the world in 1521, brought home the first cargo of cloves to come straight from the Moluccas to Europe. By 1640, about three million pounds of these dried flower-buds, often called "brown gold," were being imported annually by the Europeans.

Elements of Indian culture began to enter both the insular and continental parts of Southeast Asia in the early centuries of the Christian era. Notable among the ideas and practices adopted from India were: concepts of royalty based on Hindu or Buddhist beliefs, the use of the Sanskrit and Pali languages, a mythology centering on traditions drawn from the Hindu classics, and the adoption of Hindu legal precepts as set down in the *Laws of Manu* and other classics. The evidence now available indicates that adoption of Indian customs and ideas took place mainly at the court level. Buddhist missionaries preached the law at court and often ended by converting the royal family and establishing Buddhist orders. Native Buddhist monks sometimes completed their religious education at famous Indian monasteries, made pilgrimages to the places associated with the life of the Buddha, and searched India and Ceylon for religious writings, relics, and images. Javanese architects and artists employed classical Indian canons of construction and taste in creating their exquisite buildings and sculptures.

The adoption of new religious or cultural attitudes did not usually extinguish older faiths or customs. In most parts of Southeast Asia, new ideas were simply combined with the old. Hinduism and Buddhism of various schools blended on the mainland with animism, ancestor worship, and other age-old beliefs. In the insular areas, Islam was superimposed on the melange of earlier cultures. Beginning in the fifteenth century, the Malay sultanate became the watershed between Buddhism and Islam. Even after their conversion to Islam, the Malaccan rulers continued to follow certain traditional Hindu practices, such as reserving to royalty the exclusive right to wear gold colors.

The history of Indochina, like those of Malacca and Java, shows vividly how foreign civilization merged with indigenous culture and how outside influences waxed and waned with changes in local conditions. Chinese influence was particularly powerful in the northern part of the Indochinese peninsula among the Annamese, or the Vietnamese. Hindu and Buddhist influences in Indochina centered historically in Cambodia. The great Khmer (Cambodian) empire, with its splendid capital of Angkor, dominated Indochina until the end of the twelfth century when Champa (the northern half of modern South Vietnam) had its brief period of glory. After Angkor fell to the Chams in 1177, a simpler Hinayana Buddhism was introduced into Cambodia. This simpler Buddhism undermined the Khmer state cult of Shaivism, which had accounted the ruler a god and had inspired the Cambodian kings to build the monumental temples and reservoirs of Angkor. The century between 1350 and the capture of the Khmer capital, Angkor, by the Siamese in 1431 climaxed a long period of almost continuous fighting between the Tais and Khmers. Gradually the monuments raised by the Khmer kings in the valley of the Mekong River were covered by jungle, and their marvelous water conservation and transportation systems fell into disrepair as the six-hundred-year old kingdom (802-1431) succumbed to the Tais.

The "cradle of Tai civilization" was Sukotai, an area in northern Siam on a tributary of the Menam River. The first use of the term "Siam" for the Tai state dates from the eleventh century; by the end of the thirteenth century Tai armies were driving southward into the Indochinese peninsula. The Tai in 1350 founded the city of Áyuthia on the lower reaches of the Menam River to the west of Angkor in the Mekong valley. A period of consolidation of the kingdom based on Ayuthia followed. Under Boromo Trailokanat (reigned 1448-1488), civil administration was definitively systematized into five departments (Interior, Local Government, Finance, Agriculture, and Royal Household) and a separate military administration was established. This political structure was in advance of other governments of the peninsula and it prevailed in its broad outlines into the nineteenth century. The King maintained and perpetuated the Tai social hierarchy by assigning land to all the people according to their status. To a successor of Trailok, Rama Tibodi II (reigned 1491-1529), who ruled when Albuquerque's emissary arrived in Ayuthia, was left the task of completing the military organization of the country. He established a system of compulsory service for all men of eighteen and over. The alphabet for writing the Tai language was borrowed from the Cambodians; otherwise Indian influence predominated, firmly based on the Buddhist religion which had come to Siam through the Mons of Burma.

The history of Burma is a story of conflicts among various warring groups. The Mon peoples and the Burmese trace the chronological foundations of their respective capitals, Pegu and Pagan, back to the early ninth century. The Burmese overwhelmed the Mons in the eleventh century, gained control of the Irrawaddy and Salween deltas, and adopted Buddhism. At first the culture of the defeated Mons pervaded the court of Pagan (1044-1287), the Mon alphabet being used for the Burmese language. When the Burmese refused to pay tribute to the Mongol dynasty, several expeditions from China brought an end to the empire of Pagan late in the thirteenth century. The Mon kingdom of Pegu in southern Burma had meanwhile escaped the clutches of the Pagan empire and reëstablished its independence when the latter was destroyed. After having fought off the Siamese, the kingdom of Pegu won for itself a period of peace and prosperity early in the fifteenth century. The ports of Martaban (recaptured from Siam), Syriam, and Bassein carried on lively traffic throughout the Bay of Bengal and even attracted daring prospectors from Europe. Very shortly after the Portuguese from India and Malacca had established a trading base at Martaban (1519), the Burmese from Toungoo, with technical assistance from the Portuguese, swallowed up Pegu and reunited all Burma under one ruler.

The Toungoo dynasty moved its capital to Pegu, and began to threaten the Siamese. After assaulting the Siamese capital of Ayuthia in 1548, the Toungoo dynasts turned on the Shan states of north Burma, bringing them into line in the 1550's. Siam and Laos both repeatedly felt the weight of Burmese power in the time of Bayinnaung (reigned 1551-1581). The latter part of the sixteenth century saw a three-cornered battle royal pitting a briefly revitalized Ayuthia against Cambodia and the declining state of Pegu.

China, like continental Southeast Asia, is a land of mountains and rivers. Except for the north China plain, the whole country is divided into distinct geographical units by a series of intersecting mountain ranges. The centers of habitation, which lie within the mountain ranges and along the seacoast, are watered by great rivers, all of which flow eastward into the sea. The Yangtze River, the dividing line between northern and southern China, is 3200 miles long, and at least half of its length is navigable. The Yellow River, which dominates the north China plain, is known as "China's Sorrow" because of its disastrous floods. The ranges of climate in China are similar to those of the eastern United States and the Caribbean: Peking is much like Philadelphia, and Canton similar to Havana, Cuba. A heavy annual rainfall provides ample water for irrigated rice cultivation in south China, while low rainfall, cold, dry winds, and periodic floods pose constant threats to agriculture and are often responsible for famine in the north. For these reasons, most of China's food has been grown in the south, while throughout most of its history China has been governed from the north.

China prides itself on having the longest continuous and independent history of any known civilization, empire, or nation. Founded in the valley of the Yellow River in about 1500 B.C., the civilization of China spread historically from north to south. In the three thousand years of its history before the advent of the Portuguese, China had experienced thirty-five dynasties. When the Europeans touched on its southern coast, China was living in the middle period of the Ming dynasty (1368-1644). The rule of the Ming, China's last native dynasty, is still remembered as a period of great internal stability and significant cultural accomplishment.

In the Ming period, as in all previous dynasties, the Chinese economy was firmly rooted in the soil. About 80 per cent of China's population worked in agriculture and related enterprises to maintain the entire population. Taxes on land and labor served as the mainstay of government; the administration evidently realized little from taxes on industrial production and trade. While attempts were made in the last century of Ming rule to make the tax system more efficient and equitable, these efforts failed to increase revenues substantially. Royal extravagance, administrative inefficiency and corruption, and the heavy expenses of the war in Korea during the 1590's combined to produce a tide of fiscal bankruptcy and popular rebellion which finally engulfed the dynasty itself by 1644.

Traditionally, the family, rather than the individual, state, or religion, provided the basis for China's social and political organization. For each individual the family was the major focus of economic and social security. The family was ordinarily governed by a patriarch who controlled its properties and other economic assets, arranged marriages, and meted out rewards and punishments. Within each household the individual was responsible for the acts of every member; within each community each family was responsible for the acts of all families in its group. The Confucian ethical system, on which society and government were based, upheld filial piety as the highest of virtues and extolled the maintenance of dutiful and loving relationships between father and son, husband and wife, and ruler and subject as the basis of society.

Confucian political ideology set the welfare and happiness of the people as the primary aim of philosophy and government. The highest duty of the true gentleman consisted in serving his fellows; the effectiveness of a ruler demonstrated his personal virtue; imperial law could be best enforced through the ministrations of carefully selected, morally upright, well-educated subordinates. Governmental office was the best way, and often the only way, to achieve economic wealth, social prestige, and political power. Ordinarily, candidates for government service had to pass a series of competitive examinations on the Confucian classics. The nation-wide examination system guaranteed the government a select body of men, with comparable training and standards of conduct, regardless of social origin. This unprecedented sponsorship of social mobility by China's "Confucian state" infused new blood into the ruling class. At the same time, the traditional ideological framework ensured the nation's stability.

Reminiscent of Hinduism in its syncretism, flexibility, and powers of survival, Confucianism continued to be recognized as the dominant school of thought, even when foreign dynasties ruled China. Once imperial patronage raised Confucianism to the stature of official state philosophy, the merit of individual officials gradually came to be judged primarily in terms of moral character and literary competence. The struggle to attain academic degrees and to pass the civil service examinations absorbed the intellectual energies of countless generations of Chinese. Under the Ming dynasty, private academies and libraries flourished, and the government sought repeatedly to extend equality of educational opportunity by encouraging the establishment of a system of public schools. The government was so successful in ferreting out and utilizing talent that it was not unheard of for the grandson of a hunter or a peddler to become prime minister. In this way, the conviction became institutionalized that all men who respond positively to proper education and moral training are suited to be members of the ruling class and that ancestry and wealth are minor criteria of status.

Mighty China's unity and determination over the ages to remain the only sun in the Oriental sky, as a Chinese proverb phrases it, long held the Europeans at arm's length. The arrival of the Portuguese on China's littoral chanced to coincide with a turn in imperial policy that discouraged foreign commerce. However impatiently the "South Sea barbarians" tried to gain admittance to the empire on equal terms, both merchants and missionaries were forced to learn Chinese etiquette and practices before they could make the slightest progress with their complacent, ethnocentric hosts. It was an accepted and time-honored fact that China was the center of the world and that one of its emperor's duties was to manage relations with rulers and peoples of the outside world.

The primary object of Peking's foreign policy was to build up a protective system of loyal buffer states that would accept vassalage and engage in trade on terms dictated by China. States willing to accept such vassal status could send embassies to the Chinese capital at stated intervals. As a rule, the "gifts" to be exchanged on these occasions were mutually determined in advance. The goods formally transferred as "gifts" actually constituted a considerable volume of foreign trade for China. Since arrivals and other arrangements were reckoned according to the Chinese calendar, its usage was enjoined upon vassals. Throughout their stay on Chinese territory, foreign ambassadors and their retainers were provided with food, lodging, transportation, and a guard for their possessions and "gifts." Among the formalities required of the ambassadors at the Emperor's reception was performance of the *kowtow,* standardized as three kneelings and nine knockings of the head on the floor. Chinese ambassadors were frequently dispatched abroad to recognize, invest, and congratulate new rulers of vassal states, although China ordinarily kept her involvement in the internal affairs of vassals to a minimum.

This paternal system of foreign relations entered a new phase in 1433 when the Ming turned from encouraging to limiting foreign commerce, and to tightening imperial control over what little trade was permitted. Three ports, usually superintended by eunuchs, were opened from time to time in the sixteenth century. Canton, in Kwangtung, often continued to function when the other two ports to the north in Fukien and Chekiang were closed. Foreign trade, the official line held, was not of prime importance in the tributary relationship because of China's vaunted self-sufficiency. As China minimized trade and tribute relations, disaffected sailors and merchants of both the foreign states and China conspired in illicit trade or, in desperation, turned to piracy. And despite the government's position, the demand in China for silver and foreign manufactures was so great and constant that the merchants of south China regularly defied imperial orders and conspired with the foreign traders to carry on an illicit commerce.

While pursuing commerce along the China coast, several Westerners inadvertently landed in Japan in 1543. One of their number soon sent a report back to Europe describing Kyushu, the southernmost of Japan's islands. He was most impressed by the temperate climate of Kyushu and the industry of its people. He had no knowledge of the other three large islands (Shikoku, Honshu, and Hokkaido) of the Japanese archipelago, but it was not long before the Jesuit missionaries who followed the traders to the ports of Japan sent word of these islands to Europe.

These Jesuits then penetrated on their own deep into the interior of the country, far from the protection of Portuguese guns.

The Jesuits soon learned that Japan was a much larger and less isolated country than they had originally supposed. Larger in area than Italy, Japan was seen to be an insular country with endless miles of rugged coastlines, great ranges of towering mountains, and isolated patches of arable land. Since only about 20 per cent of its land was suitable for cultivation, the Japanese, to a greater extent than the continental peoples of Asia, were forced to extract a substantial part of their living from the sea and from maritime commerce. Silver and copper from Japan's mines were traded abroad in the sixteenth century in exchange for textiles and spices—especially in China.

Like England, Japan is the insular daughter of its nearby continent. Most of the inhabitants of the islands are ethnically related to the peoples of northeastern Asia: Manchus, Chinese, and Koreans. The early Japanese were organized into numerous clans, each ruled over by a high priest or priestess. Clan solidarity, respect for religious and civil authority, and worship of nature (later called Shinto) were the hallmarks of primitive Japanese society. Beginning in the latter half of the sixth century, elements from the high culture of Sui and T'ang China gained increasing acceptance in Japan. The Chinese method of writing, Buddhism, governmental practices, and cultural standards were transmitted to Japan over the course of a century. This cultural transformation was followed by a political revolution (ca. 645), with the objective of creating in Japan a state and civilization designed to be a miniature replica of T'ang China.

The government and the civilization that gradually evolved was an amalgam of primitive Japanese traditions and imported Chinese practices. The chieftain of the early Japanese state was transformed into an autocratic emperor of the Chinese type, while he also retained a religious role as the high priest of the associated clans. A centralized administration on the Chinese model was created, but it existed mainly on paper. Real authority in local affairs continued to be exercised by clan leaders. Equally fruitless efforts were undertaken to superimpose the Chinese systems of land tenure and taxation on Japan. Elaborate law codes were drawn up according to Chinese models, but their enforcement was of only limited effectiveness. More fundamental than the political reforms were the changes wrought by the introduction of Buddhism and the arts associated with it.

Early in the ninth century Japan began to loose itself from the bonds of Chinese culture and to embark on the slow process of developing an independent native culture. Although respect for Chinese learning remained high, the Japanese sought, for example, to modify the imported Chinese system of writing to better suit the peculiar characteristics of the Japanese language. Japanese literature, painting, sculpture, and architecture were likewise released from subservience to Chinese artistic patterns; an independent prose literature came into being; and distinctive artistic creations became more common. Most striking was the gradual retreat of centralized authority; the Emperor was slowly forced to yield his supreme political position to court families who exercised power from behind the throne.

With the growth of government by shadow rulers, control over the political and economic life of the country returned to local leaders. Power passed into the hands of land-holding aristocrats who protected themselves, their servants, and their properties by their own military prowess. Wars between local lords, or between confederacies of warrior-aristocrats, plagued the country, and in the twelfth century the imperial city of Kyoto and the Emperor himself became subject to a victorious military clique. The faction headed by Minamoto Yoritomo emerged triumphant at the end of the twelfth century. Kyoto was left to itself as the imperial capital, and Yoritomo established a military headquarters at Kamakura, near modern Tokyo, and assumed the title of *shogun* or *generalissimo*. From Kamakura, the Minamoto, in alliance with other clans, imposed a military dictatorship upon Japan.

Shogunal society was dominated by the warrior, and the cult which adulated Spartan virtues, ascetic practices of self-discipline, and physical and mental conditioning. In contrast to the effete society of Kyoto and the imperial court, the warriors stressed personal loyalties, family ties, and the glories of warfare. As political authority passed to the provincial gentry, Buddhism spread from the court to all parts of the country and to all levels of society. The rise of new schools of thought instilled a new vigor into Buddhism as it became the popular religion of Japan.

The integrated feudal society created by the Minamoto *shoguns* declined in the fourteenth and fifteenth centuries. In the period of the Ashikaga *shoguns* (1338-1573), Japan again became divided into a large number of feudal domains, each presided over by a lord (*daimyo*). The warrior was eclipsed as the *daimyo* began to recruit peasants for his armies and as he assembled numbers of small knightly estates into a single, large domain over which he acted as manager. Cultural leadership in the Ashikaga period passed from

Kyoto to the shogunal court. The Zen form of Buddhism received the official patronage of the Ashikaga rulers, and the rich culture of the Muromachi epoch was dominated by Zen monks. Increased trade with China in this period brought new infusions of Chinese learning and art into Japan. Buddhist monasteries and great *daimyo* families sponsored overseas trading ventures. The Ashikaga *shoguns,* because of their great hopes for the trade with China, even permitted themselves to be invested as vassals of the Ming dynasty.

Tribute and trade relations between Japan and China were discontinued in 1549, shortly after the arrival of the first Europeans in Japan; and so the Europeans were able to take over as commercial intermediaries between Nagasaki and Macao. The earliest Europeans to report on the Japanese found them proud, courteous and curious, and receptive to Christianity. The local lords of the divided insular kingdom proved eager to trade and to make copies of firearms, previously unknown in the "Land of the Rising Sun." When political unification was effected at the end of the sixteenth century, the rulers of Japan resolved to minimize foreign influence by severely limiting foreign trade, cutting relations with Spain, Mexico and the Philippines, and finally expelling the Portuguese in 1636. Thus, Japan once again returned to isolation after a period of liberal experimentation with foreign contacts.

In the sixteenth century the civilizations of the East loomed before the Europeans as fantastically rich, mighty, and well-administered. To understand how such an impression developed, it will be useful to sample a variety of Asian and European writings of the discovery period, as well as a few observations by later writers. The tendencies inherent in the traditional cultures of the East naturally determined the responses of the Asians to the appearance of European strangers. The heritage of the fifteenth century, even though it is now thickly overlaid with the encrustations left by hundreds of years of contacts with the rest of the world, still continues deeply to influence Asia's response to the West. Study of a selection of primary sources for Asia's last period of independent development will help us to understand better what the East looked like and what values its peoples held most dear on the eve of Europe's expansion.

I / A SURVEY OF EASTERN MARITIME TRADE AROUND 1515

INTRODUCTION

Once they arrived in Asia, the Christians were confronted by Muslim competitors everywhere they turned. Then, in Buddhist Siam, they first encountered the Chinese sphere of economic and political influence. And in Malacca, they found the Gujaratis and Klings of India and the Javanese dominating trade.

To appreciate Portuguese daring in seeking to penetrate and control the widespread and distant commercial centers of the East, we should realize that the major entrepôts of the East were larger and more active in business than Lisbon. ". . . no trading port as large as Malacca is known," writes Tomé Pires, "nor any where [do] they deal in such fine and highly-prized merchandise. Goods from all over the east are found here; goods from all over the west are sold here."

Tomé Pires disembarked in Portuguese India in 1511, just thirteen years after Vasco da Gama had opened the sea route. As an apothecary to a member of Portugal's royal family, Pires also managed to serve his king in the East as secretary, accountant, and

From Tomé Pires, *The Suma Oriental*, ed. and trans., Armando Cortesão. Works issued by the Hakluyt Society, Second series, Nos. LXXXIX-XC; Vol. I, pp. 41-47, 104, 107-9, 122-27, 174-75, 180, 182, 214-16, 219-20; Vol. II, pp. 269-74. Reprinted by permission of the Hakluyt Society.

controller of drugs. Even before taking up a post at Malacca, he set about collecting data in India for a comprehensive report to King Manuel of Portugal. While Pires was stationed at Malacca from 1513 to 1517, he witnessed the return visit of members of the first European expedition to the fabled Spice Islands, as well as the return of the first Portuguese known to have visited the China coast (ca. 1514). In 1517, shortly after completing The Suma Oriental *(Account of the East), Pires himself was dispatched by the Governor of India as Portugal's first ambassador to China. He and his delegation were the first Westerners in centuries to reach Peking. Soon, however, complaints by the ruler of Malacca (whom the Portuguese had deposed) to his Chinese suzerain against the Portuguese "sea-robbers," supplemented by reports from Canton that the unruly Europeans were carrying people off as slaves, led the Chinese to imprison the ambassador and his attendants. Pires died in China.*

While at Malacca, Pires was in a position to describe and analyze Eastern commerce from its hub. Indian textiles from Gujarat (also called Cambay) and Bengal, he quickly learned, were in great demand in Malacca, in densely populated Java, and in islands as distant as the Liu Ch'ius and the Moluccas. To pay for these and other finished goods, the one-crop economies of Timor, Banda, and the Moluccas supplied the world with sandalwood, mace, and cloves, respectively, all channeled through Malacca. Slaves from various territories in the archipelago were traded at Malacca, especially for dispatch to Siam. Raw materials like wax, honey, and gold poured out of Sumatra. Except for some exchange of silks for pepper, China, singled out by Pires as large, wealthy, and militarily weak, seemed self-sufficient and indisposed to trade. Japan loomed as no more than a shadow on the horizon to Pires and his companions.

Pires, the astute Portuguese observer, was able to indicate the areas of rice deficit and surplus in Asia—for example, he notes that "beautiful" Ceylon, favored in every other respect, is forced to import its rice. He also shows that the demand for gold and/or silver, fluctuated from place to place. Pires specifies the items of trade supplied and demanded by each region, describes the cultivation of important plants, itemizes weights and measures, currencies, and duties, and catalogs the distances and periods of favorable winds. He comments on each of the countries involved in the trade of Asia, from Cambay in western India, to the Moluccas far to the east, and shows in remarkable detail how merchants and products from these places funneled through Malacca, the "city that was made for merchandise."

1 / THE SUMA ORIENTAL

Cambay or Gujarat

I now come to the trade of Cambay. These [people] are [like] Italians in their knowledge of and dealings in merchandise. All the trade in Cambay is in the hands of the heathen. Their general designation is Gujaratees, and then they are divided into various races—Banians, Brahmans and Pattars. There is no doubt that these people have the cream of the trade. They are men who understand merchandise; they are so properly steeped in the sound and harmony of it, that the Gujaratees say that any offence connected with merchandise is pardonable. There are Gujaratees settled everywhere. They work some for some and others for others. They are diligent, quick men in trade. They do their accounts with figures like ours and with our very writing. They are men who do not give away anything that belongs to them, nor do they want anything that belongs to anyone else; wherefore they have been esteemed in Cambay up to the present, practising their idolatry, because they enrich the kingdom greatly with the said trade. There are also some Cairo merchants settled in Cambay, and many Khorasans and Guilans from Aden and Ormuz, all of whom do a great trade in the seaport towns of Cambay; but none of these count in comparison with the heathens, especially in knowledge. Those of our people who want to be clerks and factors ought to go there and learn, because the business of trade is a science in itself which does not hinder any other noble exercise, but helps a great deal. . . .

They trade with the kingdom of the Deccan and Goa and with Malabar, and they have factors everywhere, who live and set up business—as the Genoese do in our part [of the world]—in places like Bengal, Pegu, Siam, Pedir, Pase, Kedah, taking back to their own country the kind of merchandise which is valued there. And there is no trading place where you do not see Gujarat merchants. Gujarat ships come to these kingdoms every year, one ship straight to each place. The Gujaratees used to have large factories in Calicut.

The Cambay merchants make Malacca their chief trading centre. There used to be a thousand Gujarat merchants in Malacca, besides four or five thousand Gujarat seamen, who came and went. Malacca cannot live without Cambay, nor Cambay without Malacca, if they are to be very rich and very prosperous. All the clothes and things from Gujarat have trading value in Malacca and in the kingdoms which trade with Malacca; for the products of Malacca are esteemed not only in this [part of the?] world, but in others, where no doubt they are wanted. . . . If Cambay were cut off from trading with Malacca, it could not live, for it would have no outlet for its merchandise.

The Gujaratees were better seamen and did more navigating than the other people of these parts, and so they have larger ships and more men to man them. They have great pilots and do a great deal of navigation. The heathen of Cambay—and in older times the Gujaratees—held that they must never kill anyone, nor must they have an armed man in their company. If they were captured and [their captors] wanted to kill them all, they did not resist. This is the Gujarat law among the heathen. Now they have many men-at-arms to defend their ships. Before the channel of Malacca was discovered they used to trade with Java round the south of the island of Sumatra. They used to go in between Sunda and the point of Sumatra island and sail to Grisee (*Agraci* in Java) whence they took the products of the Moluccas, Timor and Banda, and came back very rich men. It is not a hundred years since they gave up this route. There are keels, anchors and other parts of Gujarat ships in Grisee, which they show, saying that they are left from the time of the Gujaratees. . . .

Siam

Through the cunning [of the Siamese] the foreign merchants who go to their land and kingdom leave their merchandise in the land and are ill paid; and this happens to them all—but less to the Chinese, on account of their friendship with the king of China. And for this reason less people go to their port than would [otherwise] go. However, as the land is rich in good merchandise, they bear some things on account of the profit, as often happens to merchants, because otherwise there would be no trading.

There are very few Moors in Siam. The Siamese do not like them. There are, however, Arabs, Persians, Bengalees, many Kling, Chinese and other nationalities. And all the Siamese trade is on the China side, and in Pase, Pedir and Bengal. The Moors are in the seaports. They are obedient to their own lords, and constantly make war on the Siamese, now inland and now in Pahang. . . . There is a great abundance of rice in Siam, and much salt, dried salt fish, *oraquas*,[1] vegetables; and up to thirty junks a year used to come to Malacca with these.

[1] *Arrack*, here the distilled spirit from a palm. In some instances Pires seems to mean the palm-tree itself.

From Siam comes lac, benzoin, brazil,[2] lead, tin, silver, gold, ivory, cassia fistula; they bring vessels of cast copper and gold, ruby and diamond rings; they bring a large quantity of cheap, coarse Siamese cloth for the poor people.

They say that the chief merchandise they take from Malacca to Siam are the male and female slaves, which they take in quantities, white sandalwood, pepper, quicksilver, vermilion, opium, *azernefe* [possibly aloeswood], cloves, mace, nutmeg, wide and narrow muslins, and Kling cloths in the fashion of Siam, camlets, rosewater, carpets, brocades from Cambay, white cowries, wax, Borneo camphor, pachak which are roots like dry rampion, gall-nuts, and the merchandise they bring from China every year is also of value there.

The Siamese have not traded in Malacca for twenty-two years. They had a difference because the kings of Malacca owed allegiance to the kings of Siam, because they say that Malacca belongs to the land of Siam—They say that it is theirs and that twenty-two years ago this king lost Malacca, which rose up against this subjection. They also say that Pahang rose against Siam in the same way, and that, on account of the relationship between them, the kings of Malacca favoured the people of Pahang against the Siamese, and that this was also a reason for their disagreement.

They also say that it was about the tin districts which are on the Kedah side, and which were originally under Kedah, and were taken over by Malacca; and they quarrelled for all these reasons, and they say that the chief reason was the revolt against subjection. After this the Siamese sailed against Malacca, and the Siamese were routed by the Malays, and [they say] that the *Lasamane* was the captain—who has therefore been held in great honour ever since.

The Siamese trade in China—six or seven junks a year. They trade with Sunda and Palembang (*Palimbaão*) and other islands. They trade with Cambodia and *Champa* and Cochin China (*Cauçhy*), and with Burma (*Brema*) and *Jangoma*[3] on the main land, when they are at peace.

On the Tenasserim side Siam also trades with Pase, Pedir, with Kedah, with Pegu, with Bengal; and the Gujaratees come to its

---

[2] Brazil-wood or sappan-wood.

[3] CAUÇHY, *Cauchij* or *Cauchy Chyna*—Cochin China, called by the Malays *Kuchi*, whence the Portuguese *Cauchi* and *Cochinchina*. BREMA—Burma. Mentioned by other sixteenth-century Portuguese writers as *Berma*. JANGOMA—Mentioned by several sixteenth-century Portuguese writers. The town and state of Siamese Laos, called by the Burmese *Zimmé*, by the Siamese *Xieng-mai* or *Kiang-mai*, &c.

port every year. They trade richly outside and liberally inside the country, but they are great tyrants. . . .

China

They affirm that all those who take merchandise from Canton to the islands make a profit of three, four or five in every ten, and the Chinese have this custom so that the land shall not be taken from them, as well as in order to receive the dues on the merchandise exported as well as imported; and the chief [reason] is for fear lest the city be taken from them, because they say that the city of Canton is a rich one, and corsairs often come up to it. *Hi Taão,*[4] one of the chief people, is captain of this city, and there is a captain every year by the king's decree, and he cannot remain [in office] longer. There is another sea-captain almost like the land one, with separate jurisdiction. Both are changed yearly.

They say that the Chinese made this law about not being able to go to Canton for fear of the Javanese and Malays, for it is certain that one of these people's junks would rout twenty Chinese junks. They say that China has more than a thousand junks, and each of them trades where it sees fit; but the people are weak, and such is their fear of Malays and Javanese that it is quite certain that one [of our] ship[s] of four hundred tons could depopulate Canton, and this depopulation would bring great loss to China.

Not to rob any country of its glory, it certainly seems that China is an important, good and very wealthy country, and the Governor of Malacca would not need as much force as they say in order to bring it under our rule, because the people are very weak and easy to overcome. And the principal people who have often been there affirm that with ten ships the Governor of India who took Malacca could take the whole of China along the sea-coast. And China is twenty days' sail distant for our ships. They leave here at the end of June for a good voyage, and with a monsoon wind they can go in fifteen days. From China they have recently begun sailing to Borneo (*Burney*), and they say that they go there in fifteen days, and that this must have been for the last fifteen years.

The chief merchandise is pepper—of which they [the Chinese] will buy ten junk-loads a year if as many go there—cloves, a little nutmeg, a little more pachak, catcchu; they will buy a great deal of incense, elephants' tusks, tin, apothecary's lignaloes; they buy a great deal of Borneo camphor, red beads, white sandalwood, brazil, infinite quantities of the black wood that grows in Singapore

[4] *Hi Taão*, i.e., the Hai-tao-fu-shih, or Vice Commissioner of Maritime Affairs.

(*Syngapura*); they buy a great many carnelians from Cambay, scarlet camlets, coloured woollen cloths. Pepper apart, they make little account of all the rest.

The said junks from Malacca go and anchor off the island of *Tumon*, twenty or thirty leagues away from Canton. These islands are near the land of Nan-t'ou, a league to seaward from the mainland. Those from Malacca anchor there in the port of *Tumon* and those from Siam in the port of *Hucham*.[5] Our port is three leagues nearer to China than the Siamese one, and merchandise comes to it rather than to the other.

As soon as the lord of Nan-t'ou sees the junks he immediately sends word to Canton that junks have gone in among the islands; the valuers from Canton go out to value the merchandise; they receive their dues; they bring just the amount of merchandise that is required: the country is pretty well accustomed to estimate it, so well do they know of you the goods you want, and they bring them. . . . [This means that the Chinese traders are so well informed about the goods desired by the Europeans that they bring to the exchange exactly the right items in the required quantities.]

The chief merchandise from China is raw white silk in large quantities, and loose coloured silks, many in quantity, satins of all colours, damask chequered *enrolados* in all colours, taffetas and other thin silk cloths called *xaas*[6] and many other kinds of all colours; an abundance of seed-pearl in various shapes, mostly irregular; they also have some big round ones—this in my opinion is as important a merchandise in China as silk, although they count silk as the chief merchandise—musk in powder and in pods, plenty of this, and certainly good, which yields in nothing to that from Pegu; apothecary's camphor in large quantities, *abarute*, alum, saltpetre, sulphur, copper, iron, rhubarb, and all of it is worthless —what I have seen up to the present has been rotten when it arrived; they say it used to come fresh; I have not seen it—vases of copper and *fuseleira*, cast iron kettles, bowls, basins, quantities of these things, boxes, fans, plenty of needles of a hundred different kinds, some of them very fine and well made, these are good merchandise, and things of very poor quality like those which come to Portugal from Flanders, countless copper bracelets; gold and silver come and I did not see much, and many brocades of their kind, and

[5] Perhaps some of the islands which lie about four and a half miles south of Lin Tin island towards the sea.

[6] *Xaas*, sash or shash, from the Arab *shāsh*, muslin—'A band of a fine material worn twisted round the head as a turban by Orientals'.

porcelains beyond count. Of the things which come from China some are products from China itself and some from outside, some of them from places renowned as being better than others. You can spend your money on whatever of this merchandise you fancy, except that there is not so much musk to be found. They say that not more than one bahar comes from China each year in all junks. The land of China produces plenty of good sugar. There is a place called *Xamcy* [province of Shensi?] where there is musk; it has a little and it is good. . . .

Salt is a great merchandise among the Chinese. It is distributed from China to these regions; and it is dealt with by fifteen hundred junks which come to buy it, and it is loaded in China to go to other places. Traders in this are very rich and they say to one another among themselves 'Are you a salt merchant to speak of?'

Beyond the port of Canton there is another port which is called *Oquem* [Fukien]; it is three days' journey by land and a day and night by sea. This is the port for the *Lequjos* [Liu-Ch'iuans] and other races. It has many other ports, which it would be a long business to tell of, and they do not concern us at present, except up to Canton (*Q̃mtom*), because this is the key to the kingdom of China.

They say that there are people from Tartary (*Tartaria*) in the land of China and they call them Tartars (*tartall*), and these people are very white with red beards. They ride on horseback; they are warlike. And they say that they go from China to the land of the Tartars (*tartaros*) in two months, and that in Tartary they have horses shod with copper shoes, and this must be because China extends a long way on the northern side, and our bombardiers say that in Germany they heard tell of these people and of a city named by the Chinese *Quesechama*,[7] and it seems to them that by this route they could go to their lands in a short time; but they say that by reason of the cold the land is uninhabited.

Java

They say that the island of Java used to rule as far as the Moluccas (*Maluco*) on the eastern side and [over] a great part of the west; and that it had almost all the island of Sumatra under its dominion and all the islands known to the Javanese, and that it had all this

---

[7] *Que se chama* or *q̃ se chama*, as it appears in the manuscript, means 'which is called'. It is possible that Pires wrote some word or words corresponding to the Chinese name for a city in Tartary, which the transcriber transformed into *q̃ se chama*.

beyond count. Of the things which come from China some
ts from China itself and some from outside, some of them
s renowned as being better than others. You can spend
y on whatever of this merchandise you fancy, except that
t so much musk to be found. They say that not more
ahar comes from China each year in all junks. The land
roduces plenty of good sugar. There is a place called
vince of Shensi?] where there is musk; it has a little and
. .
great merchandise among the Chinese. It is distributed
to these regions; and it is dealt with by fifteen hundred
h come to buy it, and it is loaded in China to go to
s. Traders in this are very rich and they say to one
ong themselves 'Are you a salt merchant to speak of?'
he port of Canton there is another port which is called
kien]; it is three days' journey by land and a day and
a. This is the port for the *Lequjos* [Liu-Ch'iuans] and
It has many other ports, which it would be a long
tell of, and they do not concern us at present, except
n (*Q̃mtom*), because this is the key to the kingdom of

that there are people from Tartary (*Tartaria*) in the
a and they call them Tartars (*tartall*), and these people
te with red beards. They ride on horseback; they are
l they say that they go from China to the land of the
aros) in two months, and that in Tartary they have
vith copper shoes, and this must be because China ex-
way on the northern side, and our bombardiers say
any they heard tell of these people and of a city named
ese *Quesechama*,[7] and it seems to them that by this
uld go to their lands in a short time; but they say that
he cold the land is uninhabited.

aat the island of Java used to rule as far as the Moluccas
the eastern side and [over] a great part of the west;
d almost all the island of Sumatra under its dominion
lands known to the Javanese, and that it had all this

a or *q̃ se chama*, as it appears in the manuscript, means 'which
ossible that Pires wrote some word or words corresponding to
e for a city in Tartary, which the transcriber transformed into

From Siam comes lac, benzoin, brazil,[2] lead, tin, silver, gold,
ivory, cassia fistula; they bring vessels of cast copper and gold, ruby
and diamond rings; they bring a large quantity of cheap, coarse
Siamese cloth for the poor people.

They say that the chief merchandise they take from Malacca to
Siam are the male and female slaves, which they take in quantities,
white sandalwood, pepper, quicksilver, vermilion, opium, *azernefe*
[possibly aloeswood], cloves, mace, nutmeg, wide and narrow
muslins, and Kling cloths in the fashion of Siam, camlets, rosewater,
carpets, brocades from Cambay, white cowries, wax, Borneo camphor, pachak which are roots like dry rampion, gall-nuts, and the
merchandise they bring from China every year is also of value there.

The Siamese have not traded in Malacca for twenty-two years.
They had a difference because the kings of Malacca owed allegiance
to the kings of Siam, because they say that Malacca belongs to the
land of Siam—They say that it is theirs and that twenty-two years
ago this king lost Malacca, which rose up against this subjection.
They also say that Pahang rose against Siam in the same way, and
that, on account of the relationship between them, the kings of
Malacca favoured the people of Pahang against the Siamese, and
that this was also a reason for their disagreement.

They also say that it was about the tin districts which are on
the Kedah side, and which were originally under Kedah, and were
taken over by Malacca; and they quarrelled for all these reasons,
and they say that the chief reason was the revolt against subjection.
After this the Siamese sailed against Malacca, and the Siamese were
routed by the Malays, and [they say] that the *Lasamane* was the
captain—who has therefore been held in great honour ever since.

The Siamese trade in China—six or seven junks a year. They
trade with Sunda and Palembang (*Palimbaão*) and other islands.
They trade with Cambodia and *Champa* and Cochin China
(*Cauçhy*), and with Burma (*Brema*) and *Jangoma*[3] on the main
land, when they are at peace.

On the Tenasserim side Siam also trades with Pase, Pedir, with
Kedah, with Pegu, with Bengal; and the Gujaratees come to its

[2] Brazil-wood or sappan-wood.
[3] CAUÇHY, *Cauchij* or *Cauchy Chyna*—Cochin China, called by the Malays
Kuchi, whence the Portuguese *Cauchi* and *Cochinchina*. BREMA—Burma. Mentioned by other sixteenth-century Portuguese writers as *Berma*. JANGOMA—Mentioned by several sixteenth-century Portuguese writers. The town and state of
Siamese Laos, called by the Burmese *Zimmé*, by the Siamese *Xieng-mai* or
Kiang-mai, &c.

port every year. They trade richly outside and liberally inside the country, but they are great tyrants. . . .

China

They affirm that all those who take merchandise from Canton to the islands make a profit of three, four or five in every ten, and the Chinese have this custom so that the land shall not be taken from them, as well as in order to receive the dues on the merchandise exported as well as imported; and the chief [reason] is for fear lest the city be taken from them, because they say that the city of Canton is a rich one, and corsairs often come up to it. *Hi Taão,*[4] one of the chief people, is captain of this city, and there is a captain every year by the king's decree, and he cannot remain [in office] longer. There is another sea-captain almost like the land one, with separate jurisdiction. Both are changed yearly.

They say that the Chinese made this law about not being able to go to Canton for fear of the Javanese and Malays, for it is certain that one of these people's junks would rout twenty Chinese junks. They say that China has more than a thousand junks, and each of them trades where it sees fit; but the people are weak, and such is their fear of Malays and Javanese that it is quite certain that one [of our] ship[s] of four hundred tons could depopulate Canton, and this depopulation would bring great loss to China.

Not to rob any country of its glory, it certainly seems that China is an important, good and very wealthy country, and the Governor of Malacca would not need as much force as they say in order to bring it under our rule, because the people are very weak and easy to overcome. And the principal people who have often been there affirm that with ten ships the Governor of India who took Malacca could take the whole of China along the sea-coast. And China is twenty days' sail distant for our ships. They leave here at the end of June for a good voyage, and with a monsoon wind they can go in fifteen days. From China they have recently begun sailing to Borneo (*Burney*), and they say that they go there in fifteen days, and that this must have been for the last fifteen years.

The chief merchandise is pepper—of which they [the Chinese] will buy ten junk-loads a year if as many go there—cloves, a little nutmeg, a little more pachak, catcchu; they will buy a great deal of incense, elephants' tusks, tin, apothecary's lignaloes; they buy a great deal of Borneo camphor, red beads, white sandalwood, brazil, infinite quantities of the black wood that grows in Singapore

[4] *Hi Taão,* i.e., the Hai-tao-fu-shih, or Vice Commissioner of Maritime Affairs.

(*Syngapura*); they buy a great ...
scarlet camlets, coloured woollen ...
little account of all the rest.

The said junks from Malacca ...
Tumon, twenty or thirty leagues ...
are near the land of Nan-t'ou, a ...
land. Those from Malacca anchor ...
those from Siam in the port of *H* ...
nearer to China than the Siamese ...
rather than to the other.

As soon as the lord of Nan-t' ...
sends word to Canton that junk ...
the valuers from Canton go out ...
ceive their dues; they bring jus ...
is required: the country is pret ...
so well do they know of you th ...
them. . . . [This means that t ...
formed about the goods desirec ...
to the exchange exactly the rigl ...

The chief merchandise from ...
quantities, and loose coloured ...
colours, damask chequered *en* ...
other thin silk cloths called ...
colours; an abundance of seec ...
regular; they also have some b ...
as important a merchandise ir ...
silk as the chief merchandise— ...
of this, and certainly good, w ...
Pegu; apothecary's camphor ...
saltpetre, sulphur, copper, irc ...
—what I have seen up to t ...
arrived; they say it used to cc ...
copper and *fuseleira,* cast irc ...
these things, boxes, fans, ple ...
kinds, some of them very fin ...
chandise, and things of very ...
Portugal from Flanders, cou ...
come and I did not see much ...

[5] Perhaps some of the islands v ...
Lin Tin island towards the sea.

[6] *Xaas,* sash or shash, from the ...
worn twisted round the head as a ...

porcelains ...
are produ ...
from plac ...
your mon ...
there is n ...
than one ...
of China ...
Xamcy [p ...
it is good. ...

Salt is a ...
from Chin ...
junks whi ...
other plac ...
another ar ...

Beyond ...
Oquem [F ...
night by se ...
other races ...
business to ...
up to Cant ...
China.

They say ...
land of Chi ...
are very wh ...
warlike. An ...
Tartars (*tai* ...
horses shod ...
tends a lon ...
that in Gerr ...
by the Chir ...
route they c ...
by reason of ...

Java

They say ...
(*Maluco*) on ...
and that it h ...
and all the ...

[7] *Que se char* ...
is called'. It is ...
the Chinese na ...
q̃ se chama.

for a long time past until about a hundred years ago, when its power began to diminish until it came to its present state, as will be described below.

It is because of this power and great worth that Java had, and because it navigated to many places and very far away—for they affirm that it navigated to Aden and that its chief trade was in *Bonuaquelim,* Bengal and Pase [in Sumatra]—that it had the whole | of the trade at that time. All the navigators were heathens, so that it thus gathered together such great merchants with so much trade along its sea coasts, that nowhere else so large and so rich was known. Some of them were Chinese, some Arabs, Parsees, Gujaratees, Bengalees and of many other nationalities, and they flourished so greatly that Mohammed and his followers determined to introduce their doctrines in the sea-coasts of Java [together] with merchandise.

The island of Java is a large country, four hundred leagues round, beginning at Chi Manuk and going along the Blambangan side and turning along the other side to the other end. We will not speak of the sea-coast now, but only of the hinterland. It is well shaded country, not marshy but of the same type as Portugal, and very healthy.

The king of Java is a heathen; he is called *Batara Vojyaya.*[8] These kings of Java have a fantastic idea: they say that their nobility has no equal. The Javanese heathen lords are tall and handsome; they are lavishly adorned about their person, and have richly caparisoned horses. They use krises, swords, and lances of many kinds, all inlaid with gold. They are great hunters and horsemen —stirrups all inlaid with gold, inlaid saddles, such as are not to be found anywhere else in the world. The Javanese lords are so noble and exalted that there is certainly no nation to compare with them over a wide area in these parts. They have their head shorn—half tonsured—as a mark of beauty, and they always run their hands over their hair from the forehead upwards and not as we do, and they are very proud of this.

The lords of Java are revered like gods, with great respect and deep reverence. The land of Java is thickly peopled in the interior, with many cities, and very large ones, including the great city of *Dayo* where the king is in residence and where his court is. They

---

[8] *Batara Vojyaya,* or *Batara Vigiaja* as spelt farther on, corresponds to Batara Browijaya. *Browijaya* was one of the titles assumed by the sovereigns of Majapahit, the last Hindu kingdom of Java before the advent of Mohammedanism in the island. At the end of the thirteenth century the Browijaya assumed also the title of Batara, from the Sanskrit *Avatara,* the incarnation.

say that the people who frequent the court are without number. The kings do not show themselves to the people except once or twice in the year. They stay in their palace, like the kings of Cochin in the cave (?), and there they are with all the pleasures and with feasts, with great quantities of wives and concubines. They say that the king of Java has a thousand eunuchs to wait on these women, and these eunuchs are dressed like women and wear their hair dressed in the form of diadems.

And because the Javanese, trusting in themselves and given to this life, have lost a great part of their lands, the kings do not command, nor are they taken into account, but only the viceroy and chief captain, which each of them has; and the one who is ruling now in Java is *Guste Pate*,[9] his viceroy and his chief captain. This man is known and honoured like the [real] king. All the lords of Java obey him. Him they honour. This governor commands in every thing; he holds the king of Java in his hands; he orders him to be given food. The king has no voice in any thing, nor is he of any importance. Do not make a gesture towards a Javanese from the navel upwards, nor make as if to touch its head; they kill for this. . . .

The land of Java has only heathen [merchandise]: infinite quantities of rice of four or five kinds, and very white, better than that anywhere else; it has oxen, cows, sheep, goats, buffaloes without number, pigs certainly—the whole island is full [of them]. It has many deer of great size, many fruits, much fish along the sea coast. It is a land with beautiful air, it has very good water; it has high mountain ranges, great plains, valleys—a country like ours. The people are very sleek and splendid, without blemish, with strong bodies, such as the said country demands. They are not black men, but rather white than black; and just as we stroke hair downwards they do it in the opposite way for elegance—this is not very appropriate for this chapter. Java also has delicious wines of its own kind, and many oils; it has no butter nor cheese; they do not know how to make it.

Java has a goodly quantity of gold, eight and eight and a half *mates* proof; it has many topazes; it has cubeb, up to thirty bahars a year, and there is none anywhere else; it has long pepper; it has tamarinds, [enough] to load a thousand ships. There is very good cassia fistola in the jungles; there is cardamon, not much, rice,

---

[9] *Guste* was an honorary title given to a high personage, such as a regent or prince of the blood.

which is the chief merchandise, vegetables, slaves. For merchandise they have countless Javanese cloths, which they take to Malacca to sell. There is also a topaz mine in Java. They have enough copper and *fruseleira* bells for the needs of these parts. It is a great merchandise. . . .

The Moluccas

The chief island of all the five [Moluccas] is the island of Ternate. The king is a Mohammedan. He is called Sultan *Bem Acorala*.[10] They say he is a good man. His island produces at least a hundred and fifty bahars of cloves every year. Two or three ships can anchor in the port of this island; this is a good village. This king has some foreign merchants in his country. They say that the island must contain up to two thousand men, and up to two hundred will be Mohammedans. This king is powerful among his neighbours. His country is abundant in foodstuffs from the land, although many foodstuffs come to the Molucca kings from other islands, as will be told later. Only the king of Ternate is called Sultan; the others are called Raja. He is at war with his father-in-law, *Raja Almançor*,[11] king of the island of Tidore. He has as many as a hundred *paraos* [war canoes]. The island must be six leagues round. There is a mountain in the middle of this island, which yields a great deal of sulphur, which burns in great quantities.[12] This king has half the island of Motir (*Motei*) for his own, whence he gets many foodstuffs. [The people of] Ternate are more tractable than those in any of the other [islands], although another has a better port, and more trade because of it. They say that this king dispenses justice. He keeps his people obedient. He says he would be glad to see Christian priests, because if our faith seemed to him good he would forsake his sect and turn Christian. . . . The people of Ternate are knights among those of the Moluccas. They are men who drink wines of their kind. Ternate has good water. It is a healthy country with good air. The king of Ternate has four hundred women within his doors, all daughters of men of standing; he has many daughters by them. When the king goes to

[10] Barros says that 'the name of this kind of Ternate (who helped Serrão) was *Cachil Boleise*, a man of great age and much prudence, whom the Moors held almost for a prophet in what he said'.

[11] Barros refers extensively to *Almançor*, king of Tidore, and his quarrels with the Portuguese. Pigafetta calls him *raia sultan Manzor*.

[12] Actually Ternate island, eight miles long from north to south, and six miles broad, is composed almost exclusively of a conical volcano, 5184 feet (1580 m) in height, which has been in a state of constant activity for more than 300 years.

war he rallies forth with a crown of gold, and his sons wear them also as a mark of dignity. These crowns are of moderate value.

The country produces cloves. A great deal of iron comes from outside, from the islands of Banggai (*Bemgaia*),[13] iron axes, choppers, swords, knives. Gold comes from other islands. It has some little ivory; it has coarse native cloth. A great many parrots come from the islands of Morotai (*Mor*),[14] and the white parrots come from Ceram. . . .

Cloves have six crops a year; others say that there are cloves all the year round, but that at six periods in the year there are more. After flowering it turns green and then it turns red; then they gather it, some by hand and some beaten down with a pole, and red as it is they spread it out on mats to dry, and it turns black. They are small trees. Cloves grow like myrtle berries, a great many heads grow together. All this fruit is in the hands of the natives, and it all comes through their hands to the seacoast. . . .

Do not say that the navigation from Malacca to the Moluccas is dangerous, for it is a good route and convenient for our ships, and with monsoon winds you can sail to Banda or Amboina in a month, and from there to the Moluccas in a day or two. Our well-equipped ships will not linger in Amboina; they must go on to the Moluccas, especially anyone who has been able to learn and investigate how to come from Portugal to the Moluccas in such a short time; anyone will be able, as is known, when his turn comes and if he works —anyone who is zealous that things should be accomplished in the service of the King our lord—to make the journey of the Moluccas not by way of the coast of Java, but by Singapore, and from Singapore to Borneo and from Borneo to the island of Buton (*Butum*)[15] and then to the Moluccas. Anyone who has sailed to the Moluccas has always found this a very good way, in a monsoon, and quick. . . .

Malacca

Finally, in the port of Malacca very often eighty-four languages have been found spoken, every one distinct, as the inhabitants of

[13] Banggai Island is one of the more important in the Banggai archipelago, which lies 300 miles southwest of Ternate, off Banggai peninsula, on the east coast of central Celebes.

[14] Morotai or Morti island lies thirteen miles east of the northeastern point of Gillolo, with the small Rau island and some islets close by.

[15] Buton island appears like a prolongation of the southeastern peninsula of Celebes. Banda lies due east of the north part of Buton.

Malacca affirm; and this in Malacca alone, because in the archipelago which begins at Singapore and Karimun up to the Moluccas, there are forty known languages, for the islands are countless.

Because those from Cairo and Mecca and Aden cannot reach Malacca in a single monsoon, as well as the Parsees and those from Ormuz, and *Rumes,* Turks and similar peoples such as Armenians, at their own time they go to the kingdom of Gujarat, bringing large quantities of valuable merchandise; and they go to the kingdom of Gujarat to take up their companies in the said ships of that land, and they take the said companies in large numbers. They also take from the said kingdoms to Cambay, merchandise of value in Gujarat, from which they make much profit. Those from Cairo take their merchandise to Tor, and from Tor to Jidda, and from Jidda to Aden, and from Aden to Cambay, where they sell in the land things which are valued there, and the others they bring to Malacca, sharing as aforesaid.

Those from Cairo bring the merchandise brought by the galleasses of Venice, to wit, many arms, scarlet-in-grain, coloured woollen cloths, coral, copper, quicksilver, vermilion, nails, silver, glass and other beads, and golden glassware.

Those from Mecca bring a great quantity of opium, rosewater and such like merchandise, and much liquid storax.

Those from Aden bring to Gujarat a great quantity of opium, raisins, madder, indigo, rosewater, silver, seed-pearls, and other dyes, which are of value in Cambay.

In these companies go Parsees, Turks, Turkomans and Armenians, and they come and take up their companies for their cargo in Gujarat, and from there they embark in March and sail direct for Malacca; and on the return journey they call at the Maldive Islands.

Four ships come every year from Gujarat to Malacca. The merchandise of each ship is worth fifteen, twenty, or thirty thousand *cruzados,* nothing less than fifteen thousand. And from the city of Cambay one ship comes every year; this is worth seventy or eighty thousand *cruzados,* without any doubt.

The merchandise they bring is cloths of thirty kinds, which are of value in these parts; they also bring pachak, which is a root like rampion, and catechu, which looks like earth; they bring rosewater and opium; from Cambay and Aden they bring seeds, grains, tapestries and much incense; they bring forty kinds of merchandise. The kingdom of Cambay and that of Deccan as far as Honawar are called First India, and so each of these kings calls himself in his titles 'King of India.' They are both powerful, with large forces of horse and foot. For the last 300 years these two kingdoms have had Moorish kings. The kingdom of Cambay is superior to that of Deccan in everything.

The principal merchandise brought back is cloves, mace, nutmeg, sandalwood, seed-pearls, some porcelain, a little musk; they carry enormous quantities of apothecary's lignaloes, and finally some benzoin, for they load up with spices, and of the rest they take a moderate amount. And besides they take gold, enormous quantities of white silk, tin, much white damask—they take great pains to get this—coloured silks, birds from Banda for plumes for the *Rumes,* Turks and Arabs, which are much prized there. These have the main Malacca trade. They pay in dues six per cent; and if they will have their ships assessed by valuers, they pay on their valuation. This is the custom with the Gujaratees, in order to avoid extortions by the mandarins; for besides the six per cent, they pay the *Bemdara, Lasamane, Tumunguo* and *Xabamdar*[16] one cloth per hundred, and each one according to who he is, which the merchants regard as a great oppression, and therefore they have the ship valued; at the lowest a Gujarat ship is valued at seven *cates* of *timas,* which is twenty-one-thousand *cruzados,* and on this they pay at the rate of six per cent.

Those from Chaul, Dabhol and Goa come and take up their companies in Bengal, and from there they come to Malacca; and they also take them up at Calicut. . . .

The Malabars come to Pulicat to take their companies. They bring merchandise from Gujarat, and those from Choromandel bring coarse Kling cloth. There come every year to Malacca three or four ships, each one must be worth twelve to fifteen thousand *cruzados;* and from Pulicat come one or two ships, each worth eighty or ninety thousand *cruzados,* or a junk worth no less. They bring thirty kinds of cloths, rich cloths of great value. They pay in Malacca six per cent. These Klings have all the merchandise and more of the Malacca trade than any other nation. . . .

It is an old custom in Malacca that as soon as the merchants arrive they unload their cargo and pay their dues or presents, as will be said. Ten or twenty merchants gathered together with the owner of the said merchandise and bid for it, and by the said merchants the price was fixed and divided amongst them all in proportion. And because time was short and the merchandise considerable, the merchants were cleared, and then those of Malacca took the merchandise to their ships and sold them at their pleasure; from

---

[16] Titles of Malay officials.

which the traders received their settlement and gains, and the local merchants made their profits. And through this custom the land lived in an orderly way, and they carried on their business. And that was done thus orderly, so that they did not favour the merchant from the ship, nor did he go away displeased; for the law and the prices of merchandise in Malacca are well known.

The entire East does not pay dues on merchandise, but only presents to the king and to the persons mentioned above—[the entire East,] to wit, Pahang and all the places as far as China, all the islands, Java, Banda, Moluccas, Palembang, and all [places] in the island of Sumatra. The presents are a reasonable amount, something like dues. There were taxing officials who made the estimation. This was the general custom, but the presents from China were larger than from all other parts. And these presents amount to a great deal because the number of sea-traders who paid presents is considerable. And if they sold junks in Malacca, the dues paid were two or three *tundaias* of gold per hull; and this goes to the king of Malacca. And afterwards [that is, after the capture of Malacca] it was decreed that on each 300 *cruzados* 15 should be paid in dues, and this the *xabandares* of the different nations collected for the king. All provisions pay presents and not dues.

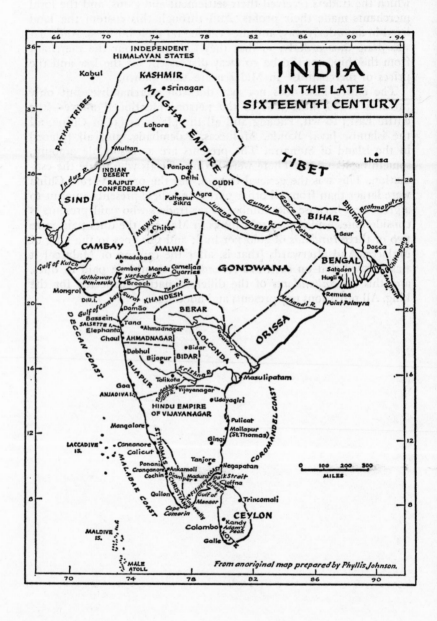

THE GOAN PRIESTHOOD

while the nobles re-lived their adventures and vice, and the petty merchants made their profits that cornered his riches; the best

INDEPENDENT
HIMALAYAN STATES

INDIA
IN THE LATE
SIXTEENTH CENTURY

Kabul

KASHMIR
Srinagar

PATHAN TRIBES

MUGHAL EMPIRE

Lahore

TIBET

Lhasa

Multan

INDIAN
DESERT
RAJPUT
CONFEDERACY

Panipat
Delhi
OUDH

BHUTAN

SIND

MEWAR
Fathepur
Sikra
Agra

Chitor

Gumti R.

Gogra R.

BIHAR

Brahmaputra

Patna

CAMBAY

MALWA

Ahmadabad
Cambay
Mandu
Carnelian
Quarries

GONDWANA

Gaur

BENGAL

Dacca

Gulf of Kutch

Kathiawar
Peninsula

Narbada R.
Broach

Satgdon
Hugli

Chittagong

Mongrol

DIU I.

Surat

Tapti R.

KHANDESH

BERAR

Mahandi R.

Remuna
Point Palmyra

Sundarbans

Gulf of Cambay
Bassein
SALSETTE I.
Elephanta

Damão
Tana
Ahmadnagar

Godavari R.

ORISSA

DECCAN COAST

Chaul

AHMADNAGAR

GOLCONDA

Dobhul

Bijapur

Bidar

BIDAR

Krishna R.

Masulipatam

BIJAPUR

Talikota

Goa

ANJADIVA I.

Vijayanagar

CORAMANDEL COAST

Uddayagiri

Mangalore

HINDU EMPIRE
OF VIJAYANAGAR

Pulicat

Mailapur
(St.Thomas)

LACCADIVE
IS.

Cannanore
Calicut

Gingi

ST. THOMAS

Tanjore
Negapatan

Penani
Cranganore
Cochin

Ankamali
Dampier
Madura

Palk Strait
Jaffna

Gulf of
Manaar

Trincomali

Quilon

Cape
Comorin

CEYLON

MALDIVE
IS.

Kandy
Adam's
Peak

Colombo

KOTE

Galle

MALE
ATOLL

From an original map prepared by Phyllis Johnson.

II / INDIA

INTRODUCTION

The following readings from European and Indian sources shed
light on the prevailing political, economic, social, and religious life
of sixteenth-century India. The Indian people, except for the Muslims, have traditionally displayed little interest in historical studies,
and have preserved no comprehensive native record of the past.
Consequently the accounts of foreign observers contribute significantly to the existing fund of knowledge about the subcontinent.
The Muslim sources on India, which will be treated in another
volume of this series, are not included in these selections. We have
limited ourselves to those territories, historical periods, and topics
in India's complicated history that are best described in extant
Hindu and European writings of the sixteenth century. Although
the omissions are inevitably numerous, the following sections show
that India, even though politically fragmented, possessed great
states, brilliant cultural centers, and dynamic religious movements
of its own when the Europeans first arrived.

2 / THE HINDU EMPIRE OF VIJAYANAGAR

*Several comparatively brief histories of the royal houses of Vijay-
anagar, such as the anonymous* Rāyavācakam *(see below) composed early in the seventeenth century, have come down to us. Indian collections of saints' lives, such as those* Krishnādēvarāya *drew
on for characterization of the heroes in his* Āmuktamālyadā *(see below), must also be considered source materials, even though it is*

33

difficult to separate the factual from the miraculous in those accounts. A court-oriented literature in the Telugu language likewise helps to keep the record straight in the history of Vijayanagar. Leading Hindu authors and scholars, as well as kings with a literary bent, made it a practice to add short histories of the reigning family as dedicatory introductions to poems, drama, and works of music. An oral tradition, which paralleled the written in its laudatory tone of the court, was carried on by succeeding generations of royal and noble servitors. And as time passed, some of these oral histories were written down in whole or in part. Numerous inscriptions recording the offerings made by kings and high officials to temples and Brahmans survive on copper and stone. Most broadly inclusive of all native source materials are the village registers that have been preserved, for they provide insights into the political, economic, social, and religious conditions of the ordinary people. In their early portions legend predominates, but as the era of Vijayanagar is approached the village records yield valuable factual data.

The European writers on India, from the Greeks to the British, make many additions to the other sources of Indian history, and especially contribute to precision in dating. On Vijayanagar specifically, they are very useful indeed. Nikitin, the Russian traveler of the later fifteenth century, covered Vijayanagar in his rounds, as did the Italian, Ludovico Varthema, in the early sixteenth century. With the surveys of Duarte Barbosa and Tomé Pires, the Portuguese began to show an interest in the Hindu empire; in time Italians, English, Dutch, French, and Germans all turned their pens to describing in prose and poetry their observations or fantasies about India north and south.

Social Life and Customs at the Capital

Domingo Paes, a Portuguese merchant who visited Vijayanagar around 1520, prepared and sent to Portugal a description of those things that most impressed him in the Hindu empire. The following excerpt from his narrative concentrates on the physical landscape, temple architecture, the ruler, and a Hindu religious festival which Paes witnessed. Navatra, the fast and festival he describes, lasted for nine days and nights, each day of the fasting period being sacred to a manifestation of the mother goddess Durga. On the afternoon of the last day a thanksgiving sacrifice was performed in commemoration of Rāma's triumph over the fiend Rāvan. It will be noticed that in general the accounts of European visitors like

*Paes describe Indian life only superficially, for the observers were
severely handicapped by their own prejudices and preconceptions
and by their ignorance of the native languages and traditions.*

Of the Things Which I Saw and Contrived
to Learn Concerning the Kingdom of
Narsimga,[1] Etc.

On leaving India[2] to travel towards the kingdom of Narsymga
from the sea-coast, you have (first) to pass a range of hills (*serra*),
the boundary of the said kingdom and of those territories which
are by the sea. This *serra* runs along the whole of the coast of India,
and has passes by which people enter the interior; for all the rest
of the range is very rocky and is filled with thick forest. The said
kingdom has many places on the coast of India; they are seaports
with which we are at peace, and in some of them we have factories,
namely, Amcola, Mirgeo, Honor, Batecalla, Mamgalor, Bracalor,
and Bacanor. And as soon as we are above this *serra* we have a plain
country in which there are no more ranges of hills, but only a few
mountains, and these small ones; for all the rest is like the plains of
Santarem.[3]

It [Vijayanagar] is a country sparsely wooded except along this
serra on the east,[4] but in places you walk for two or three leagues under groves of trees; and behind cities and towns and villages they
have plantations of mangoes, and jack-fruit trees, and tamarinds and
other very large trees, which form resting-places where merchants
halt with their merchandise. I saw in the city of Recalem[5] a tree
under which we lodged three hundred and twenty horses, standing
in order as in their stables, and all over the country you may see
many small trees. These dominions are very well cultivated and
very fertile, and are provided with quantities of cattle, such as
cows, buffaloes, and sheep; also of birds, both those belonging to
the hills and those reared at home, and this in greater abundance
than in our tracts. The land has plenty of rice and Indian-corn,

"Narrative of Domingo Paes." From *A Forgotten Empire (Vijayanagar)*, ed. and
trans. Robert Sewell (London: Swann Sonnenschein, 1900), pp. 236-43, 245-47,
262-63, 265-75.

[1] The "kingdom of Narsinga" is the name often given by the Portuguese and
others to Vijayanagar. This spelling, and other variants in the text, all refer to
Vijayanagar.

[2] The term here is limited to the small territory of Portuguese India immediately round the city of Goa.

[3] In Portugal.

[4] That is, on the east of Portuguese India, west of the territory of Vijayanagar.

[5] Unidentified. The great tree was of course a banyan.

grains, beans, and other kinds of crops which are not sown in our parts; also an infinity of cotton. Of the grains there is a great quantity, because, besides being used as food for men, it is also used for horses, since there is no other kind of barley; and this country has also much wheat, and that good. The whole country is thickly populated with cities and towns and villages; the king allows them to be surrounded only with earthen walls for fear of their becoming too strong. But if a city is situated at the extremity of his territory he gives his consent to its having stone walls, but never the towns; so that they may make fortresses of the cities but not of the towns.

And because this country is all flat, the winds blow here more than in other parts. The oil which it produces comes from seeds sown and afterwards reaped, and they obtain it by means of machines which they make. This country wants water because it is very great and has few streams; they make lakes in which water collects when it rains, and thereby they maintain themselves. . . . The water in these lakes is for the most part muddy, especially in those where there are no springs, and the reason why it is so muddy is because of the strong wind and the dust that is in this country, which never allows the water to be clear; and also because of the numbers of cattle, buffaloes, cows, oxen, and other small cattle that drink in them. For you must know that in this land they do not slaughter oxen or cows; the oxen are beasts of burden and are like sumpter-mules; these carry all their goods. They worship the cows, and have them in their pagodas made in stone, and also bulls; they have many bulls that they present to these pagodas, and these bulls go about the city without any one causing them any harm or loss. . . .

You must know that this kingdom of Narsymga has three hundred *graos* of coast, each *grao* being a league, along the hill-range (*serra*) of which I have spoken, until you arrive at Ballagate and Charamãodel,[6] which belong to this kingdom; and in breadth it is one hundred and sixty-four *graos;* each large *grao* measures two of our leagues, so that it has six hundred leagues of coast, and across it three hundred and forty-eight leagues . . . across from Batacalla to the kingdom of Orya.[7]

And this kingdom marches with [borders] all the territory of Bengal, and on the other side with the kingdom of Orya, which is

---

[6] Coromandel. This name was applied by the Portuguese to the Eastern Tamil and Southern Telugu countries.

[7] Orissa.

to the east, and on the other side to the north with the kingdom of Dakhan, belonging to which are the lands which the Ydallcão[8] has, and Ozemelluco.[9] Goa is at war with this Ydallcão, because that city was his, and we [the Portuguese] have taken it from him. . . .

[The city] Darcha[10] has a pagoda [temple], which is the monument I speak of, so beautiful that another as good of its kind could not be found within a great distance. You must know that it is a round temple made of a single stone, the gateway all in the manner of joiners' work, with every art of perspective. . . . It has three entrance gates, which gates are very large and beautiful, and the entrance from one of these sides, being towards the east and facing the door of the pagoda, has some structures like verandahs, small and low, where sit some *Jogis;*[11] and inside this enclosure, which has other little pagodas of a reddish colour, there is a stone like the mast of a ship, with its pedestal four-sided, and from thence to the top eight-sided, standing in the open air. I was not astonished at it, because I have seen the needle of St. Peter's at Rome, which is as high, or more.[12]

These pagodas are buildings in which they pray and have their idols; the idols are of many sorts, namely, figures of men and women, of bulls, and apes, while others have nothing but a round stone which they worship. In this temple of Darcha is an idol in the figure of a man as to his body, and the face is that of an elephant with trunk and tusks,[13] and with three arms on each side and six hands, of which arms they say that already four are gone, and when all fall then the world will be destroyed; they are full of belief that this will be, and hold it as a prophecy. They feed the idol every day, for they say that he eats; and when he eats women dance before him who belong to that pagoda, and they give him food and all that is necessary, and all girls born of these women belong to the temple. These women are of loose character, and live in the best streets that there are in the city; it is the same in all their cities, their streets have the best rows of houses. They are very much esteemed, and are classed amongst those honoured ones who are the mistresses of the captains; any respectable man may go to their houses without any blame attaching thereto. . . .

[8] The Âdil Khân, Sultan of Bîjapûr.
[9] For Nizâm-ul-Mulkh, or the Nizâm Shâh, the Sultan of Ahmadnagar.
[10] The spelling of this name in the original is very doubtful. It may refer to Dhárwár.
[11] *Yogis,* Hindu ascetics.
[12] This probably refers to the Egyptian obelisk at St. Peter's.
[13] Evidently the god *Ganesa.*

Afterwards, going from this city of Darcha towards the city of Bisnaga,[14] which is eighteen leagues distant, and is the capital of all the kingdom of Narsymga, where the king always resides, you have many cities and walled villages; and two leagues before you arrive at the city of Bisnaga you have a very lofty *serra* which has passes by which you enter the city. These are called "gates" *(portas)*. You must enter by these, for you will have no means of entrance except by them. This range of hills surrounds the city with a circle of twenty-four leagues, and within this range there are others that encircle it closely. . . . Between all these enclosures are plains and valleys where rice is grown, and there are gardens with many orange-trees, limes, citrons, and radishes *(rabãos)*, and other kinds of garden produce as in Portugal, only not lettuces or cabbages. Between these hill-ranges are many lakes by which they irrigate the crops mentioned, and amongst all these ranges there are no forests or patches of brushwood, except very small ones, nor anything that is green. For these hills are the strangest ever seen, they are of a white stone piled one block over another in manner most singular, so that it seems as if they stood in the air and were not connected one with another; and the city is situated in the middle of these hills and is entirely surrounded by them. . . .

[Their] Brahmans are like friars with us, and they count them as holy men—I speak of the Brahman priests and the lettered men of the pagodas—because although the king has many Brahmans, they are officers of the towns and cities and belong to the government of them; others are merchants, and others live by their own property and cultivation, and the fruits which grow in their inherited grounds. Those who have charge of the temples are learned men, and eat nothing which suffers death, neither flesh nor fish, nor anything which makes broth red, for they say that it is blood. Some of the other Brahmans whom I mentioned, who seek to serve God, and to do penance, and to live a life like that of the priests, do not eat flesh or fish or any other thing that suffers death, but only vegetables[15] and butter and other things which they make of fruit[16] with their rice. They are all married, and have very beautiful wives; the wives are very retiring, and very seldom leave the

[14] "Bisnaga," the Portuguese rendering of *Vijayanagar,* the "city of victory." The spellings adopted by different writers have been endless.

[15] *Bredos,* "blites," an insipid kitchen vegetable. But as the word is not common, and as Brahmans make use of most vegetables, we have preferred the more general term.

[16] *Maçaas,* literally "apples."

house. The women are of light colour, and in the caste of these
Brahmans are the fairest men and women that there are in the
land. . . .

This new city that the king made bears the name of his wife for
love of whom he made it,[17] and the said city stands in a plain, and
round it the inhabitants make their gardens as the ground suits,
each one being separate. . . . Before you enter the place where the
king is there are two gates with many guards, who prevent any one
from entering except the captains and men who have business
there; and between these two gates is a very large court with its
verandahs round it, where these captains and other honoured
people wait till the king summons them to his presence.

This king [Krishnādēvarāya] is of medium height, and of fair
complexion and good figure, rather fat than thin; he has on his
face signs of small-pox. He is the most feared and perfect king that
could possibly be, cheerful of disposition and very merry; he is one
that seeks to honour foreigners, and receives them kindly, asking
about all their affairs whatever their condition may be. He is a
great ruler and a man of much justice, but subject to sudden fits of
rage, and this is his title—"Crisnarão Macaçāo,[18] king of kings,
lord of the greater lords of India, lord of the three seas and of the
land." He has this title[19] because he is by rank a greater lord than
any, by reason of what he possesses in (?) armies and territories, but
it seems that he has (in fact) nothing compared to what a man like
him ought to have, so gallant and perfect is he in all things. . . .

When the time of the principal festival arrives the king comes
from the new city to this city of Bisnaga, since it is the capital of
the kingdom and it is the custom there to make their feasts and to
assemble. For these feasts are summoned all the dancing-women of
the kingdom, in order that they should be present; and also the
captains and kings and great lords with all their retinues,—except
only those whom the king may have sent to make war. . . . These
feasts begin on the 12th of September, and they last nine days, and
take place at the king's palace. . . .

You must know that when it is morning the king comes to this
House of Victory, and betakes himself to that room where the idol
is with its Brahmans, and he performs his prayers and ceremonies.
. . . After the king has entered inside he comes out, and with him

[17] It was generally called Nâgalâpur.
[18] A mixture, apparently, of Mahâ, "great," and "Shâh."
[19] The passage that follows is not very clear in the original.

a Brahman who takes in his hand a basket full of white roses and approaches the king on the platform, and the king, taking three handfuls of these roses, throws them to the horses, and after he has thrown them he takes a basket of perfumes and acts towards them as though he would cense them; and when he has finished doing this he reaches towards the elephants and does the same to them. And when the king has finished this, the Brahman takes the basket and descends to the platform, and from thence puts those roses and other flowers on the heads of all the horses, and this done, returns to the king. Then the king goes again to where the idol is, and as soon as he is inside they lift the curtains[20] of the room, which are made like the purdahs of a tent, and the king seats himself there where these are, and they lift them all. Thence he witnesses the slaughter of twenty-four buffaloes and a hundred and fifty sheep, with which a sacrifice is made to that idol; you must know that they cut off the heads of these buffaloes and sheep at one blow with certain large sickles which are wielded by a man who has charge of this slaughter; they are so sure of hand that no blow misses. When they have finished the slaughter of these cattle the king goes out and goes to the other large buildings, on the platforms of which is a crowd of Brahmans, and as soon as the king ascends to where they stand they throw to the king ten or twelve roses—those (that is) who are nearest to him. Then he passes all along the top of the buildings, and as soon as he is at the end he takes the cap from his head, and after placing it on the ground turns back (to the place) where the idol is; here he lies extended on the ground. . . . And the king withdraws to the interior of his palace by that gate which I have already mentioned—that which stands between the two buildings that are in the arena (terreyro); the courtesans and bayadères[21] remain dancing in front of the temple and idol for a long time. This is what is done during the morning of each day of these nine days, with the ceremonies I have mentioned, and each day more splendid (than the last).

Now, returning to the feasts. At three o'clock in the afternoon every one comes to the palace. They do not admit every one at once (they allowed us to go into the open part that is between the gates), but there go inside only the wrestlers and dancing-women, and the elephants, which go with their trappings and decorations,

---

[20] *Paredes*, probably for "purdahs" (Persian, *parda*), curtains or screens. The Portuguese word means a "wall."

[21] *Molheres solteiras e baylhadeiras*, *i.e.* the dancing-girls of the temple and palace.

those that sit on them being armed with shields and javelins, and wearing quilted tunics. . . . Many other people are then at the entrance-gate opposite to the building, namely Brahmans, and the sons of the king's favourites, and their relations; all these are noble youths who serve before the king. . . .

Salvatinica,[22] who is the principal person that enters the building, supervises the whole, for he brought up the king and made him king, and so the king looks on him like a father. Whenever the king calls to him he addresses him as 'Lord (senhor) Salvatinica,' and all the captains and nobles of the realm make salaam to him. This Salvatinica stands inside the arena where the festivals go on, near one of the doors, and from there gives the word for the admission of all the things necessary for the festival.

After all this is done and arranged the king goes forth and seats himself on the daïs I have mentioned, where is the throne and the other things, and all those that are inside make their salaam to him. . . . As soon as the king is seated in his place he bids to sit with him three or four men who belong to his race, and who are themselves kings and the fathers of his wives; the principal of these is the king of Syrimgapatão and of all the territory bordering on Malabar, and this king is called Cumarvirya,[23] and he seats himself as far in front as the king on the other side of the daïs, the rest are behind. . . .

As soon as the king is seated, the captains who waited without make their entrance, each one by himself, attended by his chief people, and so on, all in order; they approach and make their salaams to the king, and then take their places in the pavilions which I have previously described. As soon as these nobles have finished entering, the captains of the troops approach with shields and spears, and afterwards the captains of the archers; these officers are all stationed on the ground around the arena in front of the elephants, and they constitute the king's guard, for into such a place no man may enter bearing arms, nor near to where the king is. As soon as these soldiers have all taken their places the women begin to dance, while some of them place themselves in the circular galleries that I have said were (erected) at their gate of entrance. Who can fitly describe to you the great riches these women carry on their persons?—collars of gold with so many diamonds and rubies and pearls, bracelets also on their arms and on their upper arms, girdles

---

[22] Sâluva Timma, the minister.

[23] The king of Seringapatam at this period was Bettâda Châma Râya, who ruled the Mysore country from 1513 to 1552.

below, and of necessity anklets on the feet. The marvel should be otherwise, namely that women of such a profession should obtain such wealth; but there are women among them who have lands that have been given to them, and litters, and so many maid-servants that one cannot number all their things. There is a woman in this city who is said to have a hundred thousand *pardaos*,[24] and I believe this from what I have seen of them.

Then the wrestlers begin their play. Their wrestling does not seem like ours, but there are blows (given), so severe as to break teeth, and put out eyes, and disfigure faces, so much so that here and there men are carried off speechless by their friends; they give one another fine falls too. They have their captains and judges, who are there to put each one on an equal footing in the field, and also to adjust the honours to him who wins. . . .

When these amusements are ended, they begin to throw up many rockets and many different sorts of fires, also castles that burn and fling out from themselves many bombs (*tiros*) and rockets.

When these fireworks are finished, there enter many triumphal cars [floats] which belong to the captains, some of them sent by those captains who are waging war in foreign parts; and they enter thus. The first belongs to Salvatinica, and they come in one after the other. Some of the cars appear covered with many rich cloths, having on them many devices of dancing-girls and other human figures; there are other cars having tiers one on top of another, and others all of one kind; and so in their order they pass to where the king is. When the cars have gone out they are immediately followed by many horses covered with trappings and cloths of very fine stuff of the king's colours, and with many roses and flowers on their heads and necks, and with their bridles all gilded; and in front of these horses goes a horse with two state-umbrellas of the king, and with grander decorations than the others, and one of the lesser equerries leads it by the bridle. . . .

After this is over you will see issuing from inside twenty-five or thirty female doorkeepers, with canes in their hands and whips on their shoulders; and then close to these come many eunuchs, and after these eunuchs come many women playing many trumpets and drums and pipes (but not like ours) and viols, and many other kinds of music, and behind these women will come some twenty women-porters, with canes in their hands all covered with silver, and close to them come women clothed in the following manner.

[24] A small gold coin, of which it is very difficult to assess the exact value.

They have very rich and fine silk cloths; on the head they wear high caps which they call *collães*,[25] and on these caps they wear flowers made of large pearls; collars on the neck with jewels of gold very richly set with many emeralds and diamonds and rubies and pearls; . . . They carry in their hands vessels of gold each as large as a small cask of water; inside these are some loops made of pearls fastened with wax, and inside all this a lighted lamp. They come in regular order one before the other, in all perhaps sixty women fair and young, from sixteen to twenty years of age. Who is he that could tell of the costliness and the value of what each of these women carries on her person? So great is the weight of the bracelets and gold and jewels carried by them that many of them cannot support them, and women accompany them assisting them by supporting their arms. In this manner and in this array they proceed three times round the horses, and at the end retire into the palace. . . .

When these women retire the horses also go, and then come the elephants, and after making their salaam they too retire. As soon as they are gone the king retires by a small door which is at the end of the building. Then the Brahmans go and take an idol, and carry it to the House of Victory, where is the room of cloth that I have spoken of; and the king at once comes from within, and goes to where the idol is, and offers his prayers and performs his ceremonies. Then they bring there more buffaloes and sheep, and kill them in the same way as before, and then come the professional women to dance. As soon as the slaughter of the buffaloes and sheep is over the king retires, and goes to his supper; for he fasts all these nine days, and (each day) they eat nothing until all is finished, and their hour for food is midnight. The bayadères remain dancing before the idol a long time after all this is done.

In this way are celebrated these festivals of nine days; on the last day there are slaughtered two hundred and fifty buffaloes and four thousand five hundred sheep.

The Coronation of Krishnādēvarāya in 1509

The Hindu sources on Indian history, as contrasted to Paes' narrative, rarely deal with economic affairs and social customs in terms that are easily comprehensible to Westerners. As a rule, they are concerned with ceremonies or great military victories and are often couched in language that we find difficult to follow. The following short description is a good example of one of the types of Hindu

[25] *Kullāyi* in Telugu. These women appear to have worn men's head-dresses.

writing from which the history of India must be reconstructed. It is written by an anonymous author of the early seventeenth century, and it describes in traditional fashion a coronation that took place a century before the author's time. Because of the time lapse, the author had to reconstruct his description of the ceremony on the basis of the oral tradition and from his own knowledge of how such ceremonies were performed in his own day. The description is nonetheless an important historical source because it records a story that had been kept alive orally and because it gives us a feeling for what the Hindus themselves regarded as memorable.

Vīra Narasimha told his *dalanāyakas* [nobles] that he had become old, and that they should make arrangements for crowning Kṛṣṇarāya king of the city and the kingdom, so that he might rule the state in his place. He also gave Kṛṣṇarāya his signet-ring at an auspicious moment.

Accordingly the ministers, captains, officials, noblemen and the men of learning who were at the court gave Kṛṣṇarāya a ceremonial bath at an auspicious moment and seated him upon a golden settle placed on a platform specially erected for the occasion. At their instance, he distributed the 'ten *dānas*,' 'the sixteen *mahā-dānas*,' and performed the *svarṇa-tulā*, the *rajata-tulā* and the *mauktika-tulā*.[1] Moreover, he also performed the *mērus*, made gift of one crore of cows, and established a thousand families. Then the Brahmans chanting the Vēdic *mantras* bathed him at an auspicious moment in the water brought from the four oceans and the sacred rivers such as the Gangā, Yamunā, Sarasvatī, Gōdāvarī, Narmadā, Sindhu, Kāvēri and Tāmraparṇī, while the musicians played on the eighteen kinds of musical instruments. Next, they bathed him also in a shower of gold coins and gems. The moisture was wiped off by means of a newly washed white cloth; and a finely kneaded paste of sandal, musk and aloe-wood was smeared upon his body. He then put on a garment of golden hue, and gave permission to his courtiers to retire to their respective residences.

The *Rāyavācakam*. From K. A. Nilakanta Sastri and N. Venkataramanayya, *Further Sources of Vijayanagara History: Translations and Summaries* (Madras: Madras University, 1946), III, 94-96. Reprinted by permission of K. A. Nilakanta Sastri and N. Venkataramanayya.

[1] *Tulā* means a balance. The king weighed himself against gold, silver and pearls which he distributed among the people.

The Rāya next dined in the company of his sons-in-law, sons, relations, friends, and followers, and having washed his hands in scented water, he performed the *ācamana*.[2] He put on the jingling sandals, and reciting the abridged Rāmāyaṇa, he walked a few steps. Then he seated himself on the carpet, and summoned to his presence the *daḷanāyakas*, Appāji and the other ministers.

The Political Maxims of Krishnādēvarāya

For some three hundred years Vijayanagar stood as a sometimes extensive but often disunited power, guarding what survived of Hindu culture in southern India after centuries of encroachment by foreigners and Muslims. Krishnādēvarāya, who ruled from 1509 to 1529, spent the first fifteen years of his reign leading a succession of campaigns against his foes to the northwest, northeast, and south. The only respite Krishnādēvarāya took from military campaigning was the luxury of patronizing the arts and scholarship and of making religious pilgrimages. Himself a poet in Telugu and reputedly the author of five works in Sanskrit, the Emperor attracted literary men from all over India to his court and rewarded them generously. The most distinguished of the savants he sponsored are referred to as "The Eight Elephants" of Telugu literature.

In his own composition in the vernacular, the Āmuktamālyadā, the Emperor claims to be inspired by Vishnu, who appears in the work. The story of the Āmuktamālyadā revolves around the lives of several saints of the Vaishnava sect of Hinduism. Krishnādēvarāya entwines a traditional story of two celebrated seers with that of a famous Brahman who had been redeemed from a worldly life to become a servant of Vishnu. One of the seers has been called "one of the supreme women mystics of the world"; her hymns or song offerings, as well as those composed by her foster-father (another prominent figure in the composition), are still chanted in Vaishnava temples as expressions of the profound love experienced by devotees longing for union with Vishnu. For artistic purposes, the Emperor intensifies his religious theme dramatically by making contemporaries of saints who actually lived many hundreds of years apart.

In addition to his religious fervor, Krishnādēvarāya shows intense concern for the science of polity (Daṇḍa Nīti). He himself listened

---

[2] "Sipping water three times before religious ceremonies or meals, or after meals, or the necessities of nature, repeating at the same time the 24 principal names of Viṣṇu."

daily to readings from the classics on Hindu political ethics, enjoyed questioning and testing his ministers on the subject, and discussed the duties of the model ruler in a part of his Āmuktamālyadā. Many treatises of advice, or "mirrors of the prince," have been composed by educators, philosophers, saints, bishops, and diplomats for the benefit of young rulers the world over. In the Western tradition works by Plato, Aristotle, Machiavelli, and Erasmus spring to mind most readily. The Meditations of Emperor Marcus Aurelius and the Basilicon Doron (Kingly Gift) (1599) of James I of England hold a special place in this genre of European literature because they contain political ideas set down by reigning monarchs. The maxims of Krishnādēvarāya, a near-contemporary of King James, occupy a respected place among the various "mirrors of the prince" in Eastern literature.

The following forty-two of eighty verses by Krishnādēvarāya on polity (civil order) consist of instructions put in the mouth of Yamunacharya, a Vaishnava poet-saint, to his son and heir-apparent to the throne of Pandya, a kingdom which dominated the Tamil country of south India during the thirteenth century. The verses treating the prince's duties comprise a quarter of the whole (including these among the following: 219, 238, 240-242, 252, 277, 280, 284); half the maxims stress his responsibilities regarding the care and treatment of ministers and subordinate officers (including these among the following: 208-209, 211-213, 215, 217, 227-228, 233, 235, 248, 254, 259, 269, 272), and Brahmans (207, 209, 211, 217, 255), and their rewards. Krishnādēvarāya's decided preference for Brahmans as counselors, administrators, and military leaders stands out strongly in these recommendations. Foreign relations (241, 248-249, 251, 255), the system of espionage necessary to the conduct of foreign affairs (238, 279), and the treatment of subdued enemies (235) constitute another important branch of his instructions. Economic affairs (236, 238, 242, 262) concern the king comparatively little. Traditionally, the primary duty of a king consisted in protecting his subjects and keeping evil elements under control. In view of this, the scant attention given in the maxims to the administration of justice (four citations, including 205) is somewhat surprising. Although the following English translation of the Telugu original is awkward, most of the maxims can be deciphered by careful reading.

The *Āmuktamālyadā*. From "Political Maxims of the Emperor-Poet Krishnadeva Raya," trans. A. Rangasvami Sarasvati, *Journal of Indian History*, IV: 3 (1926), 64-77. Reprinted by permission of the *Journal of Indian History* and the University of Kerala.

Āmuktamālyadā / Canto IV

v. 205. Be always intent upon protecting your subjects. Whenever you hear complaints from people in distress, hear them and redress their sufferings. Do not entrust your affairs to mean persons.

(The people of) a country wish the welfare of the king who seeks the progress and prosperity of the country. One should not think it is no serious matter. Will not God who is in the minds of all persons grant the united wishes of the Brahman and other subjects of a king?

v. 206.—It is essential that a king should be able to enforce his commands. . . .

v. 207.—Entrust your fortresses to such Brahmans (Generals) as you are best acquainted with. Do not keep them weak, but give them such strong forces that they can be devoid of fear from enemies.

v. 208.—You should not promote a subordinate in the beginning and then once more degrade him. Such men do not generally think of their original position, but only get angry. So, promoting your subordinates step by step according to their character, you should extract work from them.

v. 209.—Do not have the following as your servants even though they are Brahmans. One born of a mean family, one living in a Kīkaṭa (a Śabara village), one who is not learned, a coward, a liar, an Ātatāyin, one who is not afraid of ignominy, a foreigner and one devoid of *Dharma*.

v. 211.—If a Brahman who is a scholar, who is afraid of *Adharma*, who is well-versed in *Rājanīti* and who is between the ages of fifty and seventy, who is healthy in body, whose connection with the king has come down from previous generations and who is not conceited accepts the ministership under a king and looks after his business, would it take more than a day for the *Aṅgas* (constituents of royalty) of such a king to increase?

vv. 212 and 213.—In the absence of such a minister if a king is not contented with ruling himself to the best of his genius according to (the science of polity) and with the help of a strong army and a full treasury, and has recourse to a minister who is devoid of virtues, the minister would prove a source of trouble like the pearl of the size of a pumpkin and the king would ultimately find himself in the hands of that minister.

v. 215.—No business can be accomplished by money alone without the co-operation of many big officers. For having them in due subordination the following are essential, absence of greed, absence of cruelty and truthfulness.

v. 217.—Because a Brahman would stand to his post even in times of danger and would continue in service though reduced to becoming a subordinate to a Kshatriya or a Śūdra, it is always advisable for a king to make Brahmans as his officers.

v. 218.—Do not entrust the temples of your kingdom to an officer who is intent upon amassing wealth (anyhow), for he would, in his thirst for money divert the money of the temples to compensate for the losses sustained by his province. Such money is not at all proper to be spent on state business. So a separate officer should be appointed to administer them. If such an officer misappropriate the property of the temples he will alone suffer for it and the king would have no share of it.

v. 219.—A king should first establish his power in his territory either being in terms of affected friendship with his enemies or relying on his land- and water-defences (fortifications). After this without external fear, he should set about rooting out the internal enemies of his kingdom, just as a farmer first lays out the boundaries of his field and constructing fencing all round, softens the soil by digging up with the spade and removing the roots and stones in the ground.

v. 221.—It is always advisable to entrust the government over wild tribes inhabiting hills and forests to heroes who have fallen from great positions. It would not affect the king much whoever succeeds in the struggle between them.

v. 222.—If the people of the forest (wild tribes) multiply in any state the trouble to the king and his people would not be small. . . .

v. 227.—In the Council when one officer proposes a particular course another would object to it as unsuitable through mere spite of the former. The king should discover their individual motives and without denying the statement of either should close the council and then follow the course proposed by the first councillor, without spite.

v. 228.—Bad ministers, on observing enmity abroad, allow the insurgent elements within the state to sprout forth and, when the king finds himself in trouble, do not do things in a decisive manner, but making themselves indispensable and spreading their influence everywhere continue fearless.

v. 233.—Are there any real friends to a king except such as would think of his ruin when a morsel is taken off from their usual rewards?

Such being the case would it be meet for the king to dispense with their services? He should carry on the business of the state without (completely) confiding in any person and with mercy.

v. 235.—If a person thinks evil of you when you are in difficulties, do not think of destroying him after you succeed in the affair, but only destroy his great power and wealth. What can a serpent do after its sharp fangs are drawn? Even an open enemy will have faith in you if you show such mercy.

v. 236.—The extent of a state is the root cause of its prosperity. When a state is small in extent then both virtue (*Dharma*) and prosperity (*Artha*) will increase only when tanks and irrigation canals are constructed and favour is shown to the poor cultivators in the matter of taxation and services.

v. 238.—A king should divide his income into four parts, use one part for extensive benefactions and for enjoyment, two parts for the maintenance of a strong army, and one part to be added to the treasury; after arranging his income and expenditure thus he should be watching by means of his spies the movements of his enemies and the movements of his ministers and other people of his own party. He should destroy all thieves in his territory.

v. 240.—A king can find out three parts out of four of all the affairs of the state. He can find out the fourth part that has been concealed from him, through his favourites and friends. . . .

v. 241.—A king should have a watchful eye over his enemies both external and internal even while he is enjoying pleasure, like the owl on the top of the tree which sleeps with one eye and keeps watch with the other.

v. 242.—If a king through his partiality for letters gives large sums of money and villages to mendicant ascetics and those of matted hairs they may (as a result of his benefactions) swerve from their necessary discipline which would increase in the state evils such as famine, disease and infantile mortality. Therefore, in the case of such people, it is sufficient if the king shows *bhakti* (respect and devotion) towards them. The only evil that might then result is their suffering, but no sin would accrue to the sovereign. Be assured of this.

v. 245.—A king should improve the harbours of his country and so encourage its commerce that horses, elephants, precious gems, sandalwood, pearls and other articles are freely imported into his country. He should arrange that the foreign sailors who land in his country on account of storms, illness and exhaustion are looked after in a manner suitable to their nationalities. He should set his own favourites to look after the gardens, herds of cattle and mines of the state.

v. 248—Collecting money by oppressing the subjects, taking the counsel of worthless people, allowing one's territory to be annexed by others, an able king should see that these things exist only with his enemies. When his enemy king is suspicious of his own feudatories and when they are suffering from his oppression a king should encourage the latter and gratify them by presents of jewels and ornaments.

v. 249.—A king should destroy the fear from his internal enemies even by granting half of his whole kingdom to an enemy when the enemy sues for it and by thus establishing a firm and everlasting friendship with him. Is not the fear from an internal foe greater than the fear from a serpent?

v. 251.—A king should not put severe constraint on an enemy who is afraid of him and consequently does not join him, but should allow him to come of his [own] accord, and get captured like a fisherman who draws ashore a big fish which has been caught in his hook.

v. 252.—Cruel punishments, want of discrimination with regard to flimsy charges, pressing an enemy without giving him an opportunity to come to terms, ruining (plundering) a foreigner who goes to him after seeing the wrongs in other states, doing things so as to be plain to the enemy ministers, mixing much with the people knowing that they are not favourably disposed to him, looking with estrangement [at] men who can be relied upon, admitting too many into counsel as a result of their flattery, neglecting to punish a councillor who reveals the secret counsels, not looking about carefully for remedies when any strange mishap happens, not caring for (looking towards) worthy people, associating with bad people [and thus] getting addicted to the *vyasanas* (intense desires) and obstinacy. All these should never be with a king.

v. 254.—Kings should increase the jealousies among the lords and warriors under him. Then their actions good or bad, can never be concealed. In trying to get over each other and become famous they will not entertain any idea of treachery to the sovereign.

v. 255.—The king should not go personally anywhere against the enemy country. It is meet that he appoints one as his lord and sends him on the business. . . .

v. 258.—Make the merchants of distant foreign countries who import elephants and good horses attached to yourself by providing them with villages and decent dwellings in the city, by affording them daily audience, presents and allowing decent profits. Then those articles will never go to your enemies.

v. 259.—A king should freely converse in his court with the ambassadors from the kings of neighbouring states and speak to him about administration and war that understands the situation. He should so speak about administration and war that his followers may understand his point. What his counsellors say through attachment, the king should not take as offences.

v. 269.—False persons approach a king and by skilful flattery look to the fulfilment of their own purpose. They serve their masters when he is powerful and happy, but when he is in difficulties, desert him. A king should behave like a merchant in determining the relative worths of his servants.

v. 270.—A king should rule collecting round him people skilled in statecrafts, should investigate the mines yielding precious metals in his kingdom and extract the same, should levy taxes from his people moderately, should counteract the acts of his enemies by crushing them with force, should be friendly, should protect one and all of his subjects, should put an end to the mixing up of the castes among them, should always try to increase the merit of the Brahmans, should strengthen his fortresses and lessen the growth of the undesirable things and should be ever mindful of the purification (?) of his cities and thus strengthen himself and increase his longevity just as a man strengthens his own body and increases his longevity by consulting good doctors. . . .

v. 272.—A king's followers (subordinates) are of three classes, those who are favourable to him, those who are favourable as well as not favourable, and those who are unfavourable. . . .

v. 277.—The wife's attachment to her husband, the proper relations between men and women, the ascetic subduing his *indriyas* [senses], the lower castes showing deference to the higher, the servant looking carefully to the interests of the master, you should know that all these are brought about (ultimately) by the fear of the king's punishment.

v. 279.—A spy should be one who resides in your town (capital), should be conversant with languages, should be acquainted with the spies of other countries, should not have any special marks, and should be one who has got from the king more money than he expected. Others should never enter the profession.

v. 280.—A king should get the merit of severe fasting and subduing the body only by giving money and not by giving up the enjoyment derivable from the anointments, baths, feasts, smearings, clothes and flowers in the several seasons.

v. 284.—You should not think that ruling a kingdom is a sin and get embarrassed how to get rid of the sin. The scriptures do not ordain any impossible thing. Therefore you should rule the kingdom to the best of your ability.

v. 285.—Manu, Dhaṇḍadhara and others became known as addicted to *Dharma* only by finding out the mistakes of the subjects and punishing them. The anointed king who is equal to God and who is created by God (*Prajāpati*) in various forms for the purpose of ruling the subjects is known by various terms which are sanctioned by the Vēdas as *Virāṭ, Samrāṭ*, and should put up with the trouble and relieve the sufferings of the world. If he does not do this, the purpose of his creation is not fulfilled. . . .

3 / THE DECCAN AND GOA

The Portuguese lovingly called it "Goa the Golden" after they made it the capital of their Eastern conquests. Located midway between Surat in Cambay and Cochin on the Malabar coast, Goa commands a fine natural harbor at the confluence of two rivers. The port and the rich strip of coast it serves (known as the Konkan) had, according to legend, been recovered from the sea after Parashurama, an incarnation of Vishnu, drove the waters back with a single arrow shot.

Early in the fourteenth century, Muslim invaders captured the ancient Hindu city of Goa. Thereafter they engaged in a seesaw battle to hold Goa, and by 1370 were forced to yield suzerainty for a century of the Hindu state of Vijayanagar. Bijapur, one of the Islamic sultanates of the Deccan, gained control over the island when the Bahmani kingdom disintegrated late in the fifteenth century. At that time, Goa reportedly produced annual revenues of more than one million dollars, mostly from duties on trade.

The succession struggle that ensued when a minor became Shah of Bijapur in 1510 gave the Portuguese an opportunity to take their first parcel of Indian territory. Affonso de Albuquerque took advantage of Bijapur's internal crisis to advance Portuguese influence in India by taking a giant step northward from Cochin to Goa. His

Foral dos Usos e Costumes (Roll of the Subsidiary Rights and Customs) for the Villages of Goa, ca. 1526. From "The Villages of Goa in the Early Sixteenth Century," by B. H. Baden-Powell, *Journal of the Royal Asiatic Society* (1900), pp. 262-77. Reprinted by permission of the Royal Asiatic Society.

attack on Goa ultimately utilized twenty-eight vessels and 1700 men, not counting his Hindu allies. Once the city was in Portuguese hands, Albuquerque inaugurated a policy of conciliating the Hindu population and of dispossessing the Muslims ruthlessly. Twenty years later Goa became the administrative seat and military head-quarters of the Portuguese East and the commercial entrepôt with the most frequent and direct connections with western Europe. The Portuguese ruled Goa and its environs for 451 years, finally sur-rendering it to a resurgent India in 1961.

During the 1520's, six governors in quick succession supervised Portuguese affairs in India from their station in Cochin. Because of their short tenures of office, however, little continuity of policy was possible. A move toward a more enlightened colonial administration was made shortly after Lopo Vaz de Sampaio took office as governor in 1526 when he tried to place government finances on solid founda-tions, taking existing practices and conditions into account. He ordered the Portuguese administration in Goa to prepare a sum-mary of the accepted or customary rules for governing the thirty-one villages sprinkled over the islands and to determine traditional practices governing land tenure, inheritance, and taxation. On the basis of the facts and figures collected, a charter was prepared and a revenue assessment list was drawn up to accompany it. The Foral *dos usos e costumes that follows is, then, "the earliest known account of a local group of Indian villages written by a European observer."*

As in the pre-European past, taxes in Portuguese Goa were not levied on each citizen or household. Hereditary village headmen (Gancars) *were responsible for raising a specified sum annually. The burden of providing the annual levy was apportioned among the landholders according to the decisions of the headmen. The amount due the authorities was calculated arbitrarily, rather than on the basis of careful periodic land surveys. The Portuguese continued this policy, which gave authority to the village headmen. Originally, at least, the Portuguese were more interested in obtaining customs duties from Goa than revenue from agriculture.*

In the following translation of the Foral, *the various clauses of the charter of 1526 have been topically rearranged to increase their in-telligibility.*

Preamble

The Roll (*Foral*) purports to be granted to the 'Gancars' or village headmen, cultivators, and taxpayers, dwellers in, and [permanent] residents of, the [thirty-one] villages in the several islands that make up Goa. The facts, i.e. the amount of revenue, "the rights [of possession], 'usos' [subsidiary rights], and customs," are declared to have been recorded after inquiry, and by ascertaining what the people "paid to the kings and lords of the soil before it was ours." The figures of the Revenue Assessment were set down in a separate roll: the rights and customs are recorded in what follows.

I. The Village Headmen, Their Origin and Privileges

(Clause 1.) Every village has certain 'Gancars'; in some there are more, in others fewer, according to the custom of the village. The said word (Gancar) means governor, administrator, and benefactor, and was given because *in the old times there were four men to establish new cultivation in an island or other waste place.* These improved and cultivated the land so that in time there grew up a large inhabited site. And the founders, for their good government, administration, and work at the spread of cultivation, were called 'Gancar' and became lords and superiors over the others, who agreed to pay rent and taxes so that they might remain possessed of their heritable rights and customs. *But the true origin of this is unknown.* . . .

(Clause 8.) In order to secure the position of the Gancars, because they are leaders and their office is hereditary, no Gancar (in his own village) can be removed from office—no matter what fault he may commit. Neither can the writer [Kulkarni, or secretary], since he also holds an hereditary post and was appointed by the said headmen. . . . If either class commits a crime, there may be a penalty in person or goods; and if the punishment is death, the office passes on to the son or next heir. . . .

(Clause 17). Should a Gancar *abscond* to avoid payment of his revenue, an assembly of the village called Gancaria (Gāṅwkaria) must be held, and a proclamation made for the fugitive. Should this be disregarded, his property will be taken over by the other Gancars [who are jointly liable with him], and they can transfer it to others. . . .

(Clause 18). But an absconding Gancar's heritable property [i.e. his *watan* or special holding as headman] cannot be taken from him. His heirs must be asked if they will take up the absconder's obligations; if they refuse, or if there are no heirs, *the other Gancars* take over the property, but not the moveable property which in the absence of [direct] heirs escheats to the Crown. . . .

II. The Headmen's Precedence (among themselves)

(Clauses 41, 42.) At a festival when piçhauris [small scarfs] and betel are distributed, the chief Gancar takes first, and the others in order of their grades; and in calling the roll of names, the order of precedence is to be observed.

(Clause 46.) At seed-time and at harvest, the first field to be taken in hand shall be that of the chief Gancar: and so with thatching the roofs with *olhas* (leaves of *Borassus* palm); the chief Gancar shall have his house thatched before the other houses. . . .

Gancars of *equal rank* are to receive betel, etc., standing side by side with their arms crossed so that the right hand of one may be below the left hand of the other: (then) if one says "I received it with my right hand," the other will be able to say, "My left hand was held above your right" [so that your right hand was not superior to mine].[1]

III. The Status of the Villages

(Clause 2.) In the Goa territory there are 31 villages (a list is given); eight are placed at the head of the list, as "these are the chief for their privileges and pre-eminence."

(Clauses 43, 44.) When a formal resolution regarding some matter is come to by all the villages assembled, and the decision is written down by the 'writer,' a formal reading and confirmation is called *'Nemo.'* This *nemo* is made by the chief headman present of the village Neura Kalān, because it is the chief village: in his absence the 'writer' makes it.

Clause 45.) The village of Taleigão has this pre-eminence, that it *commences the rice harvest.* The headmen carry a bundle of rice to present it at the High Altar of the Cathedral. [This association of the village with the religion of the conquerors is very curious.] The Vicar of the Cathedral after this function accompanies the headmen to the Factory, and the Factor will spend 4 *pardaos* in piçhauris, which he will put round the necks of the headmen: the other villages can then begin to cut their rice.

[1] As no Oriental would receive with his left hand, the explanation is confusing. What is perhaps meant, is that, as the betel-giver is one person, he must necessarily approach one of the two right hands first, and so seem to give one a preference; whereas by arranging that one of the right hands is in a position of some inferiority, the difference is ceremonially neutralized.

IV. The Headmen's Duties in Connection with the Revenue and the Cultivation

(Clause 3.) Each of the villages is bound to pay a certain rent (or revenue) as entered in a separate roll.

The headman assisted by the 'writer' *will distribute and assign the amount among the cultivators and those having lands,* according to their customs and conditions of this charter. The headmen are bound to *distribute, collect, and pay the revenue or rent,* whether it increases or decreases, *and the loss or profit shall remain with them and with the village,* in order that the persons may bear the loss or share in the profit, who by custom (as before set forth) are entitled. Loss occasioned by war they shall be exempt from accounting for, according to the proportion of loss sustained by each holder.

(Clause 4.) The said profit and loss of each year shall be distributed, in proportion to each person's rent, on the palm or garden cultivation, or rice-land, which he holds.

V. "Watan" Grants for Village Service

(Clause 12.) Gancars can *give rent-free lands,* be they waste, or cultivated, but vacant, lands, *to the village servants,* i.e. the temple Brahman, the gate-keeper (*porteiro*), the *'rendeiro,'* [2] the washerman, cobbler, carpenter, blacksmith, temple-sweeper, dancing girls, and the *'chocarreiro.'* [3] These persons *get rent-free holdings of garden or other land as the recompense of their services. . . .*

(Clause 13.) Headmen cannot, without express orders, make a rent-free grant to any person not a resident of the village.

VI. Disposition of Village Lands That Are Vacant

(Clause 9.) Headmen can *grant land which is waste or fallow within the boundaries of their village* to any applicant who wishes to cultivate vegetables ['garden' land] or a grove, or for "other profitable use." [4] The grant is conditioned for the payment of such

[2] *Rendeiro* in Portuguese may mean either one who receives, or one who pays, a rent or other charge or dues. I am unable to suggest definitely what person, regarded as one of the village staff, is meant. But it is quite possible that some 'bailiff' or other collector of the various imposts and levies was required (though not belonging to the original 'balute' staff), and so was put in and rewarded with a 'watan.'

[3] "Chocarreiro" means a buffoon or jester—always implying jests of a low and coarse character.

[4] Apparently wet land (suited for rice) is not included, as that is disposed of in another way (clause 20, *post*). Apparently also the 'dry' crop of the Dakhan

rent-rate as may seem fair [presumably a favourable or reduced rate] up to twenty-five years, after which the full customary rate will be payable. The customary rate is for each plot (grove) of twelve paces broad, that is, from palm-tree to palm-tree, up to one hundred trees; for the whole of it, five *'tanga'* of four *'barganim'* to the *tanga*. . . .

(Clause 10). Land granted to make a betel-garden[5] will be given at the following rates:—5 cubits × 5 cubits (which is from one betel-vine to another) up to 100 plants: if irrigated by well, 4 *barganim* [i.e. 1 *tanga*] annually; if irrigated by running stream, 6 *barganim* [i.e. 1½ *tanga*].

Once granted, all such lands become hereditary possessions: this is the general rule, but if there is in any village some special custom in the matter, it will be given effect to.

(Clause 20). The rice-lands[6] of each village, according to the custom, will be put up to auction and knocked down to the highest bidder; this *does not apply to such lands when they are private property as heritable lands.* The bidding is to be among residents of the village, unless any special custom allows non-residents to bid.

[Bidding was, by custom, for many years, confined to headmen.]

VII. Failure of a Whole Village

(Clause 6.) Should any village be so destroyed that it can no longer pay us [the Portuguese] the revenue assessed on it, the Gancars shall notify the 'Chief Thānadār' and the 'writer of the Island,' who will inquire into the causes of the failure; if they find it to be true, *they will call the headmen of the eight principal villages.* Other headmen may be present, but, by custom, the affairs of the Island lie with the headmen of the eight. To such an assembly, the headmen of the disabled village may relinquish the management. The eight must accept the charge as they are bound, and will put the village up to auction (in presence of the officials mentioned) and make it over to the highest bidder.

The deficiency [difference between the sum bid and the normal revenue] is to be made good by distributing the amount *over the*

(jirāit) is not known in the Goa climate; rice, vegetables, etc., palm-groves, and betel-gardens are the staple.

[5] These gardens for the aromatic leaf (betel) (*Piper betle*), used with areca-nut for chewing, can only be made in favourable soil and with careful irrigation. They are very profitable. The (climbing) plants are often protected overhead with mats.

[6] Low-lying and flooded lands only suited for rice, which is here the chief crop.

eight villages, *or over the whole* island, viz. on those properties which are liable to make good losses, in such way that the full amount of our revenue shall in any case be made good to us.[7]

The lessee or lessees of the village are bound to improve and restore the disabled lands during the term of their lease, and for this purpose they shall hold the office of Gancar.

(Clause 7.) But the regular hereditary Gancars are not by this means permanently ousted; they must be restored whenever they ask for restitution and offer to pay the revenue-demand. When the lease has expired, the lessees have no further claim.

VIII. Rules of Inheritance

(Clause 30.) The order of succession is from father to son and grandson, etc., and [failing the direct descending line] upwards to father, grandfather, etc. No female can inherit.

(Clause 27.) If a man [however] has no sons, etc., *his property will escheat to the Crown, and not go in the ascending line even if his father is alive;* unless, indeed, the deceased was holding undivided with his father.[8]

Among sons the division is equal; if partition takes place in the father's lifetime, the father is entitled to maintenance.

If one son dies without heirs, his share lapses to the Crown, unless it is an undivided share, when it falls to the surviving co-sharers. A share of revenue-free land in any case lapses to the Crown. Should one of the brothers turn Mussulman or abandon the world and become a yogi, "which is the same as the gipsies (*ciganos*)" in Portugal (!), the property lapses to the Crown; but, *if it is revenue-paying land,* it will be sold and the private debts first discharged.

(Clause 32) The principle of division when there are sons by two wives is, to divide *per stirpes* [= jorubānṭ in N.W. India, or cūṇḍavanḍ in the Panjāb] and not *per capita;* [so that four sons of one wife would get one-half between them, and one son of the other wife the whole of the other share. This was modified by a later order allowing either rule according to custom as established.]

---

[7] Nothing is said as to *when* 'the eight' and when the whole body of cultivators in the island (not holding free, or at any fixed rates) can be called on. Probably the headmen will decide, according to which gives the best prospect of making up the deficit.

[8] No notice is taken of the ordinary rule, that failing the downward or upward direct line, the collaterals come in, brothers and brothers' sons. These are thus disinherited by the rules, which claim everything for the Crown.

IX. Rules about Alienation of Land

(Clause 15.) Should a Gancar *or other person* desire to sell *any heritable property* in the village, he must obtain the consent of all the Gancars of the village in question. And no one can purchase without similar permission.

Any bargain made without such consent is *ipso facto* voidable, and can be set aside if the Gancars so desire in the interest of the revenue collection for which they are responsible. A purchaser is to receive a written slip, noting the revenue on the land bought, to save mistakes and discontent.

(Clause 16.) It is not sufficient that the sellers of heritable property sign the deed of sale: all his heirs must sign also; and if one of them is a minor, there must be a consent signed by his guardian or next friend on his behalf.

X. Rules of Procedure

(Clause 11.) The writer of the 'Camara' (Chamber or State Council?) of the Island, must be present at the passing and establishing, called 'Nemo,' of all agreements and resolutions such as are issued by the Chief Gancars of all the island together with the Chief Thānadār and writer, etc. Without the writer of the Island nothing can be done; for he takes note and assents to all, so that he may decide any doubts or question that may afterwards arise. In like manner [in a village matter] the village writer must be present. The writer's records (village books) regulate all the villages in the islands.

(Clause 14.) When the chief officers summon a general meeting of Gancars in the Island, all must attend or at least get a local meeting to choose a deputy to appear in their stead. At such a local meeting (*Gancaria*) every Gancar must attend, or at least an heir of an absent member. The "usual penalty" will be exacted from anyone intentionally absent.

Money loans are next regulated. A larger sum than 50 *tangas* must not be lent except on a written bond. If otherwise the parties may agree to refer the matter to "two selected men" for decision.

Interest is allowed at one *barganim* for every six *tangas*. [One in 24, or a little over 4 per cent., if it is *per annum;* but more probably it is *per mensem,* in which case it is nearly 50 per cent.]

But interest can never be more than double the principal. [The other clause excludes, as do the Hindu law books, certain persons from giving evidence; among them children under 16, 'gardeners,'

day-labourers, sons of a prostitute, variously defective persons:
these, though incompetent in serious cases, may testify in minor
ones.]

XI. Miscellaneous

(Clause 21.) The village headmen are liable to provide (unpaid)
labour (begāri) from any dwellers (*pelos moradores*) in the village,
to clear away bushes and weeds from the city walls and '*cavas*'
(ditches?), also "to meet other necessities as occasion may arise."

(Clauses 37, 38, 39.) The village must feed the Chief Thānadār
and his clerks, when visiting the place officially. Also "our factor"
and his officials. Every 'peon' sent on official message is to be allowed (during his stay) two measures of rice daily and one *real* to
buy betel.

(Clause 34.) Officials must not take bribes, nor accept lands, nor
trade within their jurisdiction, etc.

(Clause 49.) Use of the torch, palankeen, or umbrella, is a privilege requiring license of the Governor, unless it is an hereditary
honour. When granted as an honour, the grant may either leave the
grantee to employ his own servants and buy his own oil (for the
torch), or may grant the oil and servants at cost of the State. Each
emblem may be granted by itself—or all together—in either way.

Commentary

General Observations.—The villages, throughout the Bombay
country and the Dakhan, and Koṇkan generally, are in the raiyat-
wāri or 'severalty' form, marked by distinctive (and ancient) features,
viz.: (i) The allotment of a separate (heritable) holding to every
cultivating family (i.e. there is nothing in the nature of a unit
estate or property shared in fractional proportions among a body
of the same descent). (ii) It is marked by the existence of certain
privileged holdings (*watan*) which are the reward of village service,
or are also the special heritable property (along with rights of
precedence) of the village officers in virtue of their position. (iii) By
the influence and power of the headman (and his family). Such an
officer has a real indigenous title in the local languages. I make
this observation because it is clear from every part of the *Foral*
of 1526 that the villages (of the old Goa territory) therein described
were *then* in the same form, and that every mark or feature of this
constitution is mentioned. . . .

From all we know of the 'Hindu' kingdoms and overlordships
(whether of Dravidian or of partly Aryan connection) it is certain

that the royal revenue was derived from a share (in kind) of the grain produce of every holding or allotment (except certain privileged ones). The share (as such) was fixed by custom, and was not increased till comparatively late times, when rulers assumed the right to take such proportion as they appointed; and even then they sometimes tried to conceal the fact. In any case it depended on the harvest; it was a share of what was actually produced and no more. But the Muhammadan system (of the Dakhan Kings) had been in force about seventy-five years, of which the last ten or twelve before the Portuguese conquest represented the more defined and stricter system of the 'Ādil Shāhi kings. This system, besides assessing the revenue-demand in money, created a *liability for a total sum from each village*, which before was unknown; and it accordingly must have given the headman so extensive a power of arranging this and that holding—leasing this and charging that—that in time, although the system never permitted the headmen actually to buy up or appropriate the holdings in their own right, every plot of land (except a few favoured with freehold or fixed rates) must have been so charged with levies and imposts, that its possession was more a burden than a profit.

4 / THE MUGHUL EMPIRE

The consolidation of Muslim power in north India, achieved under the Delhi Sultanate by the mid-fourteenth century, disintegrated under the impact of Mughul pressure from central Asia. Using Samarkand as his base, Tamerlane, a Turkish Muslim who posed as the heir and successor to Genghis Khan, swept into India, sacked Delhi, and had himself declared ruler shortly before his death in 1405. His descendant, Babur, following a similar course from Kabul in the Afghan country, reasserted his family's claim to north India by defeating a Hindu host at the battle of Panipat in the spring of 1526. After years of strife, the contest between the Afghans and Mughuls, who both had Hindu supporters, was resolved when the Mughuls won the second battle of Panipat (1556).

The task of reconstruction thereafter fell to a teen-aged emperor, Abul-fath Jalāl-ud-din Muhammad Akbar Pādshāh Ghāzi, better known as Akbar the Great. A grandson of Babur, Akbar finally

Father Monserrate, S.J., *Commentary on his Journey to the Court of Akbar from 1580 to 1583.* From *The Commentary of Father Monserrate . . .*, ed. S. N. Banjerjee, trans. J. S. Hoyland (London, 1922), pp. 196-204, 207, 213-14, 219. Reprinted by permission of Oxford University Press.

*made good the Mughul bid for supremacy and extended his rule
as far south as the Godavari River. In the latter half of the sixteenth century Mughul territory stretched from the Arabian Sea to
the Bay of Bengal, and Akbar continued pushing steadily southward.
At the foot of the northern plains, a belt of Muslim kingdoms in
the Deccan stubbornly resisted incorporation into the Mughul
empire. Under Aurangzeb, a grandson of Akbar, the Mughul empire
reached its greatest extent in the late seventeenth century when
only a negligible portion of the tip of the Indian peninsula escaped
the direct administration of Delhi.*

*Akbar's political acumen helped him to lay a firm foundation for
the Mughul empire. In the half century of his reign (1556-1605),
he successfully curbed the power of the* vazir *or* vakil *(prime minister) who had traditionally exercised far-reaching civil, military,
and judicial authority. Financial administration was entrusted to a
chief* divan *and military matters were transferred to the office of the*
mir bakhshi. *The maintenance of Mughul power obviously required a steady flow of revenue and a dependable army ready for
aciton. With the population of the empire approaching 100 million
inhabitants, Akbar divided it into 15 provinces, each with numerous subdivisions. The provincial governors exercised supreme civil
and military power; the only officer independent of the governor at
the provincial level was the revenue* divan.

*The empire's main source of revenue came from an assessment
on the produce of the land (one quarter to one half) paid either in
kind or in cash. Apparently, Akbar's intention of remeasuring and
reclassifying all the land in order to reassess taxes more equi-
tably, on the basis of a system of averages for both production and
prices, failed to materialize. Instead of supporting officials as before,
by allotting them a share of the revenue due the state, Akbar paid
them in cash from the imperial treasury whenever possible.*

*Midway in his reign, the emperor attempted to replace tribal or
other traditional allegiances among his followers with an administrative bureaucracy of his own creation. To this end he instituted
ranks of imperial officials whose advancement depended on demonstrated ability, fidelity, and honesty.* Mansabdars *("place-holders")
in the civil or military administration were moderately well paid,
according to government schedules. Each official performed stipu-
lated services and was also held responsible for maintaining specified quotas of animals for transport and cavalry ready for action.
The ranks of officialdom were open to all and they served as the
only avenue to honor. Yet neither titles nor personal wealth could*

be passed on from generation to generation. On the death of the owner, all the titles and properties of officials reverted to the state. There was no standing army, and we have no way of telling with any certainty the size of the total available forces. It is also virtually impossible to correlate the sources and translate the government's income into valid and understandable terms. We can conclude, however, that by the end of Akbar's reign in 1605, the Mughul empire was the greatest, wealthiest, and most powerful state of India, second only to China in power and influence among the Asian states.

Akbar is distinguished in the annals of world religion as a great exponent of toleration and as the founder and creator of his own eclectic religion. Political historians sometimes attribute his tolerance to an overweening desire to bring peace and stability to the numerous religious groups within the empire. Others feel that he was personally dissatisfied with all of the established creeds, and that he longed for a religion that would give him a comfortable feeling of spiritual certainty. Whatever his motives, Akbar encouraged a lively and constant religious debate at his court. He outraged the orthodox of all faiths by his bland skepticism. At the same time he never tired of listening to and asking questions of Muslim teachers of all persuasions, Hindu holy men, Parsees, Zoroastrians, Jains, and even Jesuit priests from Goa.

We are indebted to the Jesuits for several eye-witness accounts of the arresting majesty and benevolent disposition of one of the world's richest potentates. The earliest of the European missionaries to write in detail about Akbar was Father Antonio Monserrate, a Jesuit who made a mission to Akbar's court from 1580 to 1583. This priest kept notes of his experiences in the Mughul empire, and used them as the basis of his extended Latin "Commentary" on Akbar's realm. The following excerpt gives a realistic portrayal of Akbar and his court as seen through European eyes and it is notable that Monserrate's estimate of Akbar is far less flattering than those given by the Persian chroniclers of his reign. Monserrate's "Commentary," excerpts of which were published in Europe in several languages by the end of the sixteenth century, ranks as a major source for the reign of Akbar.

". . . How Accessible He [Akbar] Makes Himself to All . . ."

This Prince [Akbar] is of a stature and of a type of countenance well-fitted to his royal dignity, so that one could easily recognise, even at the first glance, that he is the King. He has broad shoulders, somewhat bandy legs well-suited for horsemanship, and a light-brown complexion. He carries his head bent towards the right shoulder. His forehead is broad and open, his eyes so bright and flashing that they seem like a sea shimmering in the sunlight. His eyelashes are very long, as also are those of the Sauromates,[1] Sinae,[2] Niphones[3] and most other north-Asiatic races. His eyebrows are not strongly marked. His nose is straight and small, though not insignificant. His nostrils are widely opened, as though in derision. Between the left nostril and the upper lip there is a mole. He shaves his beard, but wears a moustache like that of a Turkish youth who has not yet attained to manhood (for on reaching manhood they begin to affect a beard). Contrary to the custom of his race he does not cut his hair; nor does he wear a hat, but a turban, into which he gathers up his hair. He does this, they say, as a concession to Indian usages, and to please his Indian subjects. He limps in his left leg, though indeed he has never received any injury there. His body is exceedingly well-built and is neither too thin nor too stout. He is sturdy, hearty and robust. When he laughs, his face becomes almost distorted. His expression is tranquil, serene and open, full also of dignity, and when he is angry, of awful majesty. When the priests first saw him he was thirty-eight years of age. It is hard to exaggerate how accessible he makes himself to all who wish audience of him. For he creates an opportunity almost every day for any of the common people or of the nobles to see him and converse with him; and he endeavours to show himself pleasant-spoken and affable rather than severe toward all who come to speak with him. It is very remarkable how great an effect this courtesy and affability has in attaching to him the minds of his subjects. For in spite of his very heterodox attitude towards the religion of Muhammad, and in spite also of the fact that Musalmans regard such an attitude as an unforgivable offence, Zelaldinus [Jalāl-ud-din, a part of Akbar's title] has not yet been assassinated. He has an acute insight, and shows much wise foresight both in avoiding dangers and in seizing favourable opportunities for carrying out his designs. Yet all these fine qualities both of body and mind lose the greater part of their splendour because the lustre of the True Faith is lacking.

[1] A sub-division of the Scythian tribe inhabiting lands above the Danube and the Black Sea and north of the Caucasus.

[2] Chinese. "Seres was the name of the great nation in the far east as known by land, and Sinae as known by sea" (Yule's *Marco Polo*, Introduction, p. 11).

[3] Japanese.

Zelaldinus is greatly devoted to hunting, though not equally so to hawking. As he is of a somewhat morose disposition, he amuses himself with various games. These games afford also a public spectacle to the nobility and the common people, who indeed are very fond of such spectacles. They are the following:—Polo, elephant-fighting, buffalo-fighting, stag-fighting and cock-fighting, boxing contests, battles of gladiators, and the flying of tumbler-pigeons. He is also very fond of strange birds, and indeed of any novel object. He amuses himself with singing, concerts, dances, conjurer's tricks, and the jokes of his jesters, of whom he makes much. However, although he may seem at such times to be at leisure and to have laid aside public affairs, he does not cease to revolve in his mind the heavy cares of state. He is especially remarkable for his love of keeping great crowds of people around him and in his sight; and thus it comes about that his court is always thronged with multitudes of men of every type, though especially with the nobles, whom he commands to come from their provinces and reside at court for a certain period each year. When he goes outside the palace, he is surrounded and followed by these nobles and a strong body-guard. They have to go on foot until he gives them a nod to indicate that they may mount. All this adds greatly to the wonderful majesty and greatness of the royal court. . . .

Magnificently Built Palaces

The splendour of his palaces approaches closely to that of the royal dwellings of Europe. They are magnificently built, from foundation to cornice, of hewn stone, and are decorated both with painting and carving. Unlike the palaces built by other Indian kings, they are lofty; for an Indian palace is generally as low and humble as an idol-temple. Their total circuit is so large that it easily embraces four great royal dwellings, of which the King's own palace is the largest and the finest. The second palace belongs to the queens, and the third to the royal princes, whilst the fourth is used as a store house and magazine. The roofs of these palaces are not tiled, but are dome-shaped, being protected from the weather on the outside by solid plaster covering the stone slabs. This forms a roof absolutely impervious to moisture. The palaces are decorated also with many pinnacles, supported on four columns, each of which forms a small covered portico. Not a little is added to the beauty of the palaces by charming pigeon-cotes, partly covered with rough-cast, and partly showing walls built of small blue and white bricks. The pigeons[4] are cared for by eunuchs and servant-maids. Their evolutions are controlled at will, when they are flying, by means of certain signals, just as those of well-trained soldiery are controlled by a competent general by means of bugles and drums. It will seem little short of miraculous when I affirm that when sent out, they dance, turn somersaults all together in the air, fly in orderly rhythm, and return to their starting point, all at the sound of a whistle. They are bidden to perch on the roof, to conceal themselves within their nesting-places, or to dart out of them again; and they do everything just as they are told. . . .

A Great Patron of Letters

He is a great patron of learning, and always keeps around him erudite men, who are directed to discuss before him philosophy, theology, and religion, and to recount to him the history of great kings and glorious deeds of the past. He has an excellent judgment and a good memory, and has attained to a considerable knowledge of many subjects by means of constant and patient listening to such discussions. Thus he not only makes up for his ignorance of letters (for he is entirely unable either to read or write), but he has also become able clearly and lucidly to expound difficult matters. He can give his opinion on any question so shrewdly and keenly, that no one who did not know that he is illiterate would suppose him to be anything but very learned and erudite. And so indeed he is, for in addition to his keen intellect, of which I have already spoken, he excels many of his most learned subjects in eloquence, as well as in that authority and dignity which befits a King. The wise men are wont every day to hold disputations on literary subjects before him. He listens with delight, not to actors, but to mimics and jesters, thinking their style of speaking to have a literary flavour. . . .

Zelaldinus has more than 300 wives, dwelling in separate suites of rooms in a very large palace. Yet when the priests were at the court he had only three sons and two daughters.[5] His sons' names are as follows:—the eldest is Xecus,[6] called after the Xecus by whose advice, as has been mentioned, the King built Sequiris; for this boy was the first born after the change of capital, and thus survived infancy. The second son is Paharis, and the third Danus or Danialus.

---

[4] Akbar was a great pigeon-fancier. More than 20,000 pigeons, divided into 10 classes, were kept at court.

[5] The three sons were Selim (Jahangir), Murad (Pahari) and Danyal.

[6] Selim was called by Akbar the Shaikh Baba.

Counsellors

Zelaldinus has about twenty Hindu chieftains[7] as ministers and counsellors to assist both in the work of governing the empire and in the control of the royal household. They are devoted to him, and are very wise and reliable in conducting public business. They are always with him, and are admitted to the innermost parts of the palace, which is a privilege not allowed even to the Mongol nobles. However, he is wont to entrust the provincial governorships to chiefs of the Xacattaei [Chagatai or Mongols] who are related to him. Some of these chiefs also act not only as tutors but also as guardians to his sons. His object in arranging this is to attach the chiefs to himself by a yet closer bond of affection, and also to provide protectors for his children from the malice of his life-long enemies. Their literary education is committed, according to the Persian custom, to learned old men,[8] of a spurious virtue (but really of a character as wicked as that of the most abandoned amongst these Musalmans), and of an empty and ostentatious kind of piety and excellence. The princes have also trainers to teach them the use of arms, riding-masters, and instructors in archery. He gives very great care and attention to the education of the princesses, who are kept rigorously secluded from the sight of men. They are taught to read and write, and are trained in other ways, by matrons.

The following is the method the King employs in deliberation— he asks each counsellor privately for his own opinion, and then himself decides upon the course which seems to be supported by the largest number and the most experienced. He asks their advice even about subjects upon which he has already made up his mind, saying to the nobles, 'This is what I think should be done, do you agree?' They reply 'Salaam, O King'; whereupon he says, 'Then let it be carried out.' If however any of them do not agree with him, he listens patiently, and sometimes even alters his own opinion. . . .

". . . Enormous Sums . . ."

The King exacts enormous sums in tribute from the provinces of his empire, which is wonderfully rich and fertile both for cultiva-

---

[7] It would be interesting to know the names of all these Hindu chieftains. From Abul Fazl's list (1590) it appears that there were 31 Hindus among [Akbar's] 252 [top] commanders. . . . Of 163 [lesser] commanders . . . , 26 were Hindus.

[8] Shaikh Faizi had been employed as tutor to the princes.

tion and pasture, and has a great trade both in exports and imports. He also derives much revenue from the hoarded fortunes of the great nobles, which by law and custom all come to the King on their owners' death. In addition, there are the spoils of conquered kings and chieftains, whose treasure is seized, and the great levies exacted, and gifts received, from the inhabitants of newly-subdued districts in every part of his dominions. These gifts and levies are apt to be so large as to ruin outright many of his new subjects. He also engages in trading on his own account, and thus increases his wealth to no small degree; for he eagerly exploits every possible source of profit.

Moreover, he allows no bankers or money-changers in his empire except the superintendents and tellers of the royal treasuries. This enormous banking-business brings the King great profit; for at these royal treasuries alone may gold coin be changed for silver or copper, and vice versa. The government officers are paid in gold, silver or copper according to their rank. Thus it comes about that those who are paid in one type of coin need to change some of it into another type. . . .

This empire is very beautiful and healthy, although in many places not well provided with fruit trees. On account of the diversity of the climate in different parts it produces many and various types of crops. Thus in the southern area or zone (as geographers would call it), the same crops are found as in the maritime district (near Goa). But the farther one goes towards the north the more similar does one find the staple products to those of Europe, though indeed the following are the only representatives of the long list of European fruits and trees which grow in India with real exuberance (and these only on the Himalaya range), viz. the grape, the peach, the mulberry, the fig (in a few places), and the pine tree. The whole country bears pomegranates in abundance. The Cotonian apple, the pear and similar fruits are imported from Persia. Rice, wheat, millet and pulse are produced in great quantities. Amongst a great number of non-fruit-bearing trees, I recognised as European only the plane, though there are willows in Indoscythia. In many places in the neighbourhood of the Indus flax and hemp are sown. The plant which is commonly called 'bangue,' [9] and which when used as a drink produces intoxication and stupefaction of the mind and senses, has leaves very similar to those of the hemp-plant. It does not however grow on one stalk only, but has a low stem, from which

[9] Bhang, or Indian hemp.

spring a number of other branches, like a bush. Indigo and opium are largely grown in the south, and bring no small profit to the royal revenues. Indigo is a plant from which a juice is extracted yielding a blue dye when it hardens. . . .

". . . Indian Towns Appear Very Pleasant . . ."

To say something about Indian towns:—they appear very pleasant from afar; for they are adorned with many towers and high buildings, in a very beautiful manner. But when one enters them, one finds that the narrowness, aimless crookedness, and ill-planning of the streets deprive these cities of all beauty. Moreover the houses are purposely built without windows on account of the filth of the streets. None the less the rich adorn the roofs and arched ceilings of their houses with carvings and paintings: plant ornamental gardens in their courtyards: make tanks and fish-ponds, which are lined with tiles of various colours: construct artificial springs and fountains, which fling showers of water far into the air: and lay down promenades paved with brickwork or marble. Yet such houses will show nothing in their facades or entrances by which the eye of the passer-by might be attracted, and nothing by which it might be known that inside is anything out of the ordinary. The Brachmanae have another style of architecture; but they also beautify their houses with cleverly executed statues and sculptures of fabulous heroes and monsters either in wood or stone. They never forget to carve or paint somewhere on their buildings (generally on the capitals of the columns) the crested snake, which is called by the Portuguese the 'cuckoo-serpent,' and which I believe to be the Egyptian asp.

The common people live in lowly huts and tiny cottages: and hence if a traveller has seen one of these cities, he has seen them all. . . .

5 / HINDUISM: THE *BHAKTI* MOVEMENT

Hinduism, a Western term, is descriptive of a way of life rather than a creed. The Sanskrit term, dharma, *which means obedience to the moral law, is the life ideal of all Hindus. Unlike a number of great religions, Hinduism has no fixed scriptural canon. Certain*

Tulasī Dās, *Rāmacaritamānasa*. From W. Douglas P. Hill, trans., *The Holy Lake of the Acts of Rāma* (Calcutta: Oxford University Press, 1952), pp. 216-19, 355-59, 445-52. Reprinted by permission of Oxford University Press.

ancient Sanskrit writings, notably the Vedas *and* Brahmanas, *are the chief scriptural authorities of Hinduism and have regularly been the subject of elaborate theological commentary and debate. Cults of Hinduism developed out of these theological differences at a very early date. One of the most persistently influential of the cults is that which stresses* bhakti *(devotion) and advocates the worship of a personal deity by individual prayer and praise.* Bhakti *became extremely popular in medieval times, especially after the invasion of India by Islam, and most of the* bhakti *movements, still very influential in popular Hinduism, date from the period just before the appearance of the Europeans in the East. The* bhakti *cult held that faith, rather than the exercise of intellect or theological subtlety, would most efficaciously free man from the material and impermanent and fix his entire attention upon God. Austerity, sacrifice, penance, and fasting were thought to be of little avail. Without grace and the guidance of a devout teacher, complete absorption in the divine would elude the most ardent devotee.* Bhakti *encouraged all, irrespective of political allegiance, social position, education, wealth, or sex, to strive for liberation from the inexorable cycle of rebirth by fastening the uninterrupted attention on God. Popular response to such an otherworldly message, preached in the vernacular by dedicated men, was enthusiastic and widespread, particularly in troubled times.*

Medieval bhakti *succeeded in focusing the attention of the devout on a single god. Thus the two major divisions of Hinduism owe their names to the god that each considers supreme: the Vaishnavites place Vishnu at the apex and the Shaivites Shiva. Shiva was the deity most revered by the Brahmans; Vishnu, the personification of preservation, was more popular with the lower castes. Vishnu inspires his votaries by descending to earth in times of stress in any one of the ten classical incarnations. The two most important and popular of the incarnations of Vishnu are Krishna and Rāma. The exploits of these traditional exemplars have long inspired the respect and admiration of the Indian people. The two great epics embodying the traditional ethical beliefs of Hinduism are the* Mahābhārata *(seven times the length of the* Iliad *and* Odyssey *combined) and the* Rāmayāna. *Authorship of both the "Great Poem of the Descendants of Bharata" and the "Adventures of Rāma" is attributed to sages. In their original forms these Sanskrit poems antedate Christ by several centuries.*

In popular Hinduism by the sixteenth century Rāma had become the incarnation of Vishnu most highly esteemed among the lower castes. A number of famous Vaishnavites of the thirteenth and fourteenth centuries had begun to bring the deeds of Rāma into the vernacular through commentaries and poems written in the popular dialects. Tulasī Dās (1532-1623), one of the greatest and most famous of India's poets, began to prepare his own Hindi version of the deeds of Rāma in 1574. His Rāmacaritamānasa (The Holy Lake of the Acts of Rāma) *completed early in the seventeenth century, quickly came to be considered in northern India as the most inspired and authoritative guide to religion and the conduct of life. His verses became popular proverbs, and were as widely quoted among Hindus as Bible verses in the West.*

Although Tulasī Dās does not neglect the myriad of gods in the Hindu pantheon, his principal desire is to inculcate bhakti *through celebrating the moral example of Rāma. In the cult of Rāma the relation of the worshipper to the deity (Rāma) is that of child to father. The deference and reverence a student shows his* guru, *or teacher, should surpass even that of a child toward his parents, for the teacher directs man to fasten his affection fully on God. Other praiseworthy loyalties are those of brother to brother and wife to husband, but the practice of right conduct* (dharma) *at the familial level is transcended by the ultimate bond of love and faith uniting a servant to his master, or a* bhakta (devotee) *to his chosen deity. The means of attaining liberation or deliverance* (moksha) *from the world of the senses are within the grasp of anyone capable of selfless devotion. Instinctively all the creatures of the universe, including the gods, love and trust Rāma. The poet repeatedly affirms the boundless grace that Rāma freely bestows on all, even to his arch-foe, the demon Rāvan. Rāma's highest gift, delivery from the curse of rebirth, plays like a beloved refrain throughout the* Rāmacaritamānasa.

Tulasī Dās opens his lengthy poetic pean to Rāma, Lord of grace, with invocations to myriads of gods, saints, men, and poets, and concludes the introduction with stories relating the heavenly origin and background of Rāma and of Rāvan and the demons. The Holy Lake proper unfolds the virtues and acts of Rāma in seven sections, which describe his descent from heaven, his childhood as Prince of Kosala, his marriage to Princess Janaki (Sītā), his banishment and retirement to the forest, and his earth-shaking confrontation with the stubborn Rāvan, king of the demons and kidnapper of Rāma's bride. Rāma assumed the form of man in order to slay the demon king in battle, thus granting even to him a final release from perpetual rebirth. Then Rāma ruled as "sole monarch of the land engirdled by seven seas," and indescribable bliss and prosperity filled the world.

The thrilling deeds of gracious, gentle Rāma can only be suggested in the excerpts below. The love borne him by his family in particular and all who know him illumines the entire narrative. Although the ecstatic tenor of the poem may become monotonous in prose translation, the poet's unerring sense of good taste and his boundless compassion for humanity and nature convey to us some feeling of how The Holy Lake of the Acts of Rāma *has won a place of distinction among the great works of world literature.*

The Exile of Rāma

When the Kols and Kirāts [forest peoples] heard the news [that Rāma had come away from the city of Avadh to them], they were as happy as though the Nine Treasures[1] had come to their homes. They filled leaf-platters with bulbs and roots and fruit and ran as beggars run to plunder stores of gold. Others who met them on the road questioned those among them who had seen the two brothers, and discoursing together of Raghubīr's beauty, they all came and saw Raghurāī.[2] With profound obeisance they laid their offerings before him and gazed upon the Lord with great devotion. They stood there all about him like painted figures, trembling with emotion, and their eyes overflowed with tears. When Rāma perceived that they were all beside themselves with love, he received them with honour and spoke to them kindly. Again and again they did obeisance to the Lord and addressed him humbly with folded hands. . . .

That Lord whom the Veda [the sacred books] cannot define nor the mind of the sage comprehend, the home of compassion, listened to the words of the Kirāts as a father to the prattling of his child. Nothing but love is dear to Rāma; let him who will understand this understand.

Rāma then contented all the forest-dwellers with gentle words and so dismissed them. Bowing their heads, they departed and went home, discoursing of the Lord's perfections as they went.

---

[1] *nava nidhi:* the Nine Treasures are attendant on Kuvera or on Lakṣmī. They are called *padma, mahāpadma, śaṅkha, makara, kacchapa, mukunda, nīla, kunda* and *varcca.* (Another list has *nanda* and *kharba* for the last two.) The possession of any of these brings a man wealth of its peculiar kind; e.g. *padma* brings gold, silver and copper and success in business dealings; *mahāpadma,* all sorts of precious stones.

[2] Patronymics of Rāma as lord of the rynasty of Raghu.

Thus the two brothers, with Sītā [Rāma's bride], took up their abode in the forest and brought happiness to gods and sages. From the day when Raghunāyak came and dwelt there the forest brought blessing to all. . . .

All creatures that had eyes, gazing on Raghubar, forgot their sorrows, glad that they had been born. Happy, too, was motionless creation as it touched the dust of his feet, and all were heirs of his high realm. That forest and hill, in all their native loveliness, brought blessing to all and even sanctified the holy. How can one describe the majesty of that spot where the ocean of delight made his abode? The glory of that wood where Sītā, Lakṣman and Rāma came to dwell, leaving the Ocean of Milk[3] and abandoning Avadh, not even a hundred thousand Śeṣas, each with his thousand tongues, could tell; then how can I declare it? Can a mere tortoise in a pond lift up Mount Mandara?

Lakṣman did them service in thought and word and deed; his loving-kindness and affection cannot be described. Moment by moment beholding the feet of Sītā and Rāma and recognizing the love they bore him, Lakṣman never even in his dreams regretted brothers, mother, father or home. Living happily with Rāma, Sītā quite forgot her city, family and home. Moment by moment gazing on her husband's face, she was as enraptured as the partridge looking on the moon. . . .

So Rāma dwelt glorious with Lakṣman and Sītā in their hut of leaves, as Indra dwells in Amarāvatī with Śacī and Jayanta. The Lord watched over Sītā and Lakṣman as the eyelid guards the pupil of the eye, while Lakṣman looked after Sītā and Raghubīr as carefully as an undiscerning fool tends his own body. In this manner the Lord dwelt at ease in the forest, a friend of birds and beasts and gods and anchorites. . . .

"As Soon as Any Creature Enters My Presence, the Sins of Ten Million Lives Are Blotted Out"

In this manner the gracious Lord marched on and halted on the shore of the sea, and all around the hosts of bear and monkey warriors[4] began to devour fruit.

Meanwhile, the demons had been in a state of great anxiety ever

---

[3] *paya payodhi*, or *kṣīrasāgara*: here, as often, Sītā is identified with Lakṣmī, and Rāma with Viṣṇu, who as Nārāyaṇa dwells on the Ocean of Milk resting on Śeṣanāga, of whom Lakṣman is the incarnation.

[4] While in exile Rāma allied himself with Hanumān, the king of the monkeys, who helped him defeat Rāvan and the demons.

since the monkey had burnt Lankā and departed. Each in his own home was thinking that there was no hope of salvation for the demon race. If Rāma's envoy, they thought, is of such indescribable might, how can we escape if he enters our city himself? When Mandodarī heard from her spies what the citizens were saying, she was greatly disquieted; with folded hands she approached her lord alone, and touching his feet spoke words full of sound sense: 'Cease, husband, to strive against Hari; take my advice to heart, it is for your good. Lord, if you value your security, summon your minister and send back the wife of him whose envoy performed such feats of valour that the demons' wives give birth before their time when they recall them. Sītā has come like a cold winter night to shrivel up the lotus-bed of your race. Hearken, husband; unless you surrender Sītā, there is no hope for you, though Śambhu and Brahmā should help you. Rāma's arrows are like a host of serpents and the demon throng as frogs; forgo your obstinate intent and take wise steps or ever they swallow us up.'

The senseless fool, whose arrogance the whole world knew, laughed when he heard her advice: 'Of a truth,' he said, 'women are timorous by nature, afraid when things go well, weak-minded too! If the army of monkeys does come, our poor demons will eat them up and live! It is quite ridiculous that my wife should be afraid when the very guardians of the spheres fear me and tremble.' So saying, he laughed aloud and clasped her to his bosom and proceeded to the council-hall, bursting with conceit. But Mandodarī was anxious at heart, thinking that God was hostile to her husband.

When he took his seat in the council-hall, tidings were brought to him that the whole army had crossed the ocean. He asked his ministers to give him sound advice, and they all laughed and said, 'Rest easy; you have conquered gods and demons without the least trouble; of what account are men and monkeys?' If a minister or a doctor or a *guru*, these three, speak fair words for fear or hope of reward, then that spells speedy ruin for the kingdom or for health or for religion. That was the sort of help that Rāvan got; they merely broke out into repeated praises of him.

Then Vibhīṣan seized the opportunity to come to him and bowed his head before his brother's feet. Bowing again, he sat upon his throne and with his brother's leave addressed him thus: 'If you ask my counsel, gracious lord, then, brother, I will declare, as far as I am able, what is for your good. Whoever desires his own welfare and to enjoy good repute, good understanding, a good manner of life or any other happiness, he, my lord, should shun to look on the face of another's wife as men shun to look on the moon on its fourth night.[5] Though a man were sole ruler of the fourteen worlds, he could not fight with all creation and stand firm. However perfect and accomplished a man may be, if he display the slightest trace of avarice, none will speak well of him. Lust, anger, pride and greed, my lord, are all roads that lead to hell. Give them all up and worship Raghubīr, whom the saints worship.

'Rāma, brother, is not merely a king of mortal men; he is sovereign of the universe, death of Death himself, the Absolute, the perfect, the unborn, the Blessed Lord, all-pervading, invincible, without origin or end; the friend of earth and Brāhmans and cows and gods, the ocean of grace in human form, come to bless the faithful and break the power of all the hosts of evil; guardian of the Veda and of righteousness; mark this well, my brother! Cease to contend with him; bow your head before him, for Raghunāth relieves his suppliants of all their woes. Give back the princess of Videha to the Lord, O king, and worship Rāma, who loves the undeserving. The Lord forsakes not even one who is guilty of harming the universe, if only he will come to him for refuge. That Lord whose name is a cure for every ill is manifest—believe it, Rāvan! Again and again I touch your feet and beseech you, O Ten-headed, have done with pride, delusion and conceit and worship the King of Kosala! The sage Pulastya has sent this message by his own disciple, and this, my brother, I have taken immediate occasion to repeat to my lord.' . . .

Thus did Vibhīṣan offer sound advice in accord with the principles of wise men, the Purāṇas and the Vedas; but when he heard it, the Ten-headed arose in a rage and cried, 'Villain, death is at your door! You only live, you wretch, because I continually support you, and yet, you idiot, you prefer to take my enemy's part! Tell me, you scoundrel, who is there in the whole world whom I have not vanquished by the might of my arm? You live in my city, but your heart is with the ascetics. You had better go to them, you fool, and preach your moral sermons!' So saying, he gave him a kick, but his brother clasped his feet repeatedly. Umā, herein lies the greatness of a saint that he does good to one who does him ill. 'You have done well to strike me,' he said, 'for you are as my father; but still, O king, it were well for you that you should worship Rāma.' Then with his ministers he went his way through the air, crying aloud to all, 'Rāma is true to his purpose, the mighty Lord, and

[5] Hindus believe that one who looks at the moon on the fourth night of its waxing in the month of Bhādoṅ will be falsely accused of some crime.

your court is doomed to death! Now I go to seek refuge with Raghu-bīr; let no one blame me!' . . .

When the monkeys saw Vibhīṣan coming, they thought he was some special envoy from the enemy; so they put him under guard and came to the Monkey King and told him of his arrival. 'Hearken, Raghurāī,' said Sugrīva; Rāvan's brother has come to see you.' 'What do you advise?' said the Lord. 'Believe me, sire,' replied the king of the monkeys, 'demon trickery is past all understanding. Why has he come here, this fellow who can change his shape at will? The fool has come to spy out the land; I propose he be bound and kept under guard.' 'That's a very good idea of yours, my friend,' said Rāma; 'but I have vowed to reassure those who come to me for refuge.' The Lord's reply delighted Hanumān, who thought, 'How tenderly the Blessed Lord loves his suppliants!'

Then said Rāma again, 'Those who spurn a suppliant because they think he may do them an injury are vile and sinful; it is a crime even to look at them. I would not turn away from one who was guilty of the murder of ten million Brāhmans if he came to me for shelter. As soon as any creature enters my presence, the sins of ten million lives are blotted out. One who is truly a sinner abhors the worship of my person; then if this demon is evil at heart, why has he come to face me? Only a man of pure heart can find me; deceit and hypocrisy I detest. Even if the Ten-headed has sent him to spy out our secrets, we have no reason to fear, Monkey King, and nothing to lose. Why, my friend, Lakṣman could slay all the demons in the world in the twinkling of an eye! If he is frightened and has come to me for refuge, I shall protect him as I would my own life. Either way, bring him here,' said the Lord of grace with a smile. 'Glory to the Merciful!' cried the monkey, and off he went with Aṅgad and Hanumān. . . .

"Can That City Be Described Where Sītā's Lord Was King?"

All his brothers, too, did him obedient service, showing supreme devotion to Rāma's feet; and they were always watching his lotus face to see if perchance the gracious Lord had any orders to give. Rāma felt great affection for his brothers and gave them much moral instruction.

The people of the city lived very happily and all enjoyed delights to which the gods could scarce attain. Day and night they made their prayer to God, beseeching him to grant them devotion to the feet of the Lord Raghubīr. Two handsome sons were born to Sītā, Lava and Kuśa, hymned in Veda and Purāṇa, both victorious, modest and accomplished and so beautiful that they seemed the very images of Hari. Each of his brothers also had two sons, very comely, accomplished and virtuous.

He who is beyond knowledge, speech and sense-perception, the uncreated, transcending illusion, intellect and the elements of nature, the sum of True Being, Thought and Bliss, played the high part of a mortal man. Early in the morning he would bathe in the Sarayū and take his seat in the council together with the Brāhmans and nobles. Vasiṣṭha would recite the Vedas and Purāṇas while Rāma listened though he knew them all. He took his meals with his younger brothers, while all the queens watched them with great delight. The two brothers, Bharat and Śatrughna, would go into the garden with the Son of the Wind and sitting there ask him to tell them the story of Rāma's gallant deeds, and Hanumān would repeat it with profoundest wisdom; and when they heard the tale of his stainless exploits, they were so delighted that they would beg him to recite it over and over again. In every single house the Purāṇas were read, and the various sacred stories of Rāma's acts. Men and women sang Rāma's praises and heeded not the passing of night and day.

Not a thousand Śeṣas could describe the wondrous happiness and prosperity of those who dwelt in the city of Avadh where Rāma sat upon the throne.

Every day Nārada and Sanaka and other high sages all came to Ayodhyā to see the king of Kosala, and when they saw the city, they forgot they were ascetics. There were balconies inlaid with gold and jewels, with tessellated pavements of great beauty. All round the city were reared walls of wondrous charm, crowned with turrets of diverse hues, as though the nine planets had mustered an army to beleaguer Amarāvatī. The ground was paved with many-coloured crystal, so lovely that great sages who saw it were bemused. On the gleaming palaces, so lofty that they touched the sky, stood pinnacles brighter than sun or moon; the lattice windows glittered, set close with jewels, and in every house shone gem-encrusted lamps. . . .

The very sight of the city with its groves and gardens and wells and ponds was enough to put to flight all sin. Its matchless reservoirs and ponds and broad and beautiful wells with their elegant flights of steps and their pellucid water so pleased the eye that gods and sages were enchanted by the sight. The many-coloured lotuses, the cooing of innumerable birds and the murmur of the bees made the garden an entrancing spot where cuckoos and other birds with their sweet notes seemed to invite wayfarers to rest.

Can that city be described where Sītā's lord was king? Aṇimā and all the supernatural powers were filling Avadh full of gladness and prosperity. . . .

"The Numberless Marks of the Saint"

'Hear then, brother, the numberless marks of the saint, as recorded in the Vedas and the Purāṇas. The behaviour of the saint and the sinner resembles the conduct of the sandal-tree and the axe; for the axe cuts down the tree, but—mark it, brother—the sandal sheds its natural fragrance on the axe. Wherefore sandal is placed upon the heads of gods and is beloved in this world too, while the blade of the axe is heated in the fire and well hammered; this is its punishment.

'Indifferent to carnal delights, kindly and virtuous, sorrowing when they see another's sorrow and rejoicing in another's joy, equable, the enemy of none, void of pride and passion, abandoning greed and intolerance, exultation and fear, tender-hearted and merciful to the poor, unfeignedly devoted to my person in thought and word and deed, honouring all and caring not for their own dignity—such people, Bharat, are to me as my own life. Naught they desire; they think of nothing but my name; in them dwell peace and continence, humility and joy. They are contented, simple, friendly, serving the feet of Brāhmans with a devotion that brings forth righteousness. Regard him, brother, in whose heart all these marks are found as always and truly a saint. Such swerve not from self-control and continence and strict observance of the moral law. They never speak a harsh word; praise and blame are all one to them, and they love my lotus feet. Such good men are dear to me as life itself, abodes of virtue and all compact of bliss. 'Hear now the characteristics of sinners, with whom one should have no communion whatever, for their company always brings sorrow in its train, as when a vicious cow spoils its gentle companion. The heart of the wicked is ever ablaze; they burn with envy at the sight of another's prosperity, and whenever they hear another slandered, they are as happy as if they had come on treasure lying in the road. They devote themselves to lust and wrath and pride and greed; they are cruel, deceitful, perverse and utterly foul. They pick causeless quarrels with everyone and return evil for good; false about receipts and false about disbursements, false about meals and false about parched gram.[6] They speak you soft but are cruel at heart,

---

[6] This obscure verse is thus interpreted by the ṭīkā: 'they deceive others in matters of business, *or* falsely boast that they have made a lot of money

like the peacock that sings so sweetly and devours large snakes. They are bent on injuring others, they covet their neighbours' wives and wealth and slander them; such men are base and sinful, demons in human form.

'Covetousness is their dress and covetousness their bed; lechery and gluttony their only aims. They have no fear of hell, and when they hear of anyone's advancement, they heave deep sighs as though they had the fever. But when they see anyone in trouble, they are as delighted as though they were kings of the earth. Utterly selfish, quarrelsome among their kinsfolk, dissolute, greedy and prone to wrath, they pay no respect to mother, father, *guru* or Brāhman. They are lost themselves and drag down others with them. In their folly they injure their neighbours and hate the fellowship of saints and the stories of Hari. Oceans of vice, insensate, lustful, critics of the Veda, claiming a right to the property of others, doing all the harm they can to Brāhmans or any others, hypocritical and treacherous at heart but outwardly fair-seeming—such vile and wicked men are not to be found in the Kṛita or the Tretāyuga; some few there are in the Dvāpara, and there will be numbers of them in the Kaliyuga.

'Brother, there is no religious duty like doing good to others, no vileness like doing them harm. This, dear brother, is the doctrine of Veda and Purāṇa that I have disclosed to you, and the learned know it well. Those who in the body cause suffering to others must always live in deadly terror of rebirth; and those who in their folly commit many sins with an eye to their own interests lose their hope of heaven. To such, brother, I am Doom; I apportion the fruit of good and evil deeds. Those who are very wise remember this, and knowing as they do that the world is but sorrow, worship me. They give up action that bears good or evil fruit and worship only me, the Lord of gods and men and sages. Thus have I described the qualities of saints and sinners, and those who fully understand them fall not into the toils of birth and death. . . .'

---

and given thousands in charity; also, they eat a frugal meal of gram and pretend they have enjoyed a banquet, *or* eat gram and falsely explain that they have taken a vow of abstinence.'

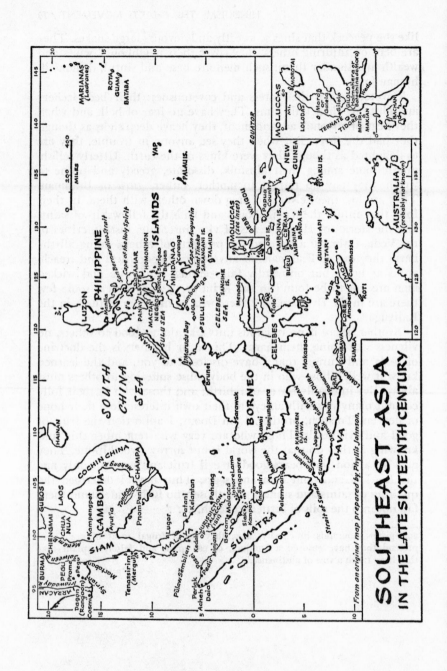

SOUTHEAST ASIA
IN THE LATE SIXTEENTH CENTURY

From an original map prepared by Phyllis Johnson.

III / SOUTHEAST ASIA

INTRODUCTION

There are few indigenous histories of Southeast Asia with any claim to veracity. The extant continental sources, as might be expected, are more numerous than those for the archipelago. Almost no native writings of the preconquest period are available for either the Philippines or Borneo. The Javanese annals are fuller and more numerous than those of any other part of Indonesia, but they are entirely unchronological and replete with legends. Continental sources are likewise sparse and unreliable, or written so long after the event as to be suspect. Most of the early Tai writings were lost in the flames that consumed Ayut'ia in 1767. The extant Siamese and Burmese chronicles dealing with the sixteenth century and earlier were first compiled in the eighteenth century from previous writings, inscriptions, and the oral tradition. They often disagree among themselves on chronology and dating. Since the native documentation is so uncertain, the history of Southeast Asia has had to be largely reconstructed from archaeological deductions and from Chinese, Indian, Muslim, and European sources.

6 / MALACCA AND ITS NEIGHBORS

The city of Malacca, founded early in the fifteenth century, prospered under Malay rule to 1511 as the center of trade for China, Indonesia, India, and the Near East. The site of Malacca was originally a settlement of a few hundred fishermen and the resort

From C. C. Brown, trans. and ed., "Sĕjarah Mĕlayu or 'Malay Annals,' a Translation of Raffles Ms 18 (in the Library of the R.A.S., London)," *Journal of the Malaysian Branch, Royal Asiatic Society*, XXV, Pts. 2 and 3, no. 159 (1953), 52, 54-55, 59, 64-66, 68, 72, 89-90, 115, 157-58, 167-69. Reprinted by permission of C. C. Brown and the Malaysian Branch, Royal Asiatic Society.

of pirates. Its founder, who capably guided the growth of the city during the port's precarious early years, had originally come from Indonesia to Singapore and had finally settled at Malacca shortly after 1400. Known as the Parameswara or "Prince Consort," he was born a prince of Palembang on Sumatra's southeastern coast. The founder first married a Javan princess, and later wed a princess of Pasei (in Sumatra) as a means of establishing good relations with the Muslims on Sumatra's northeastern coast. Parameswara's successors helped to insure the growth of trade with the Muslim merchants of India by converting to Islam themselves. From Malacca the influence of Islam spread throughout the archipelago during the fifteenth century.

In less than fifty years after its founding, Malacca began to expand significantly, especially at the expense of Siam. The seizure of Pahang, a territory rich in minerals in the interior of the Malay peninsula, brought a break in relations between Siam and Malacca. This successful move and the invasion of central Sumatra placed power in the hands of the remarkable Tun Perak for more than fifty years (1446-1498). Tun Perak, who is referred to as Paduka Raja (Viceroy) in the passages below, successfully defended the city-kingdom against Siam's assaults from land and sea. Malacca's jurisdiction in his day stretched from Kedah in the north to the tip of the peninsula, and the ships of Malacca dominated the straits from their bases in both the peninsula and Sumatra. Tun Perak held the civil offices of Viceroy and Bendahara, or Treasurer, and used his double authority to direct the other two officers, the Laksamana, or Admiral, and the Temenggong, or Security Chief. The sultans, too, were subject to Tun Perak's authority and lost real control of affairs. Not long after Tun Perak's death the Portuguese took Malacca and expelled its royal family. Descendants of the last sultan mustered allies, mounted several fierce but unsuccessful attacks on Portuguese Malacca, and finally assumed the title of sultan of Johore in 1540. The revivified Malay empire with its capital at Johore Lama in south-central Malaya retained a precarious independence until the Portuguese destroyed it in 1587.

The native story of Malacca's foundation, rise, and conquest by the Portuguese is preserved in the Sĕjarah Mĕlayu, or Malay Annals, the "best of all the Malay histories" known to us.[1] Its anonymous

---

[1] Estimate of Sir Richard Winstedt in "Malay Chronicles from Sumatra and Malaya," in D.G.E. Hall (ed.), *Historians of South East Asia* (London, 1961), p. 24.

author, evidently a courtier and noble, wrote his wonderful description at Johore in the middle of the sixteenth century. In preparing his narrative, the annalist depended on a few native chronicles and the romances that were then available, but mainly relied on contemporary folklore and oral tradition. From its title one might expect this Malay document to be as terse and factual as certain medieval chronicles. Such is not the case. The annalist, much to the dismay of the modern historian, is generally unconcerned with precise chronology and often blandly disregards consistency. Bent on telling a good story, he adopts an eclectic style, superficially similar to the stream of consciousness technique used by certain modern writers. His history is therefore an impressionistic and atmospheric appreciation of Malacca and Malaya as a great Asian center of cultural mingling and commercial activity. The author's intimacy with the life he describes enables him to show how the Malays gracefully accepted and adjusted themselves to the impact of foreign customs, values, and religious beliefs. He also, unconsciously perhaps, sheds light on characteristic Malay mores and values.

Because the Sějarah Mělayu contains a bewildering mixture of the concrete and the mythical, it must be read with care and understanding. The first chapter, for example, derives in large measure from the Malay romance of Alexander the Great, an Asian counterpart of the Alexander stories which circulated in medieval Europe. Throughout the Eastern world the Macedonian invader of India had a godlike reputation. His exploits were a part of the repertoire of every story-teller, and his deeds, real or imaginary, were soon associated with various locales and historical personages of the East. The sultans of Malacca claimed descent from Rājā Iskandar, the name given to Alexander in the Malay tradition. In the Sějarah Mělayu Alexander is soberly heralded, without any apology to chronology, as the messenger of Islam in Asia. Later the annalist unabashedly gives a contradictory version of the way in which Islam was introduced by Malacca's second ruler. Although historical consistency is maddeningly absent from the annals, the reader nonetheless obtains a view of life and history as seen through Asian eyes. Its anecdotes extoll the cleverness of the Malays and relate court ceremonies in detail. The conquest of Malacca by the Portuguese is attributed to the superiority of Portuguese artillery, to the sultan's refusal to listen to his advisers, to the disorderliness of his administration, and to his irresponsible behavior towards his subjects and allies.

The Sĕjarah Mĕlayu

Beginnings

And as the king,[1] who was hunting, stood under a tree, one of his hounds was kicked by a white mouse-deer. And Sultan Iskandar Shah said, "This is a good place, when even its mouse-deer are full of fight! We shall do well to make a city here." And the chiefs replied, "It is indeed as your Highness says." Thereupon Sultan Iskandar Shah ordered that a city be made, and he asked, "What is the name of the tree under which I am standing?" And they all answered, "It is called *Malaka,* your Highness"; to which he rejoined, "Then Malaka shall be the name of this city."

And Sultan Iskandar Shah took up his abode at Malaka, where he established a system of court ceremonial. It was he who first instituted the appointment of four ministers who were to sit in the hall of audience and hold inquiries; and the appointment of heralds who were to stand on the steps leading up to the throne, forty on either side, and transmit any command given by the king; and the appointment of youths of good family as pages, their duty being to act as bearers of the Raja's personal requisites. . . .

It was he [Sultan Muhammad Shah (1424-1444)] who first instituted royal privileges in regard to yellow, viz. that it could not be worn by commoners or used for cloths, for curtain fringes, for bolster ends, for mattresses or for any kind of wrapping. "You may not use it for stringing jewels, for the adornment of your houses or for any other purpose." It was only for three things, viz. sarongs, jackets and handkerchiefs that it could be used. It was also a royal privilege to have enclosed verandahs, pillars that hung down not reaching to the ground, posts that went right up to the roof-beam of summer-houses, while on boats only royalty could have windows and reception cabins. In regard to umbrellas white was more strictly a royal privilege than yellow, for white umbrellas were reserved for rulers while yellow umbrellas could be used by princes. Commoners might not have metal casing on the sheath of the creese, whether covering it entirely or even going only half way up the sheath. Nor was it permitted to any commoner, however high his rank, to wear anklets of gold: even with silver knobs, gold anklets were a royal privilege. Any one who disobeyed this ordnance was guilty of *Lese majesté* and the penalty was death. No one who pos-

[1] The Parameswara, ruler of Malacca from 1403 to 1424, took the Muslim name Megat Iskandar Shah.

sessed gold, however rich he might be, was permitted to wear it unless it was a present from the Raja, when he might wear it in perpetuity. No person, whoever he might be, might enter the palace without wearing his sarong in the overlap (?) fashion, his creese in front and a scarf over his shoulders. Any one wearing his creese behind would have it confiscated by the gate-keeper. The penalty for disobedience of this order was death.

When the king gave audience, principal ministers, senior war-chiefs and courtiers occupied the body of the hall of audience: princes of the blood royal occupied the gallery on the left and knights the gallery on the right: heralds and young war-chiefs stood at the foot of the dais bearing swords, the heralds on the left being descendants of ministers eligible for the appointments of Bendahara [chief minister], Treasurer or Temenggong, and the chief herald on the right being descended from a war-chief eligible for the appointment of Laksamana [Admiral] or Sri Bija 'diraja: he who bore the title of Sang Guna was Laksamana-designate: and he who bore the title of Tun Pikrama was Bendahara-designate. At the paying of homage the chief of the four or five heralds took precedence of the courtiers who sat in the body of the audience hall and of everybody except principal ministers. Cham shipmasters of high standing and young nobles (who held no office) occupied the balcony of the hall of audience. The Raja's personal requisites, such as his cuspidore, goglet and fan [and shield and bow] were put in the passage, though the betel set was placed in the gallery. The sword of state was borne by the Laksamana or the Sri Bija 'diraja, whose position was in the gallery on the left. If envoys came, the letter was received by the chief herald on the right, while the Raja's reply to the envoys was announced by the herald on the left. The ceremonial prescribed for the arrival or departure of envoys was that a large tray and a salver were to be brought in by a slave from the palace; and the large tray was to be received by the herald on the right and set down as near to the throne as the Bendahara's seat. The shoulder-cloth and the salver were given to the bearer of the letter. If it was a letter from Pasai [in Sumatra] (or from Haru?) it was received with full ceremonial equipment (? big drum,) trumpet, kettledrums and two white umbrellas side by side and the elephant was brought alongside one end of the audience hall. For the Rajas of those two countries (Pasai and Haru [in Sumatra?]) were regarded as equal (to the Raja of Malaka in greatness) and however they (the three) might stand to each other in point of age, it was 'greetings' (not 'obeisance') they sent to each other. To a letter from any other state less respect was accorded, only the big drum, the clarionet and a yellow umbrella being used. The letter was borne on elephant or on horseback as circumstances might demand, and it was taken down (from the elephant or horse as the case might be) outside the outer gate. If (it was a letter from) a Raja of some standing, the trumpet might be used and two umbrellas, one white and one yellow, and the elephant made to kneel outside the inner gate. . . .

Throughout his long reign Sultan Muhammad Shah shewed a high degree of justice in his treatment of his subjects, and Malaka became a great city. Strangers flocked thither and its territory stretched westward as far as Bruas Ujong and eastward as far as Trengganu Ujong Karang.[2] And from below the wind to above the wind Malaka became famous as a very great city, the Raja of which was sprung from the line of Sultan Iskandar Dzu'l-Karnain: so much so that princes from all countries came to present themselves before Sultan Muhammad Shah, who treated them with due respect bestowing upon them robes of honour of the highest distinction together with rich presents of jewels, gold and silver. . . .

Relations with Siam

Here now is the story of the Raja of Siam. From ancient times the country of Siam was known as Shahru'n-nuwi, and all princes of these regions below the wind were subject to Siam, the Raja of which was called the Bubunnya.[3] And when the news reached Siam that Malaka was a great city but was not subject to Siam, the Bubunnya sent an envoy to Malaka to demand a letter of 'obeisance': but Sultan Muzaffar Shah [reigned 1446-1459] refused to own allegiance to Siam. The Raja of Siam was very angry and ordered an expedition to be made ready for the invasion of Malaka. . . .

When Sultan Muzaffar Shah heard this, he gave orders that all men of the outlying districts be assembled and come up river to Malaka. And all the men of the outlying districts foregathered in Malaka. Now Tun Perak had brought the men of Klang [a place to

[2] Ujong means point or promontory. Bruas Ujong is an area north of Malacca in the vicinity of Kedah which is rich in tin. Trengganu Ujong Karang, at the estuary of the Trengganu River on the east coast of the peninsula, was once tributary to Siam.

[3] Siam's ruler, 1448-1488, was Boromo Trailokanat. The "Bubunnya" does not correspond to the common titles signifying "majesty." It may possibly be the king's personal name, considered taboo after the coronation. Perhaps "Bubunnya" can be equated with the office *Văn nă*, known to Europeans as Second King; this official was primarily a general, usually the king's eldest son, and crown prince.

the north of Malacca] to Malaka with womenfolk accompanying them. . . . Later Tun Perak came to present himself before the Raja, and the herald who bore the title of Sri Amarat said to him, "Tun Perak, the men of Klang have made representations to his Highness the Ruler that whereas in the case of other districts it is only men who have come hither to present themselves before the Raja, the men of Klang have been brought by you before the Raja accompanied by their womenfolk. Why have you behaved thus?" But Tun Perak made no answer; and even when Sri Amarat repeated his question, Tun Perak still made no answer. It was not until Sri Amarat had said his say a third time that Tun Perak made answer, thus:—"Sri Amarat, (the Ruler has appointed you to be a herald and has given you a sword;) that sword it is your business to look after, that it may not rust or lose its edge. As for the affairs of me and my men who are on duty, what should you know about them? At the present time his Highness the Ruler here in this city has his consort with him and all that he requires. Is it right in your judgment that we should come hither just we men by ourselves, with Klang so far away? If Malaka here is in trouble, what will my men (far away in Klang) care? That is why I have brought the men of Klang along with their womenfolk so that they may battle against the enemy to the best of their powers. For they will be not so much fighting for his Highness the Ruler as using their spears with might and main for the sake of their womenfolk!" And Sultan Muzaffar Shah smiled when he heard the words of Tun Perak, and he said, "Tun Perak is right." And taking sireh from his bowl he gave it to Tun Perak, saying, "You are wasted at Klang, Tun Perak! You must come and live in the city."

Meanwhile the men of Siam arrived, and they fought with the men of Malaka. After a long battle, in which many of the soldiers of the Raja of Siam were killed, Malaka still held out and the Siamese withdrew. On their retreat they flung down in Ulu Muar [river] the rattans they had used for tying their baggage. These rattans took root and grew, and they are there to this day, known as the rattans of the Siamese. . . .

And after a while the Siamese (again) attacked Malaka, under the command of Awi Dichu. And when the news of their coming reached Malaka, Sultan Muzaffar Shah commanded Bendahara Paduka Raja [Tun Perak's titles] to make ready a fleet to repel the attack, the Sri Bija 'diraja and war-chiefs to accompany him. . . . When the fleet was ready, Bendahara Paduka Raja set out to repel the Siamese, and with him went the Sri Bija 'diraja and the war-chiefs. The Siamese by this time had almost reached Batu Pahat. . . .

Then when night had fallen Awi Dichu advanced, and Bendahara Paduka Raja ordered firebrands to be fastened to mangrove and other trees growing along the shore. And when the Siamese saw these lights, so many that no man could number them, their war-chiefs said, "What a vast fleet these Malays must have, no man can count their ships! If they attack us, how shall we fare? Even one of their ships just now was more than a match for us!" And Awi Dichu replied, "You are right, let us return home!" Whereupon the Siamese returned to their country.

Tributary Relationships

When news reached China of the greatness of the Raja of Malaka, the Raja of China sent envoys to Malaka: and as a complimentary gift to accompany his letter he sent needles, a whole shipload of them. And when the envoys reached Malaka, the king ordered the letter to be fetched from the ship with due ceremony and borne in procession. And when it had been brought into the palace it was received by a herald and given by him to the reader of the mosque, who read it out. It ran as follows:—"This letter from His Majesty the Raja of Heaven is sent to the Raja of Malaka. We hear that the Raja of Malaka is a great raja and we desire accordingly to be on terms of amity with the Raja of Malaka. Of a truth there are no rajas in this world greater than ourselves, and there is no one who knoweth the number of our subjects. We have asked for one needle from each house in our realm and those are the needles with which the ship we send to Malaka is laden."

When Sultan Mansur Shah [reigned 1459-1477] heard how the letter ran he smiled. He then gave orders that the ship should be cleared of the needles and filled with fried sago [bread made of flour of the sago palm]. Tun Perpateh Puteh, younger brother of Bendahara Paduka Raja, was then commanded by Sultan Mansur Shah to go as envoy to China. He set out and after a voyage of some length arrived at his destination. The Raja of China ordered the Malaka letter to be borne in procession, but the procession was halted at the house of the chief minister, whose name was Ling Ho. Shortly before dawn Ling Ho and the chief notables went to the palace domain to present themselves before the Raja of China, and Tun Perpateh Puteh accompanied them. And (there came a vast flock of) crows which followed them in. When they arrived at the outer gate of the palace, Ling Ho and the notables who were with him stopped, and the crows stopped also. The gong of summons then sounded and the whole party passed through the gate. This happened at each of the seven successive gates. And when it was day they entered the palace and took their seats in the hall of audience: and so many were those that were presenting themselves that they sat jammed knee to knee. And the crows spread their wings over-shadowing those who were present. Thereupon was heard the rumble of thunder and the crash of thunder-claps, and forked lightning flashed, betokening the appearance of the Raja of China. Presently he appeared, faintly visible through the glass of the drag-ons' mouth litter on which he was borne. Thereupon all those present bowed their heads and lifted not their faces. The letter from Malaka was then read and the Raja of China was well pleased to hear what it said. And the sago was brought before the Raja of China, and he asked how it was made. And Tun Perpateh Puteh answered, "After this fashion, your Highness: our Raja ordered that each of his subjects should roll out a grain of sago until there were enough to fill a ship. That will indicate how many are the subjects of our Raja, no man knows their number!" Then said the Raja of China, "Great indeed must be this Raja of Malaka! The multitude of his subjects must be as the multitude of our own. It would be well that I should marry him with my daughter!" And turning to Ling Ho the Raja of China said, "If even the Raja of Malaka can order his subjects to do such work as rolling out grains of sago, by how much the more can I! In future all rice for my eating is to be husked grain by grain, there is to be no more pounding." And Ling Ho replied, "Very well"; and that is why to this day the Raja of China eats no pounded rice but only rice that has been husked grain by grain. . . .

Ere long the Raja of the Moluccas came to Malaka to do homage; and it happened that at that time the Telanai of Trengganu and the Raja of Rekan were at Malaka doing homage. The Raja of the Moluccas was given robes of honour and other presents as befitted his rank. He was an expert at Malay football (*sepak raga*) and the young nobles of Malaka played football with him, he being the leader in each game. When the ball came to him, he would kick it himself a hundred or even a hundred and fifty times before he passed it to someone else; and he would indicate to whomsoever he proposed to give the ball and then pass it without once making a mistake. Then he would sit down on a chair to rest and be fanned by men in pairs, while the young men went on playing. Then when (? he resumed playing and) the ball came to him, the Raja of the

Moluccas would kick it himself for as long as it takes to cook pot after pot of rice and the ball would stay up in the air until he wished to pass it to someone else: such was his skill at the game. And he was possessed of great strength: with a single stroke of his sword he could cut through a coconut palm big enough to be bearing fruit. The Telanai of Trengganu could drive a spear through such a palm, and Sultan Ala'u'd-din who was even more powerful still, could shoot it away with an arrow! The Raja of the Moluccas and the Telanai of Trengganu were great favourites of Sultan Ala'u'd-din [reigned 1477-1488]. . . .

The Portuguese Conquest

Now the city of Malaka at that time [ca. 1500] flourished exceedingly and many foreigners resorted thither; so much so that from Ayer Leleh to Hulu Muar there was an unbroken line of habitations, and it was thus too from Kampong Kling to Kualá Penajeh. People journeying even as far as Jenggra had no need to take firing with them, for wherever they stopped on the way there would be a dwelling-house. Such was the greatness of Malaka at that time; in the city alone there were a hundred and ninety thousand people, to say nothing of the inhabitants of the outlying territories and coastal districts.

After a while there came a ship of the Franks [Portuguese] from Goa trading to Malaka: and the Franks perceived how prosperous and well populated the port was. The people of Malaka for their part came crowding to see what the Franks looked like; and they were all astonished and said, "These are white Bengalis!" Around each Frank there would be a crowd of Malays, some of them twisting his beard, some of them fingering his head, some taking off his hat, some grasping his hand. And the commander of the ship landed and presented himself before Bendahara Sri Maharaja, who adopted him as his son and gave him robes of honour, as befitted his rank, while the commander for his part presented Bendahara Sri Maharaja with the gold chain.

And when the season came round (for the return journey) the commander went back to Goa, where he described to the Viceroy the greatness of the city of Malaka, the prosperity of the port and the number of the inhabitants. The Viceroy at that time was one Alfonso d'Albuquerque. When he realised (? the greatness of) Malaka, the Viceroy was seized with desire to possess it, and he ordered a fleet to be made ready consisting of seven carracks, ten long galleys and thirteen foysts. When the fleet was ready, he ordered it to attack Malaka. On arrival at Malaka the ships forthwith opened fire with their cannon. And the people of Malaka were bewildered and filled with fear at the sound of the cannon, and they said, "What sound is this like thunder?" And when presently the cannon balls began to arrive and struck the people of Malaka, so that some had their heads shot away, some their arms and some their legs, the people of Malaka were more and more astonished to see what manner of thing this artillery was, and they said, "What may be this round weapon that yet is sharp enough to kill us?" The next day the Franks landed two thousand men armed with matchlocks apart from a vast horde of sailors and sepoys: and the men of Malaka under the leadership of Tun Hasan Temenggong went out to repel them. And when they encountered the Franks, battle was engaged, (the flashes of fire from the cannon being like flashes of lightning in the heaven?) and the weapons falling like heavy rain. Then Tun Hasan Temenggong and the men of Malaka charged; and the line of the Franks was broken and they gave ground. Then the men of Malaka charged again, and this time the Franks were routed and fled to the waterside, pursued by the men of Malaka. They then embarked and sailed for Goa. And when they reached Goa, they related to the Viceroy all that had happened. The Viceroy was very angry and was for ordering a fresh fleet to be made ready there and then for another attack on Malaka. But the commander of the Moors dissuaded him, saying, "As long as Bandahara Sri Maharaja is alive, Malaka will never fall." To which the Viceroy replied, "That being so, wait till I am no longer Viceroy and I will go myself and attack Malaka!"

God alone knoweth the truth.

Here now is a story of Fongso d'Albuquerque. At the end of his term of office as viceroy [1509-1515] he proceeded to Pertugal and presenting himself before the Raja of Pertugal asked for an armada. The Raja of Pertugal gave him four carracks and five long galleys. He then returned from Pertugal and fitted out a fleet at Goa, consisting of three carracks, eight galeasses, four long galleys and fifteen foysts. There were thus forty (sic) craft in all. With this fleet he sailed for Malaka. And when he reached Malaka, there was great excitement and word was brought to Sultan Ahmad [reigning in 1511 in place of his father], "The Franks are come to attack us! They have seven carracks, eight galeasses, ten long galleys, fifteen sloops and five foysts." Thereupon Sultan Ahmad had all his forces assembled and he ordered them to make ready their equipment. And the Franks engaged the men of Malaka in battle, and they fired their cannon from their ships so that the cannon balls came like rain. And the noise of the cannon was as the noise of thunder in the heavens

and the flashes of fire of their guns were like flashes of lightning in
the sky: and the noise of their matchlocks was like that of ground-
nuts popping in the frying-pan. So heavy was the gun-fire that the
men of Malaka could no longer maintain their position on the
shore. The Franks then bore down upon the bridge with their galleys and foysts. Thereupon Sultan Ahmad came forth, mounted on
his elephant Jituji. . . .

And the king went forth on to the bridge and stood there amid a
hail of bullets. . . .

When day dawned, the Franks landed and attacked. And Sultan
Ahmad mounted his elephant Juru Demang, with the Sri Awadana
on the elephant's head and Tun 'Ali Hati balancing the king on
the packsaddle. The Franks then fiercely engaged the men of
Malaka in battle and so vehement was their onslaught that the
Malaka line was broken, leaving the king on his elephant isolated
(?). And the king fought with the Franks pike to pike, and he was
wounded in the palm of the hand. And he shewed the palm of his
hand, saying "See this, Malays!" And when they saw that Sultan
Ahmad was wounded in the hand, the war-chiefs returned to the attack and fought the Franks.

And Tun Salehu'd-din called upon Orang Kaya Sogoh to fight
with the Franks pike to pike. And Tun Salehu'd-din was struck in
the chest and killed, and twenty of the leading war-chiefs were
killed. The Sri Awadana was wounded in the groin, so the elephant
was made to kneel and he was put on a litter. Sultan Ahmad ordered him to be examined by a doctor, who explored the wound
with the pointed end of a sireh leaf and said, "All is well, the wound
can be treated. But had it been half a rice grain deeper, the Sri
Awadana would have died." And Malaka fell. The Franks advanced
on the King's audience hall (?) and the men of Malaka fled. Bendahara Lubok Batu was borne off the field by one Selamat Gagah,
closely pursued by the Franks. And the Bendahara said to the man
who was bearing him, "Hurl me against the Franks!" But his
family would not allow this. Whereupon the Bendahara cried,
"What cowards these young men are! If I was still a young man, I
would die fighting for Malaka!"

7 / THE PHILIPPINES AND BORNEO

*Before the Europeans arrived in the eastern part of the archipelago
in the early sixteenth century, Islam had become important in
Borneo and was beginning to establish itself in the southern Philip-*
Antonio Pigafetta, *Magellan's Voyage around the World* (Cleveland, 1906), I,

pines. The Portuguese, who followed the Muslim invasion route from Malacca to Java and the Moluccas, made no systematic efforts in the sixteenth century to penetrate either Borneo or the Philippines. The easternmost islands of the archipelago therefore became the base of operations for Spanish endeavors in the Far East during the sixteenth century. And the Spanish, beginning with Magellan's voyage, came into southeastern Asia from across the Pacific.

The pre-European past of Borneo and the Philippines is known only through a few inscriptions and the infrequent references found in Indian, Javanese, Muslim, and Chinese writings. Although these islands were certainly visited regularly by Asian and Muslim merchants, they were not "discovered" for Europe until Magellan's visit of 1521. The following descriptions are among the earliest systematic accounts available in any language on these islands— their locations, people, products, and customs.

Antonio Pigafetta, one of eighteen men fortunate enough to return from the first circumnavigation of the world, is the author of these word portraits. A native of Vincenza in Italy, Pigafetta was at the court of Spain in 1519 when the Magellan fleet was being prepared at Seville. The young Italian had read about the discoveries and was eager, as he said, "to experience and go to see these things for myself." With the permission of King Charles I of Spain, Pigafetta sailed with Magellan as a supernumerary. This meant that he had no specific duties aboard ship, though he was used by Magellan as an emissary to the native rulers visited by the expedition. A man of considerable curiosity and a keen observer, Pigafetta had time enough to keep careful notes of what he saw or heard about. He was also sufficiently interested in the native languages to compile vocabularies of Bisayan and Malayan words, and he may have been able to speak a bit of commercial Malay before he left the archipelago.

In the following extracts Pigafetta, after a long and arduous voyage across the Pacific, is obviously pleased to be received hospitably by the chieftains of Homohon, Limasawa, and Cebu, three islands of the southern Philippines. His picturesque description of Brunei, the major port of Borneo, and his account of the reception given by its ruler is based on observations made during a two-day halt. Although Pigafetta is sometimes superficial in his observations and hasty in his conclusions, his descriptions are vivid and remarkably unbiased. Only excerpts from Pigafetta's narrative were published

99, 101, 103, 107, 109, 113, 115, 117, 119, 183; II, 29, 31, 33, 35. Reprinted by permission of the publishers, The Arthur H. Clark Company, from James Alexander Robertson's translation of *Magellan's Voyage*, by Antonio Pigafetta.

in his own lifetime; the text that we use today remained in manu-script until it was published in 1894 by an Italian scholar.

At dawn on Saturday, March sixteen, 1521, we came upon a high land at a distance of three hundred leguas from the islands of Latroni [Ladrones or Mariana Islands]—an island named Zamal [*i.e.*, Samar in the Philippines]. The following day, the captain-general [Magellan] desired to land on another island [Homonhon] which was uninhabited and lay to the right of the above-mentioned island, in order to be more secure, and to get water and have some rest. He had two tents set up on the shore for the sick and had a sow killed for them. On Monday afternoon, March 18, we saw a boat coming toward us with nine men in it. Therefore, the captain-general ordered that no one should move or say a word without his permission. When those men reached the shore, their chief went immediately to the captain-general, giving signs of joy because of our arrival. Five of the most ornately adorned of them remained with us, while the rest went to get some others who were fishing, and so they all came. The captain-general seeing that they were reasonable men, ordered food to be set before them, and gave them red caps, mirrors, combs, bells, ivory, bocasine, and other things. When they saw the captain's courtesy, they presented fish, a jar of palm wine, which they call *uraca* [*i.e.*, arrack], figs more than one palmo long [*i.e.*, bananas], and others which were smaller and more delicate, and two cocoanuts. They had nothing else then, but made us signs with their hands that they would bring *umay* or rice, and cocoanuts and many other articles of food within four days.

Cocoanuts are the fruit of the palmtree. Just as we have bread, wine, oil, and milk, so those people get everything from that tree. They get wine in the following manner. They bore a hole into the heart of the said palm at the top called palmito [*i.e.*, stalk], from which distils a liquor which resembles white must. That liquor is sweet but somewhat tart, and [is gathered] in canes [of bamboo] as thick as the leg and thicker. They fasten the bamboo to the tree at evening for the morning, and in the morning for the evening. That palm bears a fruit, namely, the cocoanut, which is as large as the head or thereabouts. Its outside husk is green and thicker than two fingers. Certain filaments are found in that husk, whence is made cord for binding together their boats. Under that husk there is a hard shell, much thicker than the shell of the walnut, which they burn and make therefrom a powder that is useful to them. Under that shell there is a white marrowy substance one finger in thickness, which they eat fresh with meat and fish as we do bread; and it has a taste resembling the almond. It could be dried and made into bread. There is a clear, sweet water in the middle of that marrowy substance which is very refreshing. When that water stands for a while after having been collected, it congeals and becomes like an apple. When the natives wish to make oil, they take that cocoanut, and allow the marrowy substance and the water to putrefy. Then they boil it and it becomes oil like butter. When they wish to make vinegar, they allow only the water to putrefy, and then place it in the sun, and a vinegar results like [that made from] white wine. Milk can also be made from it for we made some. We scraped that marrowy substance and then mixed the scrapings with its own water which we strained through a cloth, and so obtained milk like goat's milk. Those palms resemble date-palms, but although not smooth they are less knotty than the latter. A family of x [10] persons can be supported on two trees, by utilizing them week about [every other week] for the wine; for if they did otherwise, the trees would dry up. They last a century. . . .

At noon on Friday, March 22, those men came as they had promised us in two boats with cocoanuts, sweet oranges, a jar of palm-wine, and a cock, in order to show us that there were fowls in that district. They exhibited great signs of pleasure at seeing us. We purchased all those articles from them. Their seignior was an old man who was painted [i.e., tattooed]. He wore two gold earrings [schione] in his ears, and the others many gold armlets on their arms and kerchiefs about their heads. We stayed there one week, and during that time our captain went ashore daily to visit the sick, and every morning gave them cocoanut water from his own hand, which comforted them greatly. There are people living near that island who have holes in their ears so large that they can pass their arms through them. Those people are caphri, that is to say, heathen. They go naked, with a cloth woven from the bark of a tree about their privies, except some of the chiefs who wear cotton cloth embroidered with silk at the ends by means of a needle. They are dark, fat, and painted. They anoint themselves with cocoanut and with beneseed oil, as a protection against sun and wind. They have very black hair that falls to the waist, and use daggers, knives, and spears ornamented with gold, large shields, fascines, javelins, and fishing nets that resemble rizali; and their boats are like ours. . . .

When I reached shore [on the island of Limasawa, south of Leyte], the king raised his hands toward the sky and then turned toward us two. We did the same toward him as did all the others.

The king took me by the hand; one of his chiefs took my companion: and thus they led us under a bamboo covering, where there was a balanghai [barangay, or a boat] as long as eighty of my palm lengths, and resembling a fusta. We sat down upon the stern of that balanghai, constantly conversing with signs. The king's men stood about us in a circle with swords, daggers, spears, and bucklers. The king had a plate of pork brought in and a large jar filled with wine. At every mouthful, we drank a cup of wine. The wine that was left [in the cup] at any time, although that happened but rarely, was put into a jar by itself. The king's cup was always kept covered and no one else drank from it but he and I. Before the king took the cup to drink, he raised his clasped hands toward the sky, and then toward me; and when he was about to drink, he extended the fist of his left hand toward me (at first I thought that he was about to strike me) and then drank. I did the same toward the king. They all make those signs one toward another when they drink.[1] We ate with such ceremonies and with other signs of friendship. I ate meat on holy Friday, for I could not help myself. Before the supper hour I gave the king many things which I had brought. I wrote down the names of many things in their language.[2] When the king and the others saw me writing, and when I told them their words, they were all astonished. While engaged in that the supper hour was announced. Two large porcelain dishes were brought in, one full of rice and the other of pork with its gravy. We ate with the same signs and ceremonies, after which we went to the palace of the king which was built like a hayloft and was thatched with fig [i.e., banana] and palm leaves. It was built up high from the ground on huge posts of wood and it was necessary to ascend to it by means of ladders. The king made us sit down there on a bamboo mat with our feet drawn up like tailors. . . . Before we left, the king kissed our hands with great joy, and we his. One of his brothers, the king of another island, and three men came with us. The captain-general kept him to dine with us, and gave him many things.

Pieces of gold, of the size of walnuts and eggs are found by sifting the earth in the island of that king who came to our ships.[3] All the dishes of that king are of gold and also some portion of his house, as we were told by that king himself. According to their customs he was very grandly decked out [molto in ordine], and the finest looking man that we saw among those people. His hair was exceedingly

---

[1] A good description of ritual drinking.
[2] I.e., in phonetic transcription.
[3] Gold is still found in northern Mindanao.

black, and hung to his shoulders. He had a covering of silk on his head, and wore two large golden earrings fastened in his ears. He wore a cotton cloth all embroidered with silk, which covered him from the waist to the knees. At his side hung a dagger, the haft of which was somewhat long and all of gold, and its scabbard of carved wood. He had three spots of gold on every tooth and his teeth appeared as if bound with gold. He was perfumed with storax and benzoin. He was tawny and painted [*i.e.*, tattooed] all over. That island of his was called Butuan and Calagan.[4] When those kings wished to see one another, they both went to hunt in that island where we were. The name of the first king is Raia Colambu, and the second Raia Siaui. . . .

In that island are found dogs, cats, rice, millet, panicum, sorgo, ginger, figs [*i.e.*, bananas], oranges, lemons, sugarcane, garlic, honey, cocoanuts, nangcas, gourds, flesh of many kinds, palm wine, and gold. It is a large island, and has a good port with two entrances— one to the west and the other to the east northeast. It lies in x [ten] degrees of latitude toward the Arctic Pole, and in a longitude of one hundred and sixty-four degrees from the line of demarcation. Its name is Zubu [Cebu]. We heard of Malucho [Moluccas] there before the death of the captain-general. Those people play a violin with copper strings.

Words of those heathen people

For Man	lac
for Woman	paranpaon
for Young woman	beni beni
for Married woman	babay
for Hair	boho
for Face	guay
for Eyelids	pilac
for Eyebrows	chilei
for Eye	matta
for Nose	ilon

* * *

When we reached the city [Brunei], we remained about two hours in the prau, until the arrival of two elephants with silk trappings, and twelve men each of whom carried a porcelain jar covered with silk in which to carry our presents. Thereupon, we mounted the elephants while those twelve men preceded us afoot with the pres-

[4] Butuan and Caraga in northeastern Mindanao.

ents in the jars. In this way we went to the house of the governor, where we were given a supper of many kinds of food. During the night we slept on cotton mattresses, whose lining was of taffeta, and the sheets of Cambaia. Next day we stayed in the house until noon. Then we went to the king's palace upon elephants, with our presents in front as on the preceding day. All the streets from the governor's to the king's house were full of men with swords, spears, and shields, for such were the king's orders. We entered the courtyard of the palace mounted on the elephants. We went up a ladder accompanied by the governor and other chiefs, and entered a large hall full of many nobles, where we sat down upon a carpet with the presents in the jars near us. At the end of that hall there is another hall higher but somewhat smaller. It was all adorned with silk hangings, and two windows, through which light entered the hall and hung with two brocade curtains, opened from it. There were three hundred footsoldiers with naked rapiers at their thighs in that hall to guard the king. At the end of the small hall was a large window from which a brocade curtain was drawn aside so that we could see within it the king seated at a table with one of his young sons chewing betel. No one but women were behind him. Then a chief told us that we could not speak to the king, and that if we wished anything, we were to tell it to him, so that he could communicate it to one of higher rank. The latter would communicate it to a brother of the governor who was stationed in the smaller hall, and this man would communicate it by means of a speaking-tube through a hole in the wall to one who was inside with the king. The chief taught us the manner of making three obeisances to the king with our hands clasped above the head, raising first one foot and then the other and then kissing the hands toward him, and we did so, that being the method of the royal obeisance. We told the king that we came from the king of Spagnia, and that the latter desired to make peace with him and asked only for permission to trade. The king had us told that since the king of Spagnia desired to be his friend, he was very willing to be his, and said that we could take water and wood, and trade at our pleasure. Then we gave him the presents, on receiving each of which he nodded slightly. To each one of us was given some brocaded and gold cloth and silk, which were placed upon our left shoulders, where they were left but a moment. They presented us with refreshments of cloves and cinnamon, after which the curtains were drawn to and the windows closed. The men in the palace were all attired in cloth of gold and silk which covered their privies, and carried daggers with gold hafts adorned with pearls and precious gems, and they had many rings on their hands. We returned upon the elephants to the governor's house, seven men carrying the king's presents to us and always preceding us. When we reached the house, they gave each one of us his present, placing them upon our left shoulders. We gave each of those men a couple of knives for his trouble. Nine men came to the governor's house with a like number of large wooden trays from the king. Each tray contained ten or twelve porcelain dishes full of veal, capons, chickens, peacocks, and other animals, and fish. We supped on the ground upon a palm mat from thirty or thirty-two different kinds of meat besides the fish and other things. At each mouthful of food we drank a small cupful of their distilled wine from a porcelain cup the size of an egg. We ate rice and other sweet food with gold spoons like ours. In our sleeping quarters there during those two nights, two torches of white wax were kept constantly alight in two rather tall silver candlesticks, and two large lamps full of oil with four wicks apiece and two men to snuff them continually. We went elephant-back to the seashore, where we found two praus which took us back to the ships. That city [Brunei] is entirely built in salt water, except the houses of the king and certain chiefs. It contains twenty-five thousand fires [*i.e.*, families]. The houses are all constructed of wood and built up from the ground on tall pillars. When the tide is high the women go in boats through the settlement [*tera*] selling the articles necessary to maintain life. There is a large brick wall in front of the king's house with towers like a fort, in which were mounted fifty-six bronze pieces, and six of iron. During the two days of our stay there, many pieces were discharged. That king is a Moro and his name is Raia Siripada.[5] He was forty years old and corpulent. No one serves him except women who are the daughters of chiefs. He never goes outside of his palace, unless when he goes hunting, and no one is allowed to talk with him except through the speaking tube. He has x [ten] scribes, called Xiritoles, who write down his deeds on very thin tree bark. . . .

[5] "Siripada" means "His Majesty."

IV / CHINA

INTRODUCTION

No people have a more ancient past or a greater respect for historical records than the Chinese. Consequently, no country possesses a
documentation comparable to that found in their detailed annals.
History, even in ancient times, was regarded in China as a model,
guide, and warning to the reigning ruler. Many of the classics
written in the pre-Christian era were actually historical writings,
and history soon became one of the four main categories of Chinese
literature. In the first century B.C. Ssū-ma Ch'ien attempted a universal history, which set a standard for reliability and objectivity
that was probably not equaled by historical writers in the West until
the seventeenth century. In the first century A.D. Pan Ku wrote a
history of the preceding dynasty which became the prototype for
the genre of historical writing known as the "dynastic history."
Hereafter it became the traditional duty of each new dynasty to
keep the record of the past continuous by compiling a history of its
predecessor. The modern student of Chinese history is rarely ham-
pered by a lack of native source material; his problem is rather one
of evaluating, analyzing, and exploiting effectively the vast and diverse collections of available materials.

8 / A JESUIT DESCRIPTION OF 1590

The Chinese, like any other people, take for granted many things
about themselves and their country which foreigners can only learn
through long and arduous investigation and experience. And since

From Richard Hakluyt, ed., *The Principal Navigations, Voiages, Traffiques and*
Discoveries of the English Nation . . . these 1500 Yeeres . . . (London, 1598-
1600), II, Pt. 2, 88-97.

China's was one of the most advanced and complex civilizations of the sixteenth century, foreign observers and commentators of that day could hardly gain more than a series of surface impressions about its size, population, customs, and institutions. Among the best foreign sources on Ming China are accounts prepared by the European sailors, merchants, and missionaries who visited there. Although many of their comments are obviously naive and their understanding imperfect, these writings convey to us a feeling of the astonishment they felt on encountering the richest and most variegated civilization of the distant East.

Portuguese contacts with China became more numerous after 1514 and, for the next fifty years, the general public of Europe relied on the Portuguese for a contemporary, firsthand glimpse of China's mighty kingdom. This official view was continually supplemented in the latter half of the century by notices contained in letters from the field from Jesuit missionaries whose activities were supported by the Portuguese government. The Jesuit missionaries, following the lead of St. Francis Xavier, conscientiously accumulated information about China so that they would be prepared to proselytize in that immense empire, as soon as the Emperor should permit them. Beginning in the 1550's the island of Macao served as their staging ground for the penetration of China. From this vantage point they came to realize that the simple techniques of teaching and conversion, previously used elsewhere, would not gain them followers in China. To gain acceptance in China, it would be necessary to learn the language and to make a sincere effort to understand the presuppositions of Chinese civilization. A policy of cultural affiliation would be required if they were to communicate effectively with members of the influential official class of China and gain their respect. Through the pioneering efforts of Alessandro Valignano and Matteo Ricci, the Jesuits finally succeeded in penetrating China in 1583 and by 1601 they had a mission at Peking.

According to official Jesuit instructions, regular reports on missionary activities had to be sent from the field to the Society in Europe. Selections from these writings were frequently published in Europe to elicit volunteers and contributions to further the missionary work. In addition to the letters published in booklets in many languages, the Society of Jesus issued official histories of the Eastern mission. But perhaps the most sensational idea for publicizing the Eastern mission was the dispatch to Europe under Jesuit auspices of an embassy of four young Japanese converts to Christianity who spent some twenty months (1584-1586) traveling through

Iberia and Italy where they were welcomed by secular and ecclesiastical princes alike. After the return home of the Japanese envoys, the Jesuits in Macao prepared and printed a book (1590) in dialogue form intended as Latin reading for Japanese converts. It sought to describe Europe and other places, such as China, on the route followed by the Japanese embassy. A copy of this book was on its way to Europe in 1592 when the Portuguese ship carrying it was intercepted near the Azores by an English squadron.

The Jesuit book was discovered on the captured vessel "inclosed in a case of sweete cedar wood and lapped up almost an hundredfold in fine Calicut cloth, as though it had beene some incomparable jewell"; the volume was soon put into the hands of Richard Hakluyt, a great collector of travel literature who was keenly interested in promoting English participation in overseas activities. Hakluyt immediately had a part of the confiscated volume translated, entitled it "An excellent treatise of the kingdome of China . . . ," and included it in the expanded edition of his Principal Navigations *issued in 1599. As a summation of the knowledge of China available to those Westerners in the best position to know, the missionaries in China, the following excerpt is truly incomparable. That it should have been "pirated" and published in London testifies to the rising interest in overseas endeavor in northern Europe.*

**An Excellent Treatise of the Kingdome of China,
and of the Estate and Government Thereof:
Printed in Latine at Macao a Citie of the
Portugals in China, An. Dom. 1590. and
Written Dialogue-wise. The Speakers Are
Linus, Leo, and Michael.**

. . . MICHAEL. Because the report of this most famous kingdome is growen so common among us, reducing divers and manifold particulars into order, I will especially aime at the trueth of things received from the fathers of the societie,[1] which even now at this present are conversant in China. First of all therefore it is not unknowen, that of all parts of the maine continent this kingdom of China is situate most Easterly: albeit certaine Ilands, as our native Japon, & the Ile of Manilia stand more Easterly then China it selfe. As touching the limites & bounds of this kingdom, we may appoint the first towards ye West to be a certaine Ile commonly called Hainan, which standeth in 19 degrees of Northerly latitude.[2] For the continent next adjoining unto this Ile trendeth towardes the

[1] Society of Jesus.
[2] The twentieth parallel touches its north coast.

East, and that especially, where the promontorie of the citie called Nimpo or Liampo³ doeth extend it selfe. Howbeit, from that place declining Northward, it stretcheth foorth an huge length, insomuch that the farthest Chinian inhabitants that way doe behold the North pole elevated, at least 50 degrees, and perhaps more also: whereupon a man may easilie conjecture (that I may speake like an Astronomer) how large the latitude of this kingdom is, when as it containeth about more then 540 leagues⁴ in direct extension towards the North. But as concerning the longitude which is accounted from East to West, it is not so exactly found out, that it may be distinguished into degrees. Howbeit certaine it is, that according to the Map wherein the people of China describe the forme of their kingdom, the latitude thereof doeth not much exceed ye longitude. This kingdom therfore is, without all peradventure, of all earthly kingdoms the most large and spacious: for albeit divers other kings under their jurisdiction containing in dimensions more length & breadth then all China, do possesse very many kingdoms & far distant asunder: yet none of them all enjoieth any one kingdom so large and so ample, as the most puissant king of China doeth. Now, if we shall make enquirie into his revenues and tributes, true it is, that this king of all others, is endued with the greatest and the richest, both in regard of the fertilitie & greatnes of his dominions, & also by reason of the severe collection and exaction of his duties: yea, tributes are imposed upon his subjects, not onely for lands, houses, and impost of marchandise, but also for every person in each family. It is likewise to be understood, that almost no lord or potentate in China hath authoritie to levie unto himselfe any peculiar revenues, or to collect any rents within the precincts of his seigniories, alsuch power belonging onely unto the king: whereas in Europe the contrary is most commonly seen, as we have before signified. In this most large kingdom are conteined 15 provinces, every one of which were in it selfe sufficient to be made one great kingdom. Six of these provinces do border upon the sea, namely (yᵗ I may use the names of the Chinians themselves) Coantum,⁵ Foquien,⁶ Chequiam,⁷ Nanquin,⁸ Xantum,⁹ Paquin:¹⁰ the other 9 be in-land provinces

³ Ningpo in Chekiang Province.
⁴ A league is approximately four miles.
⁵ Kwangtung.
⁶ Fukien.
⁷ Chekiang.
⁸ Nanking; comprising roughly modern Anhwei and Kiangsu.
⁹ Shantung.
¹⁰ Peking; comprising roughly modern Hopeh; sometimes spoken of as Northern Metropolitan Area (Pei-chih-li).

namely, Quiansi,[11] Huquam,[12] Honan,[13] Xiensi,[14] Xansi,[15] Su-
chuon,[16] Queicheu,[17] Junan,[18] Coansi.[19] Amongst all the foresayd
provinces, two are allotted for the kings court and seat roial, that is
to say, Paquin for his court in the North, and Nanquin for his court
in the South. For the kings of China were woont to be resident altogether at the South court: but afterward, by reason of the manifold
and cruell warres mooved by the Tartars, they were constrained to
defixe their princely seate and habitation in that extreme province of
the North. Whereupon it commeth to passe, that those Northren
confines of the kingdom doe abound with many moe fortresses,
martiall engines, and garrisons of souldiers.

LEO. I have heard, amongst those munitions, a certaine strange
and admirable wall reported of, wherewith the people of China doe
represse and drive backe the Tartars attempting to invade their
territories.

MICHAEL. Certes that wall which you have heard tell of is most
woorthie of admiration; for it runneth alongst the borders of three
Northerlie provinces, Xiensi, Xansi, and Paquin, and is sayd to
containe almost three hundred leagues in length, and in such sort
to bee built, that it hindereth not the courses and streames of any
rivers, their channels being overthwarted and fortified with wonderfull bridges and other defences. Yet is it not unlikely, that the sayd
wall is built in such sort, that onely lowe and easie passages bee
therewith stopped and environed; but the mountaines running betweene those lowe passages are, by their owne naturall strength, and
inaccessible heigth, a sufficient fortification agaynst the enemie.

LINUS. Tell us (Michael) whether the kingdome of China be so
frequented with inhabitants, as wee have often bene informed, or
no?

MICHAEL. It is (Linus) in very deed a most populous kingdom,
as I have bene certified from the fathers of the societie: who having
seen sundry provinces of Europe renoumed for the multitude of
their inhabitants, doe notwithstanding greatly admire the infinite
swarmes of people in China. Howbeit these multitudes are not

[11] Kiangsi.
[12] Hukwang (includes modern provinces of Hunan and Hupeh).
[13] Honan.
[14] Shensi.
[15] Shansi.
[16] Szechwan.
[17] Kweichou.
[18] Yunnan.
[19] Kwangsi.

pel-mel and confusively dispersed over the land, but most con-
veniently and orderly distributed in their townes and famous cities:
of which assemblies there are divers kindes among the Chinians. For
they have certaine principal cities called by the name of Fu[20] other
inferior cities called Cheu[21] and of a third kind also named Hien,[22]
which be indeed walled townes, but are not privileged with the
dignities and prerogatives of cities. To these may be added two
other kindes of lesser townes, which are partly villages, and partly
garrisons of souldiers. Of the first and principall kind is that most
noble citie standing neere unto the port of Macao, called by the
Chinians Coanchefu,[23] but by the Portugals commonly termed
Cantam, which is rather the common name of the province, then a
word of their proper imposition. Unto the third kind appertaineth
a towne, which is yet nigher unto the port of Macao, called by the
Portugals Ansam, but by the Chinians Hiansanhien.[24] Al the foresayd provinces therefore have their greater cities named Fu, & their
lesser cities called Cheu, unto both of which the other townes may
be added. Moreover, in every province there is a certain principal
city which is called the Metropolitane thereof, wherein the chief
magistrates have their place of residence, as the principal citie by
me last mentioned, which is the head of the whole province called
Coantum. The number of the greater cities throughout the whole
kingdom is more then 150, and there is the same or rather a greater
multitude of inferiour cities. Of walled townes not endued with
the privileges of cities there are mo then 1120[25]: the villages &
garrisons can scarce be numbred: over & besides the which convents
it is incredible what a number of countrie farmes or granges there
be: for it is not easie to find any place desert or void of inhabitants
in all that land. Now in the sea, in rivers, & in barks there are such
abundance of people, and of whole families inhabiting, that even
the Europæans themselves doe greatly wonder thereat: insomuch
that some (albeit beyond measure) have bene perswaded that there
are as many people dwelling upon the water as upon the land.
Neither were they induced so to thinke altogether without prob-
abilitie: for whereas the kingdom of China is in all parts thereof
interfused with commodious rivers, & in many places consisteth of

[20] *Fu* or prefecture.
[21] *Chou* or sub-prefecture.
[22] *Hsien* or county.
[23] Kwangchou fu or Canton.
[24] Ao-men and Hsing-shan respectively.
[25] The *Ming-shih* records these figures for late Ming times as 159, 240, and
1,144 respectively.

waters, barges & boats being every-where very common, it might easily bee supposed, that the number of watermen was equal unto the land-inhabitants. Howbeit, that is to be understood by amplification, whereas the cities do swarme so ful with citizens & the countrie with peasants. . . .

For whereas this kingdome is most large & full of navigable rivers, so that commodities may easilie be conveyed out of one province into another: the Portugals doe find such abundance of wares within one and the same Citie (which perhaps is the greater Mart throughout the whole kingdome) that they are verily perswaded, that the same region, of all others, most aboundeth with marchandise: which notwithstanding is to be understood of the Orientall regions: albeit there are some kindes of marchandise, wherewith the land of China is better stored then any other kingdom. This region affordeth especially sundry kinds of mettals, of which the chiefe, both in excellencie & in abundance, is gold, whereof so many Pezoes[26] are brought from China to India, and to our countrey of Japon, that I heard say, that in one and the same ship, this present yeere, 2000 such pieces consisting of massie gold, as the Portugals commonly call golden loaves, were brought unto us for marchandise: and one of these loaves is worth almost 100 duckats. . . . There is also great store of silver, whereof (that I may omit other arguments) it is no small demonstration, that every yeere there are brought into the citie commonly called Cantam by the Portugal marchants to buie wares, at the least 400 Sestertium[27] thereof, and yet nothing in a maner is conveied out of the Chinian kingdom: because the people of China abounding with all necessaries, are not greatly inquisitive or desirous of any marchandise from other kingdomes. I doe here omit the Silver mines whereof there are great numbers in China, albeit there is much circumspection used in digging the silver thereout: for the king standeth much in feare least it may bee an occasion to stirre up the covetous and greedie humour of many. Nowe their silver which they put to uses is for the most part passing fine, and purified from all drosse, and therefore in trying it they use great diligence. What should I speake of their iron, copper, lead, tinne, and other mettals, and also of their quick-silver? Of all which in the realme of China there is great abundance, and from thence they are transported into divers countreys. Hereunto may bee added the wonderfull store of pearles, which, at the Ile of Hainan, are found in shell-fishes taken very cunningly by certaine Divers, and doe much

[26] A weight of gold?
[27] A weight of silver.

enlarge the kings revenues. But now let us proceed unto the Silke or Bombycine fleece,[28] whereof there is great plentie in China: so that even as the husbandmen labour in manuring the earth, and in sowing of Rice; so likewise the women doe employ a great part of their time in preserving of silke-wormes, and in keeming[29] and weaving of Silke. . . . Moreover the kingdom of China aboundeth with most costlie spices & odours,[30] and especially with cynamom (albeit not comparable to the cynamom of Zeilan[31]) with camphire also & muske, which is very principal & good. Muske deriveth his name from a beast of the same name (which beast resembleth a Bever) from the parts whereof brused & putrified proceedeth a most delicate & fragrant smel which the Portugals highly esteem, commonly calling those parts of the foresaid beasts (because they are like unto the gorges of foules) Papos, & convey great plenty of them into India, & to us of Japon. But who would beleeve, that there were so much gossipine[32] or cotton-wool in China; whereof such variety of clothes are made like unto linnen; which we our selves do so often use, & which also is conveied by sea into so many regions? Let us now intreat of that earthen or pliable matter commonly called porcellan, which is pure white, & is to be esteemed the best stuffe of that kind in the whole world: wherof vessels of all kinds are very curiously framed. I say, it is the best earthen matter in all the world, for three qualities; namely, the cleannesse, the beauty, & the strength thereof. . . . This matter is digged, not thorowout the whole region of China, but onely in one of the fifteene provinces called Quiansi, wherein continually very many artificers are imployed about the same matter. . . . Unto the marchandize above-mentioned may be added divers and sundry plants, the rootes whereof be right holesome for mens bodies, and very medicinable, which are brought unto our Iles of Japon, and unto many other Ilands, amongst the which that wood may be reckoned, which (by a synechdoche) is called The wood of China,[33] being of notable force to expell out of mens bodies those humours, which would breed contagious diseases. To these you may adde sugar-canes (for in the realme of China there is great store of excellent sugar) which is conveyed by the Portugals very plentifully, both into our countrey, and also into India. . . .

[28] From the Latin, *bombycenus,* silk-worm or silk.
[29] Combing.
[30] Perfume or incense.
[31] Ceylon.
[32] Cotton-like fiber from shrub *Bombax pentandrum.*
[33] Camphor probably.

LINUS. Tell us now (Michael) of the industry of that people, whereof we have heard great reports.

MICHAEL. There industry is especially to be discerned in manuary artes and occupations, and therein the Chinians do surpasse most of these Easterly nations. For there are such a number of artificers ingeniously and cunningly framing sundry devices out of golde, silver, and other mettals, as likewise of stone, wood, and other matters convenient for mans use, that the streets of cities being replenished with their shops and fine workemanship, are very woonderfull to beholde. Besides whom also there are very many Painters, using either the pensill or the needle (of which the last sort are called Embrotherers) and others also that curiously worke golde-twine upon cloth either of linnen or of cotton: whose operations of all kinds are diligently conveyed by the Portugals into India. Their industry doth no lesse appeare in founding of gunnes and in making of gunpowder, whereof are made many rare and artificiall fireworks. To these may be added the arte of Printing, albeit their letters be in maner infinite and most difficult, the portraitures whereof they cut in wood or in brasse, and with marvellous facilitie they dayly publish huge multitudes of books. Unto these mechanicall & illiberall crafts you may adde two more; that is to say, navigation and discipline of warre; both of which have bene in ancient times most diligently practised by the inhabitants of China: for the Chinians sailing even as farre as India, subdued some part thereof unto their owne dominion: howbeit afterward, least they should diminish the forces of their realme by dispersing them into many provinces, altering their counsell, they determined to containe themselves within their owne limits: within which limits (as I have sayd)there were in olde time vehement and cruell warres, both betweene the people of China themselves, and also against the Tartarian king, who invaded their kingdome, and by himselfe and his successours, for a long season, usurped the government thereof. Howbeit the kings of the Tartarian race being worne out, and their stocke and family being utterly abolished, the Chinians began to lift up their heads, and to advance themselves, injoying for these 200 yeeres last past exceeding peace and tranquillity,[34] and at this day the posterity of the same king that expelled the Tartars, with great dignity weareth the crowne, and wieldeth the royall scepter. . . . Howbeit in this kingdome of China there is so great regard of military discipline, that no city nor towne there is destitute of a garison, the captaines and governours keeping ech man his order; which all of them, in

[34] The Ming expelled the Yüan (*Mongol*) dynasty in 1368.

every province, are subject unto the kings lieutenant generall for the warres, whom they call Chumpin,[35] and yet he himselfe is subject unto the Tutan[36] or viceroy. Let us now come unto that arte, which the Chinians do most of all professe, and which we may, not unfitly, call literature or learning. For although it be commonly reported, that many liberall sciences, and especially naturall and morall phylosophy are studied in China, and that they have Universities there, wherein such ingenuous artes are delivered and taught, yet, for the most part, this opinion is to be esteemed more popular then true: but I will declare, upon what occasion this conceit first grew. The people of China doe, above all things, professe the arte of literature; and learning it most diligently, they imploy themselves a long time and the better part of their age therein. For this cause, in all cities and townes, yea, and in pety villages also, there are certaine schoole-masters hired for stipends to instruct children: and their literature being (as ours in Japon is also) in maner infinite, their children are put to schole even from their infancy and tender yeeres, from whence notwithstanding such are taken away, as are judged to be unfit for the same purpose, and are trained up to marchandise or to manuary sciences: but the residue do so dedicate themselves to the study of learning, that (a strange thing it is to consider) being conversant in the principall books, they will easily tel you, if they be asked the question, how many letters be conteined in every page, and where ech letter is placed. Now, for the greater progresse and increase of learning, they (as the maner is in Europe) do appoint three degrees to the attaining of noble sciences: that is to say, the lowest, the middle degree, and the highest. Graduates of the first degree are called Siusai,[37] of the second Quiugin,[38] and of the third Chinzu.[39] And in ech city or walled towne there is a publique house called the Schoole, and unto that all they doe resort from all private and pety-schooles that are minded to obtaine the first degree; where they do amplifie a sentence or theame propounded unto them by some magistrate: and they, whose stile is more elegant and refined, are, in ech city, graced with the first degree. Of such as aspire unto the second degree triall is made onely in the metropolitan or principall city of the province, whereunto, they of the first degree, every third yere, have recourse, and, in one publike house or place of assembly, doe, the second time, make an

---

[35] *Tsung-ping* or Regional Commander.
[36] *Tu-t'ung* or Viceroy.
[37] *Hsiu-ts'ai* or "budding genius."
[38] *Chü-jên* or "promoted scholar."
[39] *Chin-shih* or "entered scholar."

oration of another sentence obscurer then the former, and doe undergo a more severe examination. Now, there is commonly such an huge multitude of people, that this last yere, in the foresayd famous city of Cantam, by reason of the incredible assembly of persons flocking to that publike act or commencement, at the first entrance of the doores, there were many troden under foot, and quelled to death, as we have bene most certainly informed. More-over they that sue for the highest degree are subject unto a most severe and exact censure, whereby they are to be examined at the Kings Court onely, and that also every third yere next insuing the sayd yere wherein graduates of the second degree are elected in ech province, and, a certaine number being prescribed unto every par-ticular province, they do ascend unto that highest pitch of dignity, which is in so great regard with the king himselfe, that the three principall graduates do, for honours sake, drinke off a cup filled even with the Kings owne hand, and are graced with other solemnities. Out of this order the chiefe magistrates are chosen. . . . Neither can I here omit, that certaine men of China (albeit they be but few, and rare to be found) are excellent in the knowledge of astronomy, by which knowledge of theirs the dayes of the new moone incident to every moneth are truely disposed and digested, and are com-mitted to writing and published: besides, they doe most infallibly foretell the eclipses of the Sun and Moone: and whatsoever knowl-edge in this arte we of Japon have, it is derived from them.

LEO. We doe freely confesse that (Michael) sithens our books in-treating of the same arte are, a great part of them, written in the characters or letters of China. But now, instruct you us as touching their maner of government, wherein the Chinians are sayd greatly to excell.

MICHAEL. That, that, in very deed, is their chiefe arte, and unto that all their learning and exercise of letters is directed. Whereas therefore, in the kingdome of China, one onely king beares rule over so many provinces, it is strange what a number of Magistrates are by him created to administer publique affaires. For (to omit them which in ech Towne and City have jurisdiction over the townesmen and citizens) there are three principall Magistrates in every province. The first is he that hath to deale in cases criminall, and is called Ganchasu:[40] the second is the Kings Fosterer, and is called Puchinsu:[41] the third is the Lieutenant-generall for the warres, named, as we sayd before, Chumpin. These three therefore have

[40] *An-ch'a shih* or Investigation Commissioner.
[41] *Pu-chêng shih* or Administration Commissioner.

their place of residence in the chiefe City of the province: and the two former have certaine associates of their owne order, but of inferiour authority, appointed in divers Cities and Townes, unto whom, according to the variety of causes, the Governours of Townes, and the Maiors of Cities doe appeale. Howbeit the three forenamed Magistrates are in subjection unto the Tutan, that is, the Vice-roy, ordained in ech province. And all these Magistrates beare office for the space of three yeeres together: yet so, that for the governing of ech province, not any of the same province, but strangers, that is, men of another province, are selected: whereof it commeth to passe, that the Judges may give sentence with a farre more entire and incorrupt minde, then if they were among their owne kinsefolke and allies. Over and besides all these, there is an annuall or yeerely Magistrate, which is called Chaien,[42] whose duety it is to make inquisition of all crimes, and especially the crimes of Magistrates, and also to punish common offences: but concerning the faults of the great magistrates to admonish the king himselfe. Of this order, every yere, are sent out of the King's Court, for ech province, one; and going over all the Cities and Townes thereof, they do most diligently ransacke and serch out all crimes, and upon them which are imprisoned they inflict due punishment, or, being found not guilty, they dismisse them unpunished. Hence it is, that all Magistrates greatly fearing to be called in question by the Chaien are well kept within the limits of their callings. Besides all these Magistrates there is at either Court, namely in the North, and in the South, a Senate[43] or honourable assembly of grave counsellours, unto the which, out of all provinces, according to the neerenesse and distance of the place, affaires of greater weight and moment are referred, and by their authority divers Magistrates are created: howbeit the managing and expedition of principall affaires is committed unto the Senate of Paquin. Moreover there are every yeere certaine Magistrates appointed in ech province, to goe unto the king: and every third yeere all the Governours of Cities and of Townes do visit him at once, what time triall is made of them that aspire unto the third degree: upon which occasion there is at the same time an incredible number of people at the Kings Court. . . . Also it is not to be omitted, that for the obtaining of any dignity or magistracy, the way is open, without all respect of gentry or blood, unto all men, if they be learned, and especially if they have attained unto the third and highest degree aforesayd. . . .

[42] *Chien-ch'a yü-shih* or Investigating Censor.
[43] Imperial Council.

LINUS. You have (Michael) sufficiently discoursed of the Magistrates: informe us now of the king himselfe, whose name is so renowmed and spread abroad.

MICHAEL. Concerning this matter I will say so much onely as by certaine rumours hath come to my knowledge: for of matters appertaining unto the kings Court we have no eye-witnesses, sithens the fathers of the society have not as yet proceeded unto Paquin, who so soone (as by Gods assistance) they shall there be arrived, will by their letters more fully advertise us. The king of China therefore is honoured with woonderfull reverence and submission thorowout his whole Realme: and whensoever any of his chiefe Magistrates speaketh unto him, he calleth him VAN-SVI,[44] signifying thereby that he wisheth tenne thousands of yeeres unto him. The succession of the kingdome dependeth upon the bloud royall: for the eldest sonne borne of the kings first and lawfull wife obtaineth the kingdome after his fathers decease: neither doe they deprive themselves of the kingly authority in their life time (as the maner is in our Ilands of Japon) but the custome of Europe is there observed. . . .

But to returne unto the king himselfe, hee is most chary in observing the Chinian lawes and customes, and diligently exerciseth himselfe in learning so much as concernes his estate, sheweth himselfe dayly unto his chiefe Magistrates, and communeth of matters appertaining to the publique commodity of the Realme. . . .

LEO. I would nowe (Michael) right gladly understand, what kinde of urbanity or civill demeanour both the common people and the Magistrates doe use one towardes another: for it is not likely that where such due administration of justice is, common civility, which so well beseemeth all men, should be wanting.

MICHAEL. You have hit even the very naile on the head: for among the five vertues, which the Chinians principally regard, urbanity or courtesy is one; the rest are piety, a thankefull remembrance of benefites, true dealing in contracts or bargaines, and wisedome in atchieving of matters: with the praises and commendations of which vertues the Chinian bookes are full fraught. Now as touching their unbanity, it is much unlike unto ours in Japan, and unto that of Europe: howbeit under two principall kindes the rule of their urbanity or courtesie may be comprehended: whereof one is observed betweene equals, and the other betweene superiours and inferiours. For when men of equall dignity meet together, they stand bending their backes, and bowing their heads downe to the ground, and this they doe either once or twise, or sometimes thrise. Now,

[44] *Wan sui yeh* or Lord of Ten Thousand Years.

when the inferiour meets with his superiour, the sayd inferiour, for the most part kneeling lowly on his knees, enclineth his countenance downe to the earth. But how often and when this obeizance is to be performed it is woonderfull what a number of rules and prescriptions are set downe, which to recount would require a long time. . . .

LINUS. I perceive (Michael) that drawing to an end of these dialogues, and being weary of your long race, you begin to affect brevity: yet let it not seeme troublesome unto you to speake somewhat of the religion of China, which onely thing seemes to be wanting in this present dialogue.

MICHAEL. I confesse indeed that I endevour to be briefe, not so much in regard of wearisomnesse, as for feare least I have bene over tedious unto you: howbeit I will not faile but accomplish that which I have undertaken, and (according to your request) adde somewhat more concerning religion. Whereas therefore the kingdome of China hath hitherto bene destitute of true religion, and now the first beginnings thereof are included in most narrow bounds, that nation being otherwise a people most ingenious, and of an extraordinary and high capacity, hath alwayes lived in great errours and ignorance of the trueth, being distracted into sundry opinions, and following manifolde sects. And among these sects there are three more famous then the rest: the first is of them that professe the doctrine of one Confucius[45] a notable philosopher. This man (as it is reported in the history of his life) was one of most upright and incorrupt maners, whereof he wrote sundry treatises very pithily and largely, which above all other books, are seriously read and perused by the Chinians. The same doctrine do all Magistrates embrace, and others also that give their mindes to the study of letters, a great part whereof Confucius is sayd to have invented: and he is had in so great honour, that all his followers and clients, upon the dayes of the new and full Moone, doe assemble themselves at the common Schoole, which I have above mentioned, and before his image, which is worshipped with burning of incense and with tapers, they doe thrise bend their knees, and bow their heads downe to the ground; which not onely the common scholars, but the chiefe Magistrates do performe. The summe of the foresayd doctrine is, that men should follow the light of nature as their guide, and that they should diligently endevour to attaine unto the vertues by me before mentioned: and lastly, that they should employ their labour about the orderly government of their families and of the Common-wealth.

[45] The Latinized form of K'ung-fu-tzu or Master K'ung.

All these things are in very deed praise-woorthy, if Confucius had made any mention of almighty God and of the life to come, and had not ascribed so much unto the heavens, and unto fatall necessity, nor yet had so curiously intreated of worshipping the images of their forefathers. In which regard he can very hardly or not at all be excused from the crime of idolatry: notwithstanding it is to be granted, that none other doctrine among the Chinians approcheth so neere unto the trueth as this doeth. The second sect is of them which follow the instructions of Xaquam, or as the Chinians call him Xequiam,[46] whose opinions, because they are well knowen amongst us, it were bootlesse for me to repeat; especially sithens, in the Catechisme composed by our grave visitour, they are notably refuted. This doctrine doe all they embrace, which are in China called Cen, but with us at Japon are named Bonzi.[47] For this I doe briefly and by the way give you to understand, that all words of the Chinians language are of one sillable onely, so that if there be any word that consisteth of more sillables then one, it consisteth also of more wordes then one. These sectaries called Cen doe shave their beards and their heads, and doe for the most part, together with divers of their associates, inhabit the Temples of Xaquam, or of others which in regard of the same profession have in their Kalenders beene canonized for Saints, and doe rehearse certaine prayers after their maner, either upon books or beads, using other ceremonies after the maner of our Bonzi. These men have some inckling of the life to come, and of the rewardes of good men, and the punishments of the wicked: howbeit all their assertions are fraught with errours. The third sect is of them which are called Tauzu:[48] and those doe imitate a certaine other man, to be adored, as they thinke, for his holinesse. There also are Priests after their kinde, howbeit they let their haire grow, and doe in other observations differ from the former. Nowe, because the sect of Confucius is the most famous of all the three, and the two other sects called Cen and Tauzu are not much addicted unto learning, their religion prevailing onely among the common sort, the Priests of both the sayd sects doe leade a most base and servile life amongst the Chinians, insomuch that they kneele downe before the Magistrates, and are not permitted to sit beside them, and sometimes, if the Magistrate please, are abased unto the punishment of the bastonado: whereas in our Iles of

[46] Buddha, known as Sakyamuni or "teacher of the Sakya clan," becomes *Shih-chia-fo* or *Shih-chia-mu-ni* in Chinese.

[47] *Seng* in Chinese and *bonzō* in Japanese refer to Buddhist monks.

[48] *Tao-chiao* or Taoist faith.

Japon it is farre otherwise, Priests, even of false religion, being had in so great honour among us. . . .

9 / THE MING VOYAGES OF DISCOVERY, 1405-1433

While the Portuguese under the leadership of Prince Henry the Navigator (1394-1460) were first uncovering the west coast of Africa, Chinese ships plied the Indian Ocean, visited the Persian Gulf, and touched the east coast of Africa. The Chinese maritime expeditions of the early Ming dynasty extended to the "southern seas" the fame and authority of China more dramatically and deliberately than it had ever been done before. Seven huge fleets reconnoitered the islands, straits, and coastal regions of the "West" over a period of twenty-eight years. The moving spirit behind the overseas expeditions was the Muslim eunuch, Cheng Ho, the most famous maritime figure in China's history. The precise motivation behind the sudden inauguration and abrupt cessation of the Ming overseas expansion is not clearly understood.

The Mongol emperor of the Yüan dynasty (1279-1368), who aspired to universal rule, had made serious efforts to control by military and naval forces countries as far away from Peking as Japan, Annam, Burma, and Java. Although these military expeditions were not uniformly successful, the Mongols forced or cajoled ten foreign rulers to accept vassalage. These submissions gave substantial impetus to China's connections with the rest of maritime Asia and helped to lay the groundwork for the overseas expeditions of the fifteenth century.

When the native Ming dynasty replaced the Yüan in 1368, the new government quickly invited the surrounding states to dispatch tribute missions to the imperial court. Evidently the response to this overture failed to satisfy the Ming dynasts. As the Ming dynasty reached the apex of its power under the Yung-lo emperor (1403-1424), China took action to restore its prestige in the "southern seas." Indochina was invaded, and maritime expeditions were sent to the south and west to solicit tribute and force the recognition of China's suzerainty. The expeditions sent abroad were powerful and well-manned, designed to overawe the lesser powers of the East. The first flotilla, which was sent all the way into the Indian Ocean in 1406, included sixty-two vessels (about half the number that sailed

From J. J. L. Duyvendak, "The True Dates of the Chinese Maritime Expeditions in the Early Fifteenth Century," *T'oung Pao,* XXIV (1938), 349-55. Reprinted by permission of *T'oung Pao* and the E. J. Brill Publishing Company.

in the Spanish Armada), and a complement of 28,000 men. Later, the pride of the Ming navy was its 250 "treasure ships" of extraordinary sailing range and firepower, each of which was capable of carrying five hundred men and quantities of merchandise.

The maritime expeditions, as impressive displays of technical competence and strength, were obviously designed to give substance to China's claims of suzerainty. The Ming fleets were instructed to sweep the seas clean of pirates and to establish the conditions necessary for legitimate trade. The envoys sent with the fleets negotiated the terms for the renewal of trade under the Chinese tribute system, invested foreign kings as vassals, and invited accredited embassies to undertake regular missions to China. Those who resisted the overtures of the Ming emissaries were attacked, and some recalcitrant Asian rulers were taken off to Peking as prisoners.

For China itself, maritime venture had both temporary and lasting consequences. As the southern provinces became much more involved in overseas trade than before, an increasing number of Chinese were attracted by the opportunities offered by overseas enterprises and began to migrate into maritime Southeast Asia. The government's encouragement of shipbuilding and related endeavors helped create new enterprises along China's southeastern coast. Significant advances were made in naval technology and armament; the mariner's compass, watertight bulkheads, and brass cannon were improved and came into more common use. An imperial institute was founded in 1407 to train interpreters; four of its eight sections concentrated on the languages used on China's land frontiers, while the other four specialized in the languages used in Southeast Asia and India and by the Muslims and "Western Barbarians" (possibly Arabic and Persian).

Gifts of exotic oddities were sent to Peking from the distant places visited by its fleets and they helped to broaden the horizons of the Chinese. A bone, which was thought to be that of a unicorn (a mythical animal in Chinese as well as Western lore), was received at court with as much enthusiasm as a devout Christian ruler would have welcomed a sliver of the True Cross. A fifteen-foot giraffe from Africa inspired an artist's sketch and a poet's description of it as having "the body of a deer and the tail of an ox, and a fleshy boneless horn, with luminous spots like a red cloud or a purple mist." Such effusions are reminiscent of the enthusiastic poems written in Europe during the sixteenth century celebrating the elephant and rhinoceros.

Why, it has often been asked, did the Chinese, with their head-

start in maritime endeavor, fail to find the route around the Cape of Good Hope and "discover" Europe? For a partial answer to this question we must look at the internal history of China. When the Yung-lo emperor died in 1424, his successor immediately ordered an end to the voyages and the work of naval construction. Although one voyage was nonetheless undertaken thereafter, the successors of Yung-lo were forced to direct their energies to the more immediate threat being mounted against the inner Asian frontiers of China by revitalized tribal groups. The eunuch advisers of the early Ming emperors were temporarily eclipsed in influence at the court by mandarins who accused them of encouraging extravagant maritime ventures which turned out to be profitless and constituted an unnecessary drain on the nation's resources. China, it could be claimed, was self-sufficient and could best use her vast resources to protect her land frontiers. Whatever the complex of reasons, no more maritime expeditions were sent out after 1433, and Chinese were officially forbidden to go abroad. Had the court not decided to give up the government-sponsored voyages, it is certainly possible that Chinese junks might have circumnavigated Africa and found the sea road to Europe.

Because of the mandarins' hostility to overseas enterprises, the chroniclers of the Ming dynasty sought to suppress direct mention of them in the official histories. Nevertheless, incidental information relating to the voyages can be found in the dynastic histories and in collateral Chinese sources. The voyagers themselves left records of their expeditions in the form of commemorative inscriptions, many of these stone engravings being erected in foreign lands. The following text was prepared early in 1432 during the time of the last expedition of Cheng Ho and his cohorts. The stone on which it was engraved was found in our century at Ch'ang-lo in Fukien province by a Chinese government official who made his discovery known to the world in 1937.

A Ming Inscription on Stone

Record of the miraculous answer (to prayer) of the goddess, the Celestial Spouse.

The Imperial Ming Dynasty in unifying seas and continents, surpassing the three dynasties even goes beyond the Han and T'ang dynasties. The countries beyond the horizon and from the ends of the earth have all become subjects and to the most western of the western or the most northern of the northern countries, however far they may be, the distances and the routes may be calculated.

Thus the barbarians from beyond the seas, though their countries are truly distant, "with double translation" [1] have come to audience bearing precious objects and presents.

The Emperor, approving of their loyalty and sincerity, has ordered us (Cheng) Ho and others at the head of several tens of thousands of officers and flag-troops to ascend more than a hundred large ships to go and confer presents on them in order to make manifest the transforming power of the (imperial) virtue[2] and to treat distant people with kindness. From the 3rd year of Yung-lo (1405) till now we have seven times received the commission of ambassadors to the countries of the western ocean. The barbarian countries which we have visited are: by way of Chan-ch'eng (Champa), Chao-wa (Java), San-fo-ch'i (Palembang) and Hsien-lo (Siam) crossing straight over to Hsi-lan-shan (Ceylon) in South-India, Ku-li (Calicut), and K'o-chih (Cochin), we have gone to the western regions Hu-lu-mo-ssŭ (Ormuz), A-tan (Aden), Mu-ku-tu-shu (Mogadisho in East Africa), all together more than thirty countries large and small. We have traversed more than one hundred thousand *li* of immense waterspaces and have beheld in the ocean huge waves like mountains rising skyhigh, and we have set eyes on barbarian regions far away hidden in a blue transparency of light vapours, while our sails loftily unfurled like clouds day and night continued their course (rapid like that) of a star, traversing those savage waves as if we were treading a public thoroughfare. Truly this was due to the majesty and the good fortune of the Court and moreover we owe it to the protecting virtue of the divine Celestial Spouse. . . .

We, Cheng Ho and others on the one hand have received the high favour of a gracious commission of our Sacred Lord, and on the other hand carry to the distant barbarians the benefits of respect and good faith (on their part). Commanding the multitudes on the fleet and (being responsible for) a quantity of money and valuables in the face of the violence of the winds and the nights our one fear is not to be able to succeed; how should we then dare not to serve our dynasty with exertion of all our loyalty and the gods with the utmost sincerity? How would it be possible not to realize what is the source of the tranquillity of the fleet and the troops and the salvation on the voyage both going and returning? Therefore we have made manifest the virtue of the goddess on stone and have

---

[1] This expression, literally meaning that no one could translate their language directly into Chinese, implies that these countries were tremendously far away.

[2] This is a play on the words in the reign-title Hsüan-tê.

moreover recorded the years and months of the voyages to the barbarian countries and the return in order to leave (the memory) for ever.

I. In the third year of Yung-lo (1405) commanding the fleet we went to Ku-li (Calicut) and other countries. At that time the pirate Ch'en Tsu-yi had gathered his followers in the country of San-fo-ch'i (Palembang), where he plundered the native merchants. When he also advanced to resist our fleet, supernatural soldiers secretly came to the rescue so that after one beating of the drum he was annihilated. In the fifth year (1407) we returned.

II. In the fifth year of Yung-lo (1407) commanding the fleet we went to Chao-wa (Java), Ku-li (Calicut), K'o-chih (Cochin) and Hsien-lo (Siam). The kings of these countries all sent as tribute precious objects, precious birds and rare animals. In the seventh year (1409) we returned.

III. In the seventh year of Yung-lo (1409) commanding the fleet we went to the countries (visited) before and took our route by the country of Hsi-lan-shan (Ceylon). Its king Ya-lieh-k'u-nai-erh (Alagakkonāra) was guilty of a gross lack of respect and plotted against the fleet. Owing to the manifest answer to prayer of the goddess (the plot) was discovered and thereupon that king was captured alive. In the ninth year (1411) on our return he was presented (to the throne) (as a prisoner); subsequently he received the Imperial favour of returning to his own country.

IV. In the eleventh year of Yung-lo (1413) commanding the fleet we went to Hu-lu-mo-ssŭ (Ormuz) and other countries. In the country of Su-men-ta-la (Sumatra) there was a false king Su-kan-la (Sĕkandar) who marauding and invading his country. Its king Tsai-nu-li-a-pi-ting (Zaynu-'l-Ābidīn) had sent an envoy to the Palace Gates in order to lodge a complaint. We went thither with the official troops under our command and exterminated some and arrested (other rebels), and owing to the silent aid of the goddess we captured the false king alive. In the thirteenth year (1415) on our return he was presented (to the Emperor as a prisoner). In that year the king of the country of Man-la-chia (Malacca) came in person with his wife and son to present tribute.

V. In the fifteenth year of Yung-lo (1417) commanding the fleet we visited the western regions. The country of Hu-lu-mo-ssŭ (Ormuz) presented lions, leopards with gold spots and large western horses. The country of A-tan (Aden) presented ch'i-lin of which the native name is tsu-la-fa (giraffe), as well as the long-horned animal ma-ha (oryx). The country of Mu-ku-tu-shu (Mogadisho) presented hua-fu-lu ("striped" zebras) as well as lions. The country of Pu-la-wa

(Brawa in East Africa) presented camels which run one thousand *li* as well as camelbirds (ostriches). The countries of Chao-wa (Java) and Ku-li (Calicut) presented the animal *mi-li-kao*.[3] They all vied in presenting the marvellous objects preserved in the mountains or hidden in the seas and the beautiful treasures buried in the sand or deposited on the shores. Some sent a maternal uncle of the king, others a paternal uncle or a younger brother of the king in order to present a letter of homage written on goldlead as well as tribute.

VI. In the nineteenth year of Yung-lo (1421) commanding the fleet we conducted the ambassadors from Hu-lu-mo-ssŭ (Ormuz) and the other countries who had been in attendance at the capital for a long time back to their countries. The kings of all these countries prepared even more tribute than previously.

VII. In the sixth year of Hsüan-tê (1431) once more commanding the fleet we have left for the barbarian countries in order to read to them (an Imperial edict) and to confer presents. We have anchored in this port [Ch'ang-lo] awaiting a north wind to take the sea, and recalling how previously we have on several occasions received the benefit of the protection of the divine intelligence we have thus recorded an inscription in stone.

The sixth year of Hsüan-tê, the cyclical year *hsin-hai*, the second winter month (December 5th 1431—January 3rd 1432), on a lucky day, erected by the principal envoys, the Grand Eunuchs Cheng Ho and Wang Ching-hung, the assistant-envoys, the Grand Eunuchs Li Hsing, Chou Liang, Chou Man, Hung Pao, Yang Chen, Chang Ta and Wu Chung, and the Commanders Chu Chen and Wang Heng.

The superior resident monk Yang Yi-ch'u (whose religious name is) Cheng-yi (Correct and One), knocking down his head begs to erect this stone.

10 / GOVERNMENT: THE CENSORATE

Confucian thought holds that a primary obligation of upright men is fearless criticism of acts of commission or omission that threaten the commonweal or endanger the public welfare. To serve the dual

Shih-lu or *True Records* of the Ming Dynasty. From Charles O. Hucker, "The Chinese Censorate of the Ming Dynasty . . ." (University of Chicago: unpublished Ph.D. dissertation, Department of Oriental Languages and Literatures, 1950), pp. 220-21, 240, 242-43, 252-53, 259-60, 263, 286-87. Reprinted by permission of Charles O. Hucker.

[3] We have not been able to trace this animal.

functions of criticizing the bureaucracy and reproving the ruler himself for diverging from Confucian precepts, the unique institution called the Censorate was founded. Though the roots of the Censorate reach back into the pre-Christian era, the institution came to the fore only in Yüan times. As one of the three main branches of government, it stood immediately below the Emperor and on a plane of equality with the central civil and military administrations. When decentralization set in under the Ming, a Grand Secretariat interposed itself at the top of the hierarchy between the Emperor and the top branches of administration; on the provincial level censorial functions were performed by thirteen provincial investigation offices located at the capital, though no longer directly attached to or controlled by the central Censorate. In modern China the Censorate survives as the "Control Yüan" and "Supreme People's Control Office" under the Kuomintang and the Communists, respectively.

Censors, usually called "the eyes and ears of the Emperor," were charged with keeping both the civil and military hierarchies under surveillance. During the Ming period the Censorate employed an average of 120 officials of graded rank and many assistants. Working alone or as commissions, the appointees of the Emperor relied on personal observation, recommendations and complaints submitted to them, routine reports directed to them, and systematic checking of government records. Using the information thus gathered, they were able to expose the corrupt and the lazy, and other malefactors, and were in a position to recommend promotions for deserving civil servants. Provincial inspectors, the backbone of the system, visited as many localities under their jurisdiction as possible during a one-year's tour of duty. They inquired into the conduct of all government personnel, reviewed judicial decisions, examined government-sponsored schools and charitable activities, inspected temples, granaries, and dikes, studied the problem of taxation from the viewpoint of the taxpayer, and directed the suppression of brigands. For all their powers, the censors were themselves subject to impeachment by anyone.

The following passages, which are drawn from the True Records *(Shih-lu) compiled by the government after the demise of each Emperor, refer to the Jên Tsung (1424-1425) and Hsüan Tsung (1425-1435) periods of the Ming dynasty. The subjects covered include the main preoccupations of the Censorate: disciplinary surveillance of the government, participation in judicial administration, and substantive participation in governmental activities. Although the*

Censorate made positive contributions to effective government, it was difficult to maintain discipline and morality within the Censorate itself. The outrages committed by Liu Kuan, joint chief of the Censorate hierarchy, have long symbolized governmental corruption at its worst.

Disciplinary Surveillance of Government Officials

(1428, twelfth month, the day *chia-ch'ên*): The Provincial Inspector of Shantung, Pao Tê-huai, memorialized: "Recently in Kuang-ning, Ts'ao-chuang, I-chou, and other localities, Mongol raiders have entered the borders and killed and captured men and livestock. The Provincial Commanders Li Hsin, Lu Tê, and others were not strict in defending. When the raiders arrived, also, they did not lead troops to attack them. (I) request that their crimes be punished." The Emperor proclaimed to ministers of the . . . Ministry of War: "Frontier generals who neglect opportunities ought to be put to death, (but) just order the Provincial Inspector to threaten them with death and fine them one year's salaries. If again they miss an opportunity they must be put to death and not pardoned."

(1430, tenth month, the day *chia-wu*): The Provincial Inspector of Hukwang, Chu Chien, memorialized: "The Commander of the Ch'a Guard, Yü Ch'êng, led troops to capture the bandits Ho Ma-ko and others; (but) he privately connived with the bandits and accepted the bandits' bribe of more than five hundred ounces of silver. He seized an innocent civilian and (representing him) to be Ho Ma-ko, put him to death and displayed him to the multitudes. Yet Ho Ma-ko actually exists, and his doing harm has not ceased." The Emperor proclaimed to the Censor-in-Chief of the right, Ku Tso, and others: ". . . Order the censor urgently to try him."

Participation in Judicial Administration

(1426, seventh month, the day *i-ssŭ*): Citizens of the Li-yang District, a father, Shih Ying, and his son, presumed on their wealth to tyrannize and oppress. They beat to death a man of their village and then bribed the authorities to claim falsely that it was bandits (who committed the murder). Also, they seized his relatives and kept them in confinement. The Grand Court of Revision Chief Minister, Hu Kai, investigated and discovered the truth. He sent the father, (Shih) Ying, and his son and also more than twenty men who had received bribes to the capital. The Emperor ordered the Censorate to try them. He said: "The murderers must be put to death. But among the more than twenty (other) men, perhaps there are those who are guiltless. It is necessary to investigate the circumstances and the facts so that there will not be injustice or excessiveness." Censors tried them, and all confessed their crimes. They deserved the death penalty. (When the case) arrived at the Grand Court of Revision for ratification also, there were no irregularities. Then there was an introductory memorial. The Emperor summoned (the criminals) before him and personally interrogated them. The father, (Shih) Ying, and his son were to be put to death. The others were to perform transport labor. Those released because of innocence were seven men.

Participation in Government Activities

(1429, first month, the day *ping-tzŭ*): Rules for paying in rice to atone for crimes were fixed. At this time the Emperor wished to be lenient and take pity on criminals, causing them to pay in rice to atone for crimes. He ordered the three legal offices to deliberate on it and report. Now the . . . Censorate's Censor-in-Chief of the right, Ku Tso, and others memorialized: "As for paying in rice to atone for crimes, water transport in the Nanking (area) is excellent and advantageous, and land transport in the Peking (area) is rather difficult. (We) have deliberated and propose that, when arrested and brought to the Peking legal offices and also to the eight Prefectures of the (Northern) Metropolitan Area, Ho-chien and others, and to Honan and Shantung, officials, lesser functionaries, soldiers, and civilians (subject) for miscellaneous offenses to the death penalty on down should pay in rice to the Peking granaries in accordance with the rules herein fixed:

(For) miscellaneous offenses, the death penalty: 50 piculs
Permanent banishment, in comparison to the death penalty, reduced 10 piculs
Temporary banishment, five degrees:
   three years: 35 piculs
   the lower four degrees, successively reduced 5 piculs
Beating with the heavy bamboo, five degrees:
   one hundred blows: 10 piculs
   the lower four degrees, successively reduced 1 picul
Beating with the light bamboo, five degrees:
   fifty blows: 5 piculs [? text obscure]
   forty: reduced 1 picul
   thirty, compared to forty, reduced 5 pecks
   twenty, compared to thirty, reduced 1 picul
   ten, compared to twenty, reduced 5 pecks. . . .

(1430, fifth month, the day *ping-ch'ên*): The . . . Censorate's Assistant Censor-in-Chief of the left, Li Chün, said: "During the Hung-wu period, in the metropolitan areas, Honan, Shansi, and other localities, there were established reserve granary stores. Accordingly as the times were prosperous or frugal, they were collected or distributed to advantage. Although floods or drought occurred, the people did not starve. (But) recently in every locality the authorities have been unable to carry on (this) virtuous idea, so that the granary stores have all been dissipated. If a year's grain is not abundant, the people lose their means. I beg that the authorities be ordered according to the law to repair the granaries, that government money then be provided, and that at current prices they lay in grain to provide for needs. It would be advantageous." It was approved.

Maintenance of Discipline within the Censorate

(1428, ninth month, the day *kêng-ch'ên*): The . . . Honan Circuit Investigating Censor, Chang Hsün-li, and others memorialized an impeachment: "The Junior Guardian of the Heir Apparent and concurrent Censor-in-Chief of the left in charge of the Censorate's affairs, Liu Kuan, presumes upon (imperial) favor to toy with the law; he goes to great excess in villainy and fraud. He has associated intimately with the venal, evil, and shameless censors, Yen K'ai, and others in great corruption. Also, he has privately gone about together with (Department) Directors and Secretaries of the various Ministries, Hsü Hsing, Wang Jun, and others, singing, dancing, carousing, and sporting obscenely without restraint. Also, each time officials have been commissioned to attend to affairs and go outside (into the provinces), he has first required five ounces of silver, calling it 'departure-sanction silver'; and when they have returned he has required another five ounces, calling it 'completion-sanction silver.' When Fêng Pên and others, local bullies of Chia-hsing (Prefecture), were guilty of murder and were imprisoned pending judicial review, (Liu) Kuan accepted bribes and permitted them to escape. Also he has given free rein to his son (Liu) Fu (who has) opened a wine shop, enticed prostitutes into unrestricted lewdness, stolen and made use of utensils confiscated by the government, and connived with the clerk, An Chung, to commit wrongs that are not only of a single sort. In my opinion, (Liu) Kuan's duty is to take general charge of discipline; he ranks among the great dignitaries. But, not observing propriety or the law, he commits villainy and violates the rules. His punishment ought to be rightly (fixed) so as to purify the fundamental principles (*hsien-kang*)." The Emperor said: "I also know of it. But, because he is an official of long standing during successive reigns, (I) have just patiently endured it, hoping he would be able to reform. Yet he has not reformed and has become increasingly reckless in his aims. I recently sent him to tour and inspect the Grand Canal and changingly ordered Ku Tso (to take over Liu's duties); it was not without intent." Then he ordered the various great ministers to deliberate. Now the Junior Preceptor and Minister of Civil Service, Chien I, and others all spoke out requesting that the censors' impeachment be complied with. Thereupon it was ordered that the Ministry of Justice send men to arrest (Liu) Kuan.

Nineteen days later Liu Kuan was brought to the capital and, on Hsüan Tsung's orders, was shown the impeachment lodged by the censors. He said in his own defense:

> (I) have successively served the Emperor T'ai Tsu, the Emperor T'ai Tsung [i.e., Ch'êng Tsu], and the Emperor Jên Tsung in successive offices up to Censor-in-Chief of the left (honorifically) entitled Junior Guardian of the Heir Apparent, with two salaries both paid. Your majesty succeeded to the throne and constantly conferred gifts (upon me), and day and night I have diligently thought and schemed to make recompense. Now the Censor-in-Chief of the right, Ku Tso, seeks my being punished and (as their) master has ordered the censors of every Circuit to submit impeachments. Also he has compelled the clerk, An Chung, falsely to indicate that I received bribes and (committed) other crimes. (I) humbly hope that your majesty will sympathetically investigate the circumstances and clearly distinguish them so that there will not be injustice.

To this the Emperor replied that many officials had secretly memorialized about Liu's offenses and that Liu had not yet been punished only because of his long service, adding: "Now does he still wish to gloss over his faults?" Then he sent out some of the secret memorials for Liu's perusal. They revealed that, in all, he had accepted more than one thousand ounces of silver in "selling criminal cases." Liu confessed. The legal offices demanded that he be beheaded in accordance with the law, and he was sent to the Chin-i Guard's prison. There he apparently remained until the seventh month of 1429, when the death penalty was revoked. His son Fu was disgraced to serve as a soldier in Liaotung, and Liu Kuan was sent to live with his son in exile. [The Emperor] Hsüan Tsung confessed that, although Liu was evil, he still could not bring himself to punish him more severely.

11 / DYNASTIC CHANGE AND POPULAR REVOLT

In its three-thousand-year history before 1500 A.D., China was administered by thirty-five dynasties. Some of these ruling houses were long-lived, others passed quickly, and still others paralleled or overlapped one another chronologically. Attempts by historians to explain the rise and fall of China's dynasties by formulas built upon Confucian ideology, cyclical theories of history, and Marxian determinism have usually cracked apart under the close scrutiny of specialists. About all that can be asserted with certainty is that historically each new dynasty tried to suppress the chaos out of which it was born, that it provided orderly government and economic stability for a time, that its authority gradually weakened, that the state seemed to run for a period on stored-up energy, and that finally the country was afflicted by natural calamities, moral degeneration, widespread poverty, revolt, and civil war. A state of anarchy of long or short duration thus ordinarily accompanied a change in dynasty.

Under the early Ming Emperors the Mongols and their institutions were expelled from China or integrated into the traditional Chinese way of life, which was skillfully and quickly restored. Although the internal and external enemies of the Ming occasionally caused trouble, the Yung-lo Emperor (ruled 1403-1424) and his less distinguished successors managed for two centuries to hold the country together, to provide the conditions for material prosperity, and to keep the land and sea borders secure. The Ming dynasty, perhaps because it was bent on restoring to China the traditional glories of the T'ang and Sung eras, was content to cultivate internal peace and unity, to discourage innovations as potentially dangerous, and, after a brief excursion into overseas expansion (1405-1433), to leave its continental and maritime neighbors to their own devices.

The right of the people to revolt against a ruler who has lost the Mandate of Heaven was a time-honored Confucian principle of government. When Heaven showed its displeasure with the dynasty by permitting natural disasters or social discontent to unsettle the realm, revolt was justified and Heaven could be expected to transfer

Wen Cheng-heng (?), *K'ai-tu ch'uan-hsin*, or *The True Story of the Promulgation [of the Edict of 1626]*, originally published in the Ch'ung-chen period, 1628-1644. From Charles O. Hucker, ed. and trans., "Su-Chou and the Agents of Wei Chung-hsien: A Translation of K'ai-tu ch'uan-hsin," *Silver Jubilee volume of the Zinbun-Kagaku-Kenkyusyo* (Kyoto University, 1954), pp. 229-31, 234-43, 250-51, 254-55. Reprinted by permission of Charles O. Hucker.

*its Mandate to a new family. Late in the sixteenth century wars
against the Japanese in Korea (1592-1598) were followed by attacks
on Ming China by the Manchu peoples who lived northeast of the
Great Wall in what we today call Manchuria. When the Wan-li
emperor (1573-1620) sought to fend off the invaders, he was ham-
pered, as were his successors, by factional divisions at court, by widespread agricultural distress and banditry, and by a groundswell of
internal rebellion against the dynasty. Rebellions against the Ming
became increasingly numerous after 1600. The combination of external pressure and internal weakness eventually brought about the
downfall of the Ming in the middle of the seventeenth century.*

*Contemporary Communist scholars have focused special attention
on the numerous peasant rebellions that swept China in the last
fifteen years of Ming rule. Insurgency and antidynastic demonstrations were not, however, limited to rural uprisings. The following
narrative describes a popular uprising that occurred in 1626 in Su-
chou, one of the wealthiest and most populous metropolitan centers
of Ming China. The immediate occasion for the uprising was the
promulgation of the edict calling for the arrest of the scholar-of-
ficial, Chou Shun-ch'ang (1584-1626). More broadly seen, however,
the revolt was symptomatic of an intense partisan struggle that had
split the bureaucracy for more than twenty years. Chou belonged to
the party known as the "advocates of righteousness," a group
strongly opposed to the ascendancy at court of the eunuch, Wei
Chung-hsien (1568-1627). This long partisan struggle for control of
the bureaucracy reached a climax in 1625 and 1626 when the "advocates of righteousness" were systematically purged, arrested, and
sometimes put to death by the agents of Wei and his party. Despite
the uprising that took place in Su-chou, the local hero, Chou, was
in the end taken to Peking and secretly put to death. Wei shortly
thereafter lost imperial favor, and he committed suicide in 1627.*

The True Story of the Promulgation [of the Edict of 1626]

At the time of the arrest of Wei Ta-chung (1575-1625),[1] the
former Ministry of Civil Service departmental vice-director Chou
Shun-ch'ang was living at home in Wu-men (i.e., Su-chou). Shun-
ch'ang had long enjoyed a great reputation for purity and resolute-

[1] Wei Ta-chung, a man of Chia-shan district in Chekiang, south of Su-chou,
was . . . closely allied with the Eastern Forest Party. He was one of the most out-
spoken critics of Wei Chung-hsien and his henchmen. Consequently, he was
among the famous "six heroes" who were arrested and put to death in prison in
1625.

ness, and his whole life had been devoted to loyalty and patriotism. When Ta-chung passed through Wu, Shun-ch'ang treated him cordially and through successive days was constantly in his company. In parting, he wept bitterly and betrothed his daughter to (Wei's) grandson; and when mention was made of the new influence of the inner court (i.e., the palace eunuchs), he viciously gnashed his teeth and vigorously cursed, while everyone stared. . . .

Then he called out the name of [the palace eunuch, Wei] Chung-hsien and cursed it ceaselessly. Observers gaped at one another and put out their tongues in astonishment, and his words were reported to Chung-hsien.

Later (Wei) Ta-chung was sent to prison. The censor Ni Wen-huan then impeached Shun-ch'ang because of the marriage agreement, and he was erased from the rolls (i.e., deprived of his status and prerogatives as an official).[2] . . .

Chung-hsien's hatred was not yet exhausted. . . .

During this period guardsmen, relying upon (public dread of) Chung-hsien, all became abusive and arrogant. Wherever they went prefects and magistrates prepared official residences and food for them; and lesser local officials who in the slightest regard did not meet with their approval were forthwith given official beatings. (The guardsmen) even treated governors as equals without engaging in courtesies, and governors behaved toward them with deference. From the families of the victims of their arrests they demanded money by the thousands (of taels), utterly ruining them. . . .

Shun-ch'ang, while living at home, enjoyed going before the governmental authorities on behalf of the common people to cry out for justice and to restrain oppression; in all lightening of corvée requirements or delaying of tax collections, it always was Shun-ch'ang who was in the forefront. He associated intimately with poor scholars, praising and recommending them unstintingly. Consequently, literati and commoners alike were profoundly convinced of his virtue; and when suddenly they learned of the disaster that had come upon him, they were overcome with outraged anger and wanted to take his place. There was a great clamor, and everyone blamed the censor-in-chief. . . .

Shun-ch'ang lived on a winding lane outside the city wall, in desolate surroundings behind a poor wicker gate. When the order (for his arrest) arrived at Wu, the district magistrate Ch'en Wen-jui, who had long and highly esteemed Shun-ch'ang,[3] dismissed his

---

[2] Ni was one of the most active of Wei Chung-hsien's adherents.

[3] Ch'en Wen-jui had earlier studied under Chou Shun-ch'ang.

attendants and, braving the rain, went in the night to tell him about it. Shun-ch'ang's countenance did not change. They sat and chatted for a long time, and then the magistrate asked Shun-ch'ang to go in and prepare his baggage. . . .

At dawn Shun-ch'ang watched the magistrate consume two bowls of congee. Only then did he change into prisoner's garb. Sedan-chair bearers were called, and he got in. The road was blocked by those who watched, and all wept until they lost their voices.

When he had entered the yamen to await orders, from the governor's palace near the yamen the censor-in-chief secretly sent a man to spy around. He saw that the common people, young and old alike, were arriving in swarms, all wishing to get a glimpse of Chou Li-pu (i.e., "Chou of the Ministry of Civil Service"). Some cursed, and some prayed. Those who cursed called the censor-in-chief a traitor-partisan. Students in their (formal-dress) green collars ran about in the mud and mire. From dawn till midday and on into afternoon the streets were solidly filled. . . .

Shun-ch'ang's family was bitterly poor and lacked even a single picul of stored supplies; yet the guardsmen intimidated it ceaselessly. Shun-ch'ang, however, swore that he would not give them a single coin. Thereupon the literati and commoners all wished to pour out their possessions in his aid. Even those who ordinarily lacked good principles begrudged nothing, and there even were some who left money and departed without mentioning their names. Poor scholars borrowed against their tutorial salaries and, that being thought insufficient, handed over their poor clothes to pawnshops, and the little that they obtained they forthwith presented as gifts. The guardsmen, learning of this, ever-increasingly yearned to fill up their purses. Only after lingering for three days did they issue their summons.

On this day it again rained heavily. After the crowd had heard the summons, Shun-ch'ang was put into a caged cart. The whole city went along, everyone escorting him carrying incense. Smoke billowed up to obscure heaven, and the sound of the crying out for justice reverberated for several tens of miles (*li*). As the district magistrate accompanied Shun-ch'ang out of the district yamen, the crowd blocked the way so that the cart could not go forward. Shun-ch'ang lifted up its screen and persuasively said: "I am deeply moved that my fathers and brothers covet me and wish to retain me a little while. But it is the law of the state! It cannot be delayed for a moment! My fathers and brothers, let us here say goodbye!" At this, the crowd grieved even more. From the district yamen to the guardsmen's compound was a distance of not one mile (*li*), but every few steps the crowd hindered them so that they could not proceed, and only after a long while did they get through. . . .

After arriving at the guardsmen's compound, the crowd increased. The gates not yet having been opened, and the compound being close against the city wall, a crowd climbed atop the wall and stood round on the parapets, which all became filled. Incense burned in the rain like an array of torches. When men atop the wall called out, men below the wall answered; and when men below the wall called out, then men atop the wall similarly answered. The noise became increasingly thunderous. Shun-ch'ang himself was taken by surprise and with the utmost respect requested that they disperse. But the crowd did not make a move. Meantime, teachers and elders had all assembled, and some proposed going to the capital to submit memorials demanding justice for Shun-ch'ang. . . .

When the censor arrived, his front-runners shouted to clear the way as in ordinary times. But when the censor saw the scene he was shocked and warned them not to clear the people away. As soon as the censor-in-chief arrived, the crowd thrice cried out "An unequalled injustice!" They all repeatedly echoed it. . . .

When the two dignitaries came inside, one student, Wen Chenheng, greeted them and said: "Today, when the feelings of the people and the minds of the literati are such as this, can you honorable gentlemen alone not keep the historians in mind so as to glorify yourselves?" The censor-in-chief knit his brows and said: "I always think of such things, but today what can be done?" The student said: "This is the plan for today: We request that the opening and reading (of the edict) be delayed and that you honorable gentlemen report the true facts to the Emperor, stating that the literati and people urgently cry out for no other reason than that they wish to pray for the vast and magnificent imperial mercy in order that Li-pu might be turned over to the governor and the provincial inspector for investigation. If there is evidence that he has sought favors, then let him be arrested and put to death forthwith, and there will be no remorse."

The censor-in-chief had absolutely no intention of permitting this, but because the statement was just, he feigned a cordial manner and said: "To submit memorials on behalf of Li-pu would indeed be proper. But you students have not yet given this thorough consideration. The imperial anger being so great, if memorials are submitted, can they guarantee that he will be aided?" The student said: "Certainly, if it were a question of the imperial anger, then how could it be shirked? But nowadays edicts are actually forged by Chung-hsien, so that he might murder worthy literati and officials of the empire to satisfy his own personal anger. Chung-hsien's poison flows not only to one region, and disaster is suffered not only by one man! Li-pu, especially, is one to whom we students have long submitted our hearts. . . .

All this while the censor bent his ear to listen. Noting the ardor of the student's words, he officiously said: "Don't you students clamor so; we must deliberate about bringing affairs to a good end." The censor-in-chief said: "Accordingly, let (the edict) be opened and read!"

The student said: "Honorable sir, your words are mere mockery. After the opening and reading, it can only be that he will instantly depart; and if he departs, it can only be that he will instantly die. What can be done then?"

Now the guardsmen looked at one another and whispered: "Who is this?" They were amazed that the censor-in-chief did not take punitive action against the student. The student then said to the censor-in-chief: "We students today have already risked the more. If you honorable gentlemen sacrifice your offices, and if we students sacrifice our lives, then there may be unexpected results. . . .

On hearing this the guardsmen all shrank back. But the censor-in-chief spoke on, saying: "If you wish a memorial to be submitted, you must wait until I enter my palace and prepare a draft." The student said: "Once the honorable gentleman has entered his palace would we students be permitted to see his face again? It is necessary to prepare the memorial here; that will do."

The censor then turned to the censor-in-chief and said with spirit: "(The great remonstrators of antiquity, Kuan Lung-p'ang and Pi Kan after all, were only men. Today we two ought to exert ourselves!" And the superviser of defenses from the side also vigorously urged them on. Now there was a thread of hope in the affair!

All the while the two dignitaries and the student were talking together, back and forth, the crowd encircled them like a wall, listening. The two dignitaries were standing upright in the mud; their shoulders jarred together, and they could not even stand steadily on the ground. They no longer had any dignity of demeanor! There was such a great clamor that the crowd could not make out what the student and the dignitaries were saying.

When midday had passed and the guardsmen saw that the deliberation would still not be concluded for a long time, they threw arm-chains to the ground with a clanking noise and loudly shouted:

"Where is the prisoner?" The crowd's anger suddenly rose with the force of a landslide or the crash of waves. Grasping and snapping the (platform) railings with a wrenching noise, they attacked. In the twinkling of an eye the guardsmen and the battalion commanders all were clasping their heads and slinking away to east or west, climbing trees or scrambling up onto buildings. Some hid in privies. Some concealed themselves with brambles. When the crowd caught them, they all smote their foreheads and begged for their lives. They suffered severe bodily injuries; not one was able to escape. One clambered over the wall to get away, but the people outside the wall flogged him still more mercilessly. Someone kicked him with wooden clogs until his teeth were knocked into his throat, and he promptly died.

Now the censor-in-chief, the censor, the supervisor of defenses, the prefect, and the magistrate no longer consulted one another, and the students saw that matters were already lost. All scattered to get away. . . .

The next day was clear. The leading personages of Wu [Su-chou], wearing white mourning clothes because of the extraordinary incident, called on the two dignitaries and the supervisor of defenses, seeking some means of restoring peace to the area. The censor-in-chief had already, in the night, summoned the censor to his palace, and by lamplight they had drafted a memorial reporting the uprising. At the fifth watch they had hurriedly sent it out. Toward the local personages their attitude was very hateful. They said: "This rebellious crowd! If you gentlemen had early issued a single word, they would have been soothed! It seems to us that you gentlemen actually caused it! . . ."

. . . Suddenly one night troops were sent out to take up positions on water and on land, and (Chou) was secretly despatched to undertake his journey. The battalion commanders and the guardsmen who were lucky enough to remain alive all were happy to get out the Chin-ch'ang gate with their lives. The prefect and the magistrate proceeded in a small boat together with Shun-ch'ang. Only when they had crossed the domestic-customs barrier and anchored in a wilderness did they dare to proclaim the edict. Thus crudely was the matter terminated. When daylight came and the crowd learned of this, Shun-ch'ang was already long gone. . . .

In Wu, meanwhile, there was wild terror day and night. It was said that there were going to be pit-burials (of literati) and massacres (of commoners), and rich families all moved away. In the deliberations of the inner court, it was insistently desired that great trials be undertaken in the three Wu (i.e., Su-chou, Ch'ang-chou and Hu-chou prefectures), beginning with the students who had spoken out in opposition. Moreover, guardsmen had reported their names, and they had already been arrested!

Just at the time when Chung-hsien and his partisans were secretly plotting in the palace [at Peking], there was a sudden earthquake May 31, 1626). A roof ornament over the place where they were sitting fell without any apparent reason, and two young eunuchs whom (Wei) favored were crushed to death. In a moment there was a sound like thunder rising from the northwest. It shook heaven and earth, and black clouds flowed over confusedly. People's dwellings were destroyed to such an extent that for several miles (li) nothing remained. Great stones hurtled down from the sky like rain. Men and women died by the tens of thousands; donkeys, horses, chickens, and dogs all had broken or cracked limbs. People with smashed skulls or broken noses were strewn about—the streets were full of them! Gunpowder that had previously been stored in the Imperial Arsenal exploded. This alarmed elephants, and the elephants ran about wildly, trampling to death an incalculable number of people.

The court astrologer reported his interpretation of these events as follows: "In the earth there is tumultuous noise. This is an evil omen of calamity in the world. When noise gushes forth from within the earth, the city must be destroyed." He also said: "The reason why the earth growls is that throughout the empire troops arise to attack one another and that palace women and eunuchs have brought about great disorder." Chung-hsien promptly beat him to death. How far more worthy was this court astrologer, who though a minor minister was yet able obstinately to remonstrate about a technical matter, than those who sang praises of (Wei's) merits and virtues!

When the calamity subsided, the commander of the Imperial Guard made further requests about the Wu affair, but Chung-hsien had been awed by the disaster and ordered that the matter be set aside for the time being. Yet in the end Shun-ch'ang died in prison. Till death he cursed incessantly. When it was produced in a mixed-up group, his corpse was so mutilated that it could no longer be identified. Even passers-by were deeply moved.

Further, there was issued an edict secretly ordering the censor-in-chief immediately to put to death five men including Yen P'ei-wei and to send others into frontier military service. The education intendant was also ordered to degrade or dismiss the students, variably. Their names have been recorded elsewhere. The censor-in-chief, afraid of inciting another uprising, did not dare carry out the executions publicly. . . .

12 / THE RISE OF A POPULAR LITERATURE

Popular literature, as opposed to the classical, historical, and scholarly genres cultivated by the literati, began to appear in print during the Sung dynasty (960-1279 A.D.). Folk dramas and the novel, literary forms ordinarily viewed as vulgar by the educated, began to be published regularly as literacy, urban living, and prosperity spread. Fiction in the popular language of the streets, which dealt with themes from everyday life, grew out of the art of storytelling.

The first printed versions of the traditional tales and romances were the prompt-books designed for the use of professional storytellers. Once published, the prompt-book stories served as ready-made skeleton plots for whoever cared to elaborate on them. With the passage of time, as more learned individuals became interested in producing a vernacular literature, elaborate dramas and novels with sophisticated plots laid bare the complexities of family life or satirized manners, morals, and institutions. Anthologies, many of them compiled in the Ming dynasty, preserve a rich and variegated popular literature.

Traditional Chinese novels are about as long and involved as some Chinese plays, and they likewise employ conventional themes and plots from folklore and history. The earliest of the extant novels is the Romance of the Three Kingdoms, *a rambling historical novel that dates, in the form known today, from the fourteenth century. Other novels, such as* Monkey, *are based on Buddhist stories of wonders and remind one of the tales of Paul Bunyan. Novels reached their present form in Ming times and are usually ascribed to a single author, even though he was really no more than the compiler of a host of traditional stories.*

The Golden Lotus, *one of the greatest of Chinese novels in terms of realism and character portrayal, is usually attributed to a Ming official of the late sixteenth or early seventeenth century and was first printed in 1610. Its author was obviously a severe critic of the manners and morals of his day. While he sets his story in the Sung dynasty, he is certainly talking, and bitterly, about the depraved*

From the novel *Chin P'ing Mei*, trans. Clement Egerton, as *The Golden Lotus* (London, 1939), II, Ch. 48. Reprinted by permission of Routledge & Kegan Paul, Ltd.

state of society in the declining years of the Ming and of public officials like his rake of a hero, Hsi-mên Ch'ing. His descriptions, which are often pornographic and shocking, are as realistic as anything that ever came from the pen of Samuel Richardson or Henry Fielding. For its day, The Golden Lotus *is unsurpassed as a mirror of the social and moral degeneration of Ming China and as a repository of the customs and manners of the sixteenth century. Notice particularly, in the following excerpt, the author's implied attack on the corruption and venality of office-holders.*

The Censor's Accusation

. . . At Hsi-mên's burying-place, he had recently built a mound, an arbour, and some rooms. He had not been to worship his ancestors since he had received his official appointment. Now he sent for Hsü, the Master of the Yin Yang, to examine the site, built a gateway and made a path for the spirits. Round the gateway he planted peach-trees, willows and pines. On either side he made a small embankment. At the Festival of the Dead he proposed to visit the grave and change the tablet. He prepared pigs and sheep and food.

The festival was on the sixth day of the third month. He sent out many invitations and arranged for a number of people to take the things out to the tomb—wine, rice, vegetables and so forth. He engaged musicians and actors, and arranged for several singing-girls to be present. He invited a great number of guests, both men and women. Plum Blossom, Welcome Spring, Flute of Jade and Fragrance were to be there also. Twenty-four or more sedan-chairs would be needed. But when there was question of the nurse's taking the baby Kuan Ko, the Moon Lady said to Hsi-mên: "It will be better not to take the baby. He is not a year old yet, and old woman Liu tells me that the bones of his head have not yet grown together. He is very nervous, and, if we take him on such a long trip, I am afraid he will be frightened. We will leave him behind. The nurse and old woman Fêng can stay at home and look after him so that his mother can go."

Hsi-mên Ch'ing would not agree. "Why are we going to the tombs of my ancestors at all?" he said. "I want both the baby and his mother to go and kotow to my ancestors. You always believe everything that silly old woman tells you. If the baby's head is not strong enough he must be wrapped up more carefully. He will be quite safe with his nurse in the sedan-chair. There is nothing for you to worry about."

"Have it your own way," the Moon Lady said.

In the morning all the ladies came to Hsi-mên Ch'ing's house and they started off together. They left the city by the southern gate, and, when they had gone about eight *li*, they could see the green pine-trees that surrounded the tomb. There was the new gateway and the enbankment on both sides. Stone walls encircled the tomb, and, in the middle, were the oratory and the way of the spirits. The perfume-burners, candlesticks and utensils for the worship of the ancestral spirits were all of white alabaster. Over the gate was placed a new tablet which bore the inscription: 'The Ancestral Tombs of the valorous Commander Hsi-mên.' They went in and round beneath the interlaced branches of the trees, Hsi-mên Ch'ing, wearing his scarlet robes and girdle, set out the pigs, sheep, and food for the worship of his ancestors. First the gentlemen offered their worship, then the ladies. The musicians played. The baby was frightened and hid his face in his nurse's bosom. He whimpered, lying perfectly still.

"Sister," the Moon Lady whispered to the Lady of the Vase, "I should tell the nurse to take him away. Don't you see how terrified he is? I said we ought not to bring him, but his stupid father wouldn't listen to me. Now he is frightened into such a state."

The Lady of the Vase hurriedly told Tai An to stop the beating of the drums and gongs. They covered the baby's ears and took him away.

After a time the service was ended. Master Hsü read the oration and burned paper offerings. Then Hsi-mên Ch'ing invited the gentlemen to go to the front, and the Moon Lady invited the ladies to go to the back. They went through the gardens. There were pine-trees and pine hedges, bamboos standing beside the paths, and many flowers and grasses.

Beneath the awning the actors played for the ladies while four young actors entertained the gentlemen, playing instruments and singing in the great hall. Four singing-girls served wine in turn for the gentlemen, and the four maids for the ladies. Then they stood at Orchid's table and had soup and cakes.

Golden Lotus, Tower of Jade and Orchid went with Cassia and Silver Maid to the garden and played on the swings there. Behind the arbour, Hsi-mên had arranged three rooms with furniture and beds, curtains, and things for the toilet. Here, the ladies might dress when they came to visit the tombs. The rooms were covered with paper so white that they seemed like caves of snow. Pictures and scrolls adorned the walls. To this place the nurse,

Heart's Delight, brought the baby, and, on the gilded bed, the child lay upon a tiny blanket. . . .

By this time four acts of the play had been performed and it was beginning to grow dark. Hsi-mên Ch'ing told Pên IV to give each of the chair-men a cup of wine, four cakes, and a plate of cooked meat. When the chair-men had eaten it, they took the ladies away. The servants followed on horseback. Lai Hsing came with the cooks, bringing all the food-boxes. Tai An, Lai An, Hua T'ung and Ch'i T'ung followed behind the Moon Lady's chair; Ch'in T'ung, with four soldiers, behind Hsi-mên Ch'ing's horse. Heart's Delight had a small chair for herself and the baby who was closely wrapped in bed-clothes. The Moon Lady was still anxious about him and bade Hua T'ung accompany the nurse's chair. She was afraid that they would find the streets very crowded when they came to the city.

When all the chairs had entered the city, those of the Ch'iao family went their own way. The Moon Lady reached home, but it was some time before Hsi-mên Ch'ing and Ch'ên Ching-chi arrived.

When Hsi-mên Ch'ing dismounted, P'ing An said to him: "His Lordship Hsia has been here and gone away. He sent messengers for you twice. I don't know what he wanted."

This made Hsi-mên Ch'ing thoughtful. He went to the great hall, where Shu T'ung took his clothes. "What did his Lordship say when he was here?" Hsi-mên asked the boy.

"He didn't say anything to me," Shu T'ung said. "He only asked where you were. He suggested that I should go and ask you to come back because he had something very important to say to you. I told him that you had gone to the tombs to make offering to the dead and that you would be back this evening. He said he would come again. He has sent messengers twice but I had to tell them you had not returned."

"What is this?" Hsi-mên Ch'ing said to himself.

He was thinking over the matter when P'ing An came and said Magistrate Hsia had called once more. It was very dark. The magistrate was in plain clothes and had only two servants with him. When he entered the great hall he greeted Hsi-mên. "You have just returned from your glorious estate," he said. "To-day I have been to worship at my ancestor's tombs," Hsi-mên Ch'ing said. "I ask your forgiveness for being absent when you called."

"I have come specially to bring you news," said Hsia. "Shall we go into another room?"

Hsi-mên Ch'ing told Shu T'ung to open the door, and they went in. He ordered all the servants to leave.

"This morning," Magistrate Hsia said, "Li came to me and told me that the Censor has sent a report to the Eastern Capital accusing us both. I have had the document copied and here it is. Please read it."

Hsi-mên Ch'ing was alarmed. He paled. He took the paper to the lamp and read it. It said:

> I, the Censor and Circuit Commissioner of Shan-tung, Ts'êng Hsiao-hsü, make accusation against certain rapacious and unworthy officials, and implore the Sacred Majesty to dismiss them that the dignity of the Law may be preserved.
>
> I have been instructed that the duty of the Emperor is to go round the country and investigate the morals of the people. To check evil officials and enforce the law is the duty of the censors. In olden times it was written in the Book of Spring and Autumn that the Supreme Monarch went upon an inspection of the Empire and made the whole state subject to himself. So the morals of the people were improved and the exalted principle of the Ruler made manifest. The four peoples became obedient and all men recognised the rule of wisdom.
>
> About a year ago the duty of going round all the districts of Shan-tung was entrusted to me. I have questioned the officials and found out the truth about the capacity of them all, whether military or civil. Now my tour of duty is almost at an end: I am continuing my investigations and would make report to Your Majesty. Especially would I, with Your Majesty's gracious permission, make the following accusations. . . .
>
> Hsia Yen-ling, captain of the Royal Guard and a principal magistrate in Shan-tung, is a man of no merit. He is rapacious and a man of evil conduct. People talk about his behaviour and he is a disgrace to his position. Formerly, when he held office at the Capital, he committed many irregularities and was discovered by his subordinates. Now that he is employed in the courts of Shan-tung he is more rapacious than ever. He is always associating in evil with other officials. He has entered his son at the Military College by making false statements, and procured some other person to take the examination in his son's place, thus utterly demoralising the students. He has allowed his servant Hsia Shou to take bribes. The soldiers complain bitterly and his administration is extremely disorganised. When this Hsia receives officers visiting his district, his face is as that of a slave and his knees as those of a maid. For this reason the people call him 'Maid'. When he investigates a case his judgment is always uncertain, and his underlings call him 'Wooden Image'.
>
> His Deputy, Captain Hsi-mên Ch'ing, was originally a street-corner lounger. He obtained his position by bribery and has thus improperly

secured military rank. He cannot even distinguish between the flail and the corn. He cannot read a single character. He allows his wife and his concubines to play in the streets and there have been scandals in his household. He drinks with singing girls in wineshops, and has disgraced the official class to which he belongs. Recently he has been associating with the wife of a certain Han Tao-kuo. He gives himself up completely to a dissolute life and cares nothing about his conduct. He took bribes from a certain Miao Ch'ing and has irregularly allowed that fellow to escape the justice of the law. So Miao Ch'ing's crime has never been punished.

These two rapacious and unworthy officers have long been the talk of the common people and they should be immediately dismissed from their posts. I pray Your Majesty to hear me, and instruct the Boards to examine these men closely. If it is found that what I have said is true, I pray Your Majesty to dismiss these two men. The morale of the service depends upon it. May the virtue of Your Majesty be glorious for ever and ever.

When he had finished reading this, Hsi-mên Ch'ing could only look at Magistrate Hsia. He could find no words to say. "What shall we do?" said Hsia.

"There is a proverb," Hsi-mên Ch'ing said, "which says: 'When soldiers come against us, we send out a general. When the flood comes, we build a dyke.' So, when in trouble, we must take steps to meet the situation. We must get ready presents and send them to the Imperial Tutor in the Eastern Capital."

Magistrate Hsia hurried home and got ready two hundred taels of silver and two silver vases. Hsi-mên prepared a chest full of gold, jade, and precious things, and three hundred taels of silver. Hsia ordered his servant Shou, and Hsi-mên his man Lai Pao, to take charge of these gifts. He had a letter written to the comptroller Chai. The two men hired horses and went off, travelling as fast as they were able, to the Eastern Capital.

When the baby Kuan Ko returned from the tomb, he cried all night and would not take his food. Everything he swallowed he disgorged again. The Lady of the Vase was alarmed. She came to the Moon Lady and told her.

"I said that a baby not a year old should not be taken outside the city," the Moon Lady said, "but the foolish man would not listen to me. He said the whole purpose of going to the tombs of his ancestors was that you and the child might offer worship there. He glared and shouted at me as if he were a savage. Now, what I anticipated has happened."

The Lady of the Vase did not know what to do.

Hsi-mên Ch'ing, after talking to Hsia about the Censor's report, was getting the presents ready to send off. He felt very depressed about things in general. Now the baby was ill too.

The Moon Lady sent a boy for old woman Liu and also for a doctor who specialised in children's ailments. The gate was opened, and there was much shouting and running about all night. Old woman Liu said that the baby had been frightened and that he must have met the General of the Road. "It is of no great importance," she told them. "Burn a few paper offerings and we shall get rid of the devil, sure enough." She gave them two red pills, peppermint and lamp-wick, and, when the baby had taken them, he quietened and went to sleep. He stopped crying and did not disgorge his milk any more. But the fever did not leave him. The Lady of the Vase gave old woman Liu a tael of silver for some papers. The old woman returned with her husband and another witch-woman. They burned the papers and danced the spirit dance in the arbour.

At the fifth night-watch, Hsi-mên Ch'ing got up to see Lai Pao and Hsia Chou away on their errand. Then he went to Magistrate Hsia's, and together they went to Tung-p'ing Fu to Hu's place to hear what news there was of Miao Ch'ing.

After the Moon Lady had been told that the baby had been frightened on the way home, she reproached Heart's Delight for not looking after the child properly. "He was frightened while he was in the sedan-chair," she said. "If not, why should he not have got better?"

"I wrapped him up very carefully in the bed-clothes," Heart's Delight said, "and he was not frightened. You sent Hua T'ung to follow my chair, and he was all right then. It was only when we came into the city that he suddenly began to shiver. We were quite close to home. It was then he began to refuse his milk and to cry."

Lai Pao and Hsia Shou made all the haste they could and reached the capital in six days. They went at once to the Imperial Tutor's palace, saw Comptroller Chai, and handed over the presents to him. Chai read Hsi-mên Ch'ing's letter. "The Censor's report has not yet reached the Capital," he said. "You had better stay here for a few days. The Imperial Tutor has recently sent a memorial to his Majesty which contains seven suggestions. This has not yet been returned. By the time it does return, perhaps the Censor's report will have arrived. I will warn his Eminence, and suggest that he should do no more than send the report to the Board of Military Affairs. Then I will send word to the Minister of War, Yü, and ask him to suppress it. Tell your master there is nothing to worry about. I can promise that nothing serious will come of the matter."

He entertained the two men. Then they went to their inn to rest and wait for further news.

One day, the Memorial of the Imperial Tutor Ts'ai came back from the Court. Lai Pao asked one of the officers of the Imperial Tutor's household to copy it that he might take back a copy to Hsi-mên Ch'ing. Comptroller Chai wrote a letter of thanks and gave Lai Pao five taels of silver. The two men went home again.

When they reached Ch'ing Ho, Hsi-mên was living in a state of extreme anxiety. While they were away Magistrate Hsia had been calling every day in the hope of hearing some news of their mission. The two men went at once to the inner court and Lai Pao gave Hsi-mên an account of everything that had happened. "Master Chai," he said, "read your letter, but he said there would be nothing very serious and certainly no need for you to be anxious. This Censor's tour of duty is nearly at an end and he will be succeeded by somebody else. His report has not yet reached the Capital, and, when it does, Master Chai will speak to the Imperial Tutor and see that, however serious it may be, his Eminence sends it to the Board of Military Affairs. Chai himself will go there and persuade the Minister to register it but not to let it go any further. So, no matter how serious the report may be, you will suffer no harm from it."

This was a great relief to Hsi-mên Ch'ing. He asked how it was that the Censor's report had not yet reached the Court. "When we went to the Capital," Lai Pao said, "we travelled post-haste and got there in five days. On our way back we met the couriers with the report. At least, we saw post-horses with bells and riders with yellow wrappers. The pennants bore pheasants' feathers."

"So long as the document reached the Capital after you did," Hsi-mên said, "all will be well, but if you had been too late . . ."

"There is no need to worry," Lai Pao said. "I have other good news for you."

"What is that?" Hsi-mên Ch'ing asked.

"Recently, the Imperial Tutor sent a Memorial to the Emperor with seven suggestions which his Majesty will approve. The Imperial Tutor's relative Han, the Vice-President of the Board of Domestic Affairs, proposes to open the salt monopoly in Shên-hsi, and, in every district, to set up official granaries for the sale of rice. Wealthy people will pay their contribution of rice to these granaries and get their official receipt from them. The government will issue salt certificates. The old grain certificates will rate at seventy per cent. and the new ones at thirty. Some time ago, we and your relative Ch'iao put in to the excise office of Kao Yang thirty thousand grain certificates and thirty thousand salt certificates. The Board of Domestic Affairs has now appointed Ts'ai, the President of the Academy, to be Salt Commissioner for the Two Huais. He is to leave the Capital shortly. He will certainly make an excellent inspector."

Hsi-mên asked if this was true.

"If you do not believe me," Lai Pao said, "here is a copy of the document." He took a paper from a letter-case and handed it to Hsi-mên Ch'ing. Hsi-mên looked at it, and, as there were many unusual characters, sent for Ch'ên Ching-chi to read it for him. Ching-chi read half of it, and then stopped. So many of the characters were strange to him. Then Shu T'ung was sent for, and he read it with perfect ease from start to finish, for he had come from a wealthy household and had been well taught. The paper said:

> The humble memorial Ts'ai Ching, Great Scholar of the Hall of Supreme Authority, Prime Minister, and Duke of Lu Kuo.
>
> These foolish suggestions are put forward that he may expend his futile energies upon the securing of men of capacity; that an efficient administration may be secured; the financial state of the country strengthened, and the welfare of the people fostered.
>
> Thus may the glory of the Imperial Wisdom be made manifest:
>
> First: the public examinations should be abolished and men should be given appointments direct from the colleges.
>
> Second: the hitherto existing Board of Finance should be abolished.
>
> Third: the present trade in salt should be done away with.
>
> Fourth: the promulgation of a law upon coining.
>
> Fifth: the buying and selling of cereals should be placed upon a sound footing.

When Hsi-mên Ch'ing had heard this and had read Comptroller Chai's letter again, he knew that his present had been safely delivered, and that President Ts'ai had been appointed Salt Commissioner, and would pass through Ch'ing Ho on his way to assume office. He was delighted. He sent Hsia Shou home to give the news to Magistrate Hsia, and gave Lai Pao five taels of silver, two jars of wine and a piece of meat. Then Lai Pao went to his place to rest.

V / JAPAN

INTRODUCTION

With the coming of Chinese civilization to Japan in the seventh century, Japanese writers began to produce an official history of the islands. The early historians sought to prove by their works that Japan was an old and powerful country and a worthy rival of China. Japan was proclaimed the land of the *kami* (gods) and its emperors were alleged to be descendants of the Sun Goddess. Two compilations of the eighth century set the pattern for this pseudo-history, and the assertions made in them about the origins of the nation and its "unbroken" line of emperors remained official dogma to 1945.

Later histories and other forms of Japanese literature accepted without question the myths and legends of origins, while giving reliable data on more recent events. In times of crisis the common belief in the divine origin of the country and its people served to unite the nation against foreign ideas or invasions. It also led to the conviction that Japan was superior to other nations and that its native virtues, such as austerity and frugality, were unique and sacrosanct. The Europeans, who first arrived in Japan around the middle of the sixteenth century, comment repeatedly on the uncompromising devotion of the Japanese to their country, its gods, and its traditions.

13 / THE TRANSFORMATION OF FEUDAL INSTITUTIONS

In the early sixteenth century Japan was not a centralized state. The entire country was divided into many domains, each of which was an effective political entity governed by a daimyo *(means "great names"). Though these domains varied in size and power, the* daimyo *ordinarily ruled as a father over his subjects, without serious interference from either the Emperor or the* shogun *("generalissimo"). Effective government within each domain was conducted at its lowest levels by salaried retainers of the* daimyo. *Agriculture was the major economic base of these domains. Relationships between the lord, his retainers, and the other social classes were governed by tradition, which generally changed slowly before the sixteenth century.*

The larger daimyo, *in line with their military heritage, concentrated on developing the military potential of their domains. Particular* daimyos *became so powerful at times that they managed to extend their jurisdiction over broad areas and large numbers of people. One of these* daimyo, *Odo Nobunaga, became powerful enough by 1586 to gain control over most of central Japan and thereby set in motion a process that brought about the reunification of the country. This pattern of conquest was completed by Toyotomi Hideyoshi, who restored political unity to Japan in 1590 by finally reducing to submission the stubborn* daimyo *of Kyushu.*

Once Hideyoshi was acknowledged as the leader of all Japan, he immediately took steps to consolidate the economic power of the central government throughout the land. He ordered a complete land survey supervised by his own officials, between 1583 and 1598, in spite of stubborn and widespread resistance. The land registers recorded dimensions according to standard measurements and assessed standard yields by class of land. Thus, first-class wet land was expected to yield 1.5 koku *(almost 7.5 bushels) of unhulled rice per* shaku *(a square 6.3 feet by 6.3 feet, or nearly 40 square feet), with one* koku *representing the annual consumption of each adult. Transactions in land were thereafter described in terms of the product (the number of* koku*) and not the area. Taxes were then assessed directly on the actual cultivator, and were set at a fixed proportion of the crop. Hideyoshi's own holdings, scat-*

From *The Documents of Iriki, Illustrative of the Development of the Feudal Institutions of Japan* (late sixteenth century), K. Asakawa, ed. and trans. (New Haven: Yale University Press, 1929), pp. 326-28, 331-35. Reprinted by permission of Yale University Press.

tered throughout the country, were worth an estimated two million koku. *The land register and the census of 1590 tied at least four-fifths of the population of Japan to the soil for the next several centuries. At the same time, ultimate tax authority was transferred from feudal intermediaries to the central government.*

While the land survey and the economic reorganization were being completed, Hideyoshi was massing his vassals to launch an attack on China. When Korea refused to allow free passage to the invading force in 1592, Hideyoshi sent 160,000 men to force the way. (Compare this figure to the 130,000 men who landed in Normandy on the first day of the Allied invasion of June 6, 1944). China, as Korea's suzerain, intervened and helped force the Japanese to retreat, but a peace could not be agreed on. In 1597 Hideyoshi sent 140,000 reinforcements to-complete the task in Korea, but these forces returned home when Hideyoshi died in the following year. Peace was not restored until 1606.

Consolidation of power in the hands of Hideyoshi seriously affected the entire feudal structure of government and economy and caused a lasting transformation in feudal institutions. To illustrate the changes that took place at the local level we have documents from the Iriki family of southwestern Kyushu which show in microcosm how fortunes changed in sixteenth-century Japan.

The original holdings of the Iriki, a branch of the Shibuya family, were within view of the East China Sea and directly across it from the mouth of the Yangtze River. The terrain of this part of Kyushu is so rugged that only the land immediately bordering the river valleys can be cultivated. Though they had less than fifty-five square miles of territory under their rule, the Iriki controlled a portion of the main road leading to Kagoshima, a port within the jurisdiction of the powerful Shimadzu family. After a long rivalry, the Iriki bowed to the Shimadzu at the very end of the fourteenth century.

The lords of Iriki were able to exploit the unsettled conditions of the 1530's to more than double the family domain. Much of this gain had to be relinquished by 1570, when the Iriki became vassals of the Shimadzu. In turn the men of Shimadzu, then the chief power in Kyushu, were forced to submit to Hideyoshi in 1586, though they continued to resist centralization with all their strength. In the course of the readjustments brought about by Hideyoshi's conquest, the Shimadzu moved the Iriki off their ancestral domain. The family was allowed to return in 1613 to its former home, but its estate was repeatedly reduced in size thereafter. So overwhelming was the importance of the Shimadzu that, even after having op-

posed the Tokugawa unifiers of Japan as long as possible, they were allowed to remain as daimyo of Satsuma. Their holdings, though reduced in size, produced a rice yield which was estimated as second only to that of the Maeda who ranked as growers of rice immediately below the shogun himself.

Only a few items have been chosen from the selection of 253 representative private and public manuscripts available on the history of the Iriki. The late Professor K. Asakawa translated these into English, supplied annotations, and also provided a valuable introduction relating the documents to the general development of feudal institutions in Japan. The last set of documents below shows that in Hideyoshi's second campaign the Shimadzu contingent, reckoned on the basis of their rice production as recorded for tax purposes, was expected to number about 10 per cent of the total force.

Documents Concerning the Survey and the Grant of the Shimadzu Fiefs, 1594-1595

. . . Of the several orders containing instructions of the land survey under Hideyoshi that have been preserved, the following two relate to the Shimadzu dominion; many of the instructions given here were repeated in orders issued in other parts of Japan [Trans.].

"Regulations regarding the survey of land in the domain of the Shimadzu.

"That it shall be instructed to holders (*ryō-shu*) everywhere that, all *samurai, hyaku-shō*,[1] and others who, because of the land survey, have fled to other *kuni* [provinces], shall first be examined, arrested, and delivered.

"That the order shall be certainly circulated in all communities, by previously instructing the village elders (*otona hyaku-shō*) and village officials (*kimo-iri*), that, if, in relation to the surveying, mapping, and assessing of *ta* [rice land] and *hata* [upland fields], any one should offer presents or [receiving them] give a lenient treatment, both the giver and the receiver would, as soon as the guilt was heard of, even afterwards, be executed.

"That if any one behaved insolently toward the commissioners of land survey (*ken-chi bu-gyō*), his community would be punished for the offense.

"That if a commissioner of land survey committed an arbitrary act, the commoners (*ji-ge nin*) and *hyaku-shō* should report the matter without concealment to chiefs of the commissioners.

---

[1] Here the term probably means peasants; in the early feudal period it meant the lower warrior class.

"It should be strictly ordered that, if any violate the aforegoing regulations, not only he, but also his relatives and his community, shall be executed.

"Bun-roku 3 y. 7 m. 16 d. [31 August 1594]."

"That, in connection with this survey of land, sea-dues (ura-yaku) might be rated as an annual tax (nen-gu). Where this is not done, they shall be assessed in each special instance according to estimate. [In such cases], whatever, according to the report made in reference to the condition of the sea of a mura [peasant hamlet], should be rendered to the government, should be recorded in a separate book.

"That the mountain-dues (yama-yaku) shall be likewise dealt with.

"That silk, since it is a thing [from] which [dues] should be rendered to the government, should be registered in the book after considering the condition of the mulberry trees of the place, in such wise that the hyaku-shō would not be embarrassed because they were assessed in silk instead of rice, and also that the dues of the government would not suffer; and that, thereafter, no homestead and hata where there are mulberry trees shall be rated as first-grade hata.

"That [bamboos in] bamboo-groves shall be cut annually at the rate of one-tenth, and a tenth of the tenth shall be given to the holder (nushi) of the grove; for example, ten bamboos shall be annually cut from a grove which has 100 bamboos, and nine shall be rendered to the government and one be given to the holder of the grove, and ninety shall stand in the grove; registry shall be made accordingly.

"That, as regards iron, it should also, according to estimate, be assessed either as an annual tax [in money] or in terms of rice. Since this is a thing [from] which [dues] should be rendered to the government, care should be taken in assessing it, so that the worker also would not be embarrassed.

"That, as regards tea-gardens, they should not be assessed for an annual tax (nen-gu), for, after the survey, they are not a thing [from] which [dues] should be rendered to the government. However, some consideration should be had in surveying a homestead and hata which have tea-gardens.

"That, as for lacquer-trees, they should also, by general estimation in the mura [which have them], be assessed in terms either of rice or of money; they should, however, be recorded definitely as dues (nashi) on lacquer-trees. This refers to lacquer-trees found in places which are not homesteads. Lacquer-trees on a *hata* should also be under the control of its holder (*nushi*). They should not be assessed as first-grade. Therefore, a homestead or *hata* where lacquer-trees are shall be [valued as] first-grade *hata*.

"That, since the [Buddhist] churches and [Shintō] temples, resident houses of *samurai*, and merchant houses, which should be excluded from the survey, have been decided by a [special] report, all others shall be surveyed.

"That in each *mura*, the resident houses of the two men, the *shō-ya* and the *kimo-iri*, shall be excepted.

"That trees as heretofore shall all be under the control of the *hyaku-shō* holding the land (*ji-nushi hyaku-shō*), and should not be considered as owing dues to the government.

"That the river-dues (*kawa-yaku*) shall be estimated in the *mura*, and be fixed as an annual tax (*nen-gu*).

"Thus.

"Bun-roku 3 y. 7 m. 16 d. [31 August 1594]. Monogram of Ishida *Jibu shō-yū*.

"To the Commissioners of Satsuma."

Records of Military Service in the Korean War, 1591 and 1597

The discovery that has been made from fresh sources, of hitherto unsuspected reasons which finally prompted Hideyoshi to undertake his Korean expedition, is too recent to have found its way into works in European languages which contain accounts of the campaigns. . . . We shall not discuss with any degree of fullness the part which the Shimadzu played in the two campaigns, for the story belongs rather to the history of the family, than to a volume of Iriki-in documents. Yoshihisa being too advanced in age, his younger brother Yoshihiro, himself fifty-seven years old, led the Shimadzu contingents in Korea. Yoshihiro's service was not specially marked in the first campaign, 1592-1593, but, in the second, 1597-1598, he bore the brunt of the attack at Sö-chön delivered by one of the three immense armies of China that had come to the succor of Korea, and, on 30 October 1598, achieved a brilliant victory, thus enabling the expeditionary armies of Japan to retreat with comparative ease. Hideyoshi had died on 18 September.

In the following notes of the military service in Korea, the numbers of the contingent under the Shimadzu in each campaign is set down as 15,000 more or less. Yoshihiro's army in 1592, however, is said to have been 10,000, and even this reduced number may not have been full. In 1597, again, the same number was credited to him, besides 800 under Iéhisa. The Shimadzu had been in rather straitened circumstances after the costly wars they had waged in Kyū-shū, followed by the great reduction of their territory ordered by Hideyoshi.

Iriki-in Shigetoki was ill in 1592 when Yoshihiro had issued a hurried call to arms and started on 8 April from Kurino with only twenty-three knights. Shigetoki sent two detachments, of seventy-five men each, under his kinsmen Iriki-in Shigeoku and Tōgō Shigekage. When Umekita Kunikane, a vassal of Yoshihiro, fearing punishment for his tardy arrival at Hirado, attempted a foolish revolt in Higo, in July, the Iriki warriors under Tōgō were among the more than two thousand men who were induced to join the insurgent, and shared in the speedy defeat and death which the rebels received at the hands of local barons. The other division safely landed in Korea and joined Yoshihiro at Yŏng-p'iung Chŏng, in Kyun-geui *do* near the border of Kang-wun *do*, followed by fresh recruits sent by Shigetoki. He was able to take part in the second campaign, and returned on 30 January 1598 to Yunowo, where he had been transferred in the autumn of 1595. [TRANS.]

"The military service (*gun-yaku*) of Shimadzu *dono* in the Korean expedition:

15,000 men,— Mata-ichirō *dono*.

"300 banners; 5 hand-spears (*te-yari*). Yoshihisa.

300 spears, of which 200 are long spears (*naga yari*), and 200, hand-spears. Yoshihiro.

"Besides these, the men should provide hand-spears according to their capacity. 20 hand-spears. In a retinue or in front of a camp, it is not sightly to have nothing but long spears.

"1500 guns. 1500 men with bows.

"600 men with small banners; these should be armored.

"Only distinguished men should be mounted; however, all those who cannot go on foot should be mounted. Therefore, the number of the mounted is indefinite. The mounted men might well bear helmet and armor.

"These regulations shall be observed with zeal.

"Ten-shō 19 y. [1591]."

"At the rate of one mounted knight for each 1,020 *koku;* 95 knights in all. Total, 3,230 men of this class, being 34 men with each [knight] (*zhin-tai*).

"At the rate of one mounted knight for each 510 *koku;* 24 knights in all. Total, 408 men of this class, being 17 men with each [knight].

"At the rate of one mounted knight for each 300 *koku;* 143 knights in all. Total, 1,430 men, being 10 men with each [knight].

"300 squires on foot. 900 laborers (*fu-maru*), being three laborers with each [squire].

"500 landless (*mu-ashi*) men. 1,000 laborers, being 2 laborers with each [landless man].

"665 carriers of weapons (*dō-gu*).

"2,000 laborers from the lord's domains (*kura-iri*).

"2,000 boatmen.

"Grand total, 12,433 men.

"Provision for these men for five months, 10,522.9 *koku,* inclusive of supplies for boatmen and their chiefs.

"272 horses. Their provisions 616 *koku* of beans, being for five months, at the rate of 2 *shō* per day [for each horse].

"Rice and beans together 11,438.9 *koku.*

"*Uma no kami dono's* 9 mounted knights, with 332 men.

"*Kō-gan's* 69 mounted knights, with 2,332 men.

"Total, 350 mounted knights;
    total, 15,097 men.

"Distribution of boats: two voyages counted as one.

"10 boats with 10-*tan* sails, with 80 men per boat,—800 men;

40 boats with 9-*tan* sails, with 70 men per boat,—2800 men;

31 boats with 8-*tan* sails, with 60 men per boat,—1860 men;

4 boats with 7-*tan* sails, with 40 men per boat,—160 men;

6 boats with 6-*tan* sails, with 30 men per boat,—180 men.

"Total, 91 boats, 5,800 men.

"Distribution of horse-boats.

"15 boats with 7-*tan* sails, 80 horses, with 5 horses, 15 grooms, and
            10 boatmen, per boat;

14 boats with 6-*tan* sails, 56 horses, with 4 horses, 12 grooms, and 8 boatmen, per boat.

"Total, 30 boats, 136 horses, 680 grooms and boatmen.

"Grand total, 5,800 men,
            121 boats.

"Boats on hand.

"10 boats with 10-*tan* sails; 5 boats with 9-*tan* sails;

10 boats with 8-*tan* sails; 20 boats with 7-*tan* sails;

20 boats with 6-*tan* sails.

"Total, 65 boats.

"[Boats made].

"45 boats with 9-*tan* sails, costing 65 *kwan* per boat;

21 boats with 8-*tan* sails, costing 55 *kwan* per boat.

"Total, 66 boats made;
    total [cost], 4300 *kwan,*—in terms of rice, 2,870 *koku.*

"Bun [-roku] 5 y. 12 m. 5 d. [22 January 1597]."

14 / THE IDEALS OF JAPAN'S FEUDAL ELITE

*The following selections specify the standards of conduct expected
of members of Japan's military nobility, and represent the views
of men at three levels within that heterogeneous class. At the pin-
nacle stood the leaders of the military government, or* bakufu, *who
usually ruled from behind the throne through a* shogun. *Ashikaga
Takauji (died 1358), who gained control over the imperial city of
Kyoto in 1336, set up a military government and was quick to issue
a code* (Kemmu shikimoku) *[1]*[1] *which specified the location of the
new seat of government, outlined its administrative structure, and
set down principles of conduct for the maintenance of stable rule.
Though usually respected more in the breach than observance
during Ashikaga times, the Kemmu Code is nonetheless an interesting example of what feudal Japan regarded as good conduct in
government. It was apparently a model for the Tokugawa Code
issued in 1615, the* Buke shohatto *[2].*

*In an endeavor to calm and stabilize society, the Kemmu Code
enjoins a frugal standard of living, strict personal morality, and the
energetic suppression of crime. It denounces invasions of privacy,
recommends reasonable punishment for rebels, and urges the reconstruction of burned-out buildings as the prerequisite for a
return to normal living. The next eight articles show the government's intention to raise the standards of selection and performance
for officials at both the palace and provincial levels. They specifically attack influence-peddling, negligence, idleness, and bribery.
Only "men of principle" should expect advancement, and the important distinction between "higher and lower" was to be maintained by allowing no departures from ceremonial etiquette. In
conclusion, provisions were made for receiving the petitions and
complaints of the "poor and lowly," and for promptly announcing
governmental decisions.*

*As the Tokugawas entrenched themselves in power, they too
drew up a code, which settled firmly into usage. After the death in
1598 of Hideyoshi, Tokugawa Ieyasu became the wealthiest and
most powerful daimyo of Japan. Within five years he made him-*

The Kemmu Code and Laws for the Military Houses. From John Carey Hall,
trans., "Japanese Feudal Laws, II and III," *Transactions of the Asiatic Society
of Japan,* First Series, XXXVI (1908), 11-17; XXXVIII (1911), 288-92. Reprinted
by permission of the Asiatic Society of Japan.

[1] In this section the numbers in brackets refer to the readings that follow.

self shogun, *and within a short time he permanently crippled his strongest rivals by confiscating and redistributing their fiefs. He allotted strategically located fiefs to hereditary vassals of his family, who then co-operated with the Tokugawas in holding off unfriendly* daimyo. *Thus Ieyasu rearranged the feudal power structure to his family's advantage and set the stage for the unprecedented peace of the Edo period (1600-1867). To make certain that the discipline he had imposed would continue in force, Ieyasu employed a committee of scholars to compile ordinances to govern the conduct of his immediate vassals. Shortly before his death in 1616, Ieyasu summoned his most faithful vassals and asked them to abide by the code that follows [2]. Ieyasu's successors modified its provisions only slightly.*

The decentralization characteristic of the Ashikaga period had permitted local leaders to continue consolidating their powers at the expense of shogunal authority. The increasing helplessness of the bakufu *allowed provincial and family rivalries to go unchecked, and out of the ensuing turmoil an ambitious new set of leaders emerged. Previously these "civil war barons" had occasionally served as vassals of the great houses or were small landowners who had proved their military prowess while building up substantial territorial bases of strength. Years of constant warfare produced, by 1500, two dozen* daimyo *who ruled one or more provinces and commanded the services of almost three hundred important subordinates. Among the leading* daimyo *of the northwestern provinces was the Takeda family of Kai, which was presided over by the respected warrior Takeda Shingen (1521-1573) during the critical years of the unification struggle from 1541 to 1573.*

Family policy became more unified in the Ashikaga period as primogeniture, the practice of bequeathing the entire estate to the eldest son, developed. Effective military coördination required written codes or house laws to establish the daimyo's *indisputable hold over his* samurai *(servitors). Among the first to recognize this need was Takeda Shingen, who composed both a house law of fifty-seven articles and the following longer exhortation to his retainers [3]. The high moral tone taken by the author of these precepts on military discipline goes several steps beyond the terse injunctions of earlier, more pragmatic house laws. In fact, Takeda's code foreshadows* bushidō, *a generalized system of ethics elaborated by the* samurai *themselves.*

With the blessing of the government, the samurai *retained their primacy in society even in peaceful times, and the other classes—farmers (nō), artisans (kō), and merchants (shō)—were expected to support them unquestioningly. To justify the existence of these unemployed warriors as a leading class, learned and articulate samurai elevated martial virtues to a higher plane and charged their colleagues with the responsibility for guarding Japan's moral values. One of the earliest treatises devoted to the exposition of bushidō, or the "Way of the Warrior," was written by Yamaga Sokō (1622-1685), one of the "three great rōnin" of the Tokugawa period and a respected teacher. A student of his, Daidoji Yuzan Shigesuké (1639-1731), composed the following popular adaptation of the master's precepts [4].*

The absolute loyalty demanded by a lord from his warriors was expected to take precedence even over family obligations. A hereditary samurai perfected himself in horsemanship, fencing, archery, and jiujitsu, and he studied tactics, calligraphy, literature, history, and ethics. At the age of fifteen he was invested with two swords and treated as a man. Samurai status conferred upon the holder a meager annual stipend as remuneration for the performance of onerous duties. His superiors insisted both on unswerving bravery in the face of death and on an exemplary ascetic and "ethically activist" life. Among the diverse elements that contributed to the growth of bushidō, we can distinguish the individual self-discipline encouraged by Zen Buddhists, the belief in an innate moral sense held by the Shintoists, and the proposition that "to know and to act are one and the same" as advanced by Wang Yang-ming. Generations of peace in the Tokugawa era transformed the samurai into administrators and scholars who remained inculcated with the militantly stern and selfless ideals of bushidō.

Feudal House Laws

[1] Articles of the Kemmu Code, 1336

Whether the Army Headquarters Should Be at Kamakura as Heretofore or at Some Other Place

In antiquity, both in China and our own country, there have been frequent shiftings and changes in society, more than there is time to enumerate. When we come down to later times, we find affairs become much more complicated and troublesome, so that such transitions were probably not so easy to effect. Especially remarkable as regards local changes is the case of the district of

Kamakura, where in the year-term of Bunji (A.D. 1185-1189) His Highness the Right Commander-in-Chief (Yoritomo) for the first time established a Military Office. In the Shokiu year-term (1219-1221), Yoshitoki, in rank a second-class Court noble (*Ason*) swallowed the empire. Must it not be called a lucky place for the Baronial Houses (*Buke*)! Their incomes were ample and their power great. They became, however, luxurious and avaricious, and did not reform accumulated evils; and at last (i.e. in Takatoki's case) brought upon themselves extinction. Even though their seat were to be shifted to somewhere else, if they do not mend their ways and abandon the rut that upset the cart, can there be any doubt that they will totter and be imperiled? Both the Chow (Chou) and Tsin (Ch'in) (Dynasties of China) were within the Yao-Han barrier; yet the Tsin were overthrown in the second generation, whereas the Chow maintained their line 800 years. The Dzui (Sui) and the Tang (T'ang) dynasties both lived in Changan. The Dzui were overthrown in the second generation, whereas the Tang lasted for 300 years. Therefore the duration of a locality of power must depend on the goodness or badness of the system of government. It is not the badness of the locality but the badness of the men that counts. If any one desires to shift the locality of government, must he not follow the direction of public opinion?

The Question of the System of Government

As regards this subject, seeing that we have to ponder the circumstances of the time and frame administrative arrangements to suit, we have Japan and China to choose between; and the problem is, which methods of each should we adopt?

On the whole, succeeding as we do to the inheritance of an age in which the Baronial Houses securely flourished shall we, following in their footsteps, dispense good government? If so, we have Senators of ripe experience, the Counsellors of the Hyōjō Shu (Council of Government at Kamakura), and public servants of all grades in abundance. If we make our appeal to the realities of the old Kamakura régime, is there anything in which it can be said to have been wanting? In the ancient (Chinese) Statutes it is said:—"Virtue means exercising good government, and government consists in making the lives of the folk endurable and easy, etc." Shall we promptly put an end to the distress of the myriads and at once issue our authoritative directions to them? The most important points are, in the main, as follows:—

1. Economy must be universally practised. . . . The age may almost be said to have become demented. Those who are rich become more and more filled with pride; and the less wealthy are ashamed of not being able to keep up with them. Nothing could be more injurious to the cause of good manners. This must be strictly kept within bounds.

2. Drinking parties and wanton frolics must be suppressed. . . . Much more when, through infatuation for their mistresses, men have recourse to gambling. Besides these misdoings, under the pretext of holding tea parties or under the disguise of poetical competitions, meetings are held for the purpose of laying gambling bets. Is not the waste caused by this course of conduct incalculable?

3. Crimes of violence and outrage must be quelled.

Robberies from houses in the open daylight, armed burglaries, murders and massacres occur frequently, and highway robberies take place at all the crossways, and the cries of distress from the victims never cease. . . .

4. The practice of entering the private dwellings of the people and making inquisition into their affairs must be given up. . . .

5. In the present state of affairs, more than half the area of the capital has been reduced to vacant spaces (i.e., burnt down). Are they to be restored to their original owners and the rebuilding of their dwellings permitted?

The talk of the streets is to the effect that all who took part in the Imperial departure to the top of the mountain (Hiyeizan) are to be condemned, high and low without exception; and—without investigation as to the truth or falsity of the allegation—to have their properties confiscated, and so forth. Applying the provisions of the law to the matter, is there (not) a distinction to be made between the principals in turbulence and sedition and those who are only accomplices or merely their dependants and subordinates? Should (not) scrupulous investigations be made into each case, and the treatment be made different accordingly? Did an immense number of such confiscations (not) take place in the sequel of the Shokiu disturbance? If we are again now to take away the whole of their properties, will the Ducal Houses (*Kuge*) and the holders of Court offices (not) be reduced to cruel destitution?

6. Co-operative building clubs for the erection of substantial fire-proof houses to be promoted. . . . If the plan of having (substantial fire-proof) dwellings erected (by voluntary co-operative clubs) be carried out, will it (not) become a basis for giving a sense of security to all the people?

7. Men of special ability for government work must be chosen for the posts of Protectors of the provinces.

In a time such as the present are we (not) to call upon faithful warriors and assign to them the office of the Protectorship in the provinces; and for those who have merited rewards are we (not) to procure the grant of Manors (*Shoyen*)? The provincial Protector is an ancient military functionary; the tranquility or disturbance of the whole county depends entirely on that office. If men of unquestionable capacity and such only be chosen to fill it, will (not) the minds of the folk be set at rest?

8. A stop must be put to the practice of influential nobles and women of all sorts and Buddhist (Zen) ecclesiastics making their interested recommendations (to the Sovereign).

9. Persons holding public posts must be liable to reprimand for negligence and idleness; moreover, they should be subject to the principle of careful selection for their posts.

The above two provisions have been settled principles of government for generations; they are not at all in the nature of newfangled changes.

10. Bribery must be firmly put down.

Although this principle also (like the two preceding) is by no means now enunciated for the first time, a special injunction of more than ordinary stringency is required to deal with it. . . .

11. Presents made from all quarters to those who are attached to the Palace, whether of the Inside or Outside Services, must be sent back. . . .

12. Those who are to be in personal attendance on the rulers (Sovereign and Shogun) must be selected for that duty.

It has been said: "If you want to know what sort the prince is, look at his ministers; if you want to know what sort a man is, look at his companions." Hence, seeing that the goodness or the reverse of a sovereign is at once apparent by looking at the character of the ministers he has under him, must they (not) henceforth be chosen on the ground of their capabilities? . . .

13. Ceremonial etiquette to be the predominant principle.

For regulating a state there is nothing that surpasses a regard for ceremonial formalities. For the prince, there should be a princely style of ceremonial; for the vassal (or minister) there should be a ministerial style. In all matters the distinction between higher and lower should be maintained; and both in speech and demeanour the observance of ceremoniousness should be deemed of cardinal importance.

14. Men noted for probity and their adherence to high principles should be rewarded by more than ordinary distinction. . . .

15. The petitions and complaints of the poor and lowly must be heard and redress granted. . . .

16. The petitions and claims of temples (Buddhist) and Shrines (Shinto) are to be dealt with on their merits, and are either to be approved, or, on the contrary, to be rejected if they deserve to be rejected. . . .

17. There should be certain fixed days appointed for the rendering of decisions and issuance of government orders.

As a cause of distress to people in general nothing is more vexatious than remissness and neglect on the part of those in authority over them; and on the other hand matters should not be hastily dismissed off hand without going to the root of the questions at issue. Definite decisions should be given for one side or the other. That there should be no grievances left for the people to complain of is the chief object of authoritative instructions. . . .

[2] The Laws for the Military Houses
("Buke," i.e. The Daimyos.)

[Promulgated by Hidetada, 2nd Shogun, 1615.]

1.—Literature, arms, archery and horsemanship are, systematically, to be the favourite pursuits.

Literature first, and arms next to it, was the rule of the ancients. They must both be cultivated concurrently. Archery and horsemanship are the more essential for the Military Houses. Weapons of warfare are ill-omened words to utter; the use of them, however, is an unavoidable necessity. In times of peace and good order we must not forget that disturbances may arise. Dare we omit to practise our warlike exercises and drill?

2.—Drinking parties and gaming amusements must be kept within due bounds.

In our Instructions it is laid down that strict moderation in these respects is to be observed. To be addicted to venery and to make a pursuit of gambling is the first step towards the loss of one's domain.

3.—Offenders against the law are not to be harboured in the (feudal) domains.

Law is the very foundation of ceremonial decorum and of social order. To infringe the law in the name of reason is as bad as to outrage reason in the name of the law. To disregard the law (laid down by us) is an offence which will not be treated with leniency.

4.—Throughout the domains whether of the greater or lesser Barons (*Daimyo* and *Shōmyō*) or of the holders of minor benefices, if any of the gentry or soldiers (*shi* and *sotsu*) in their service be guilty of rebellion or murder, such offenders must be at once expelled from their domain.

Fellows of savage disposition (being retainers), are an apt weapon for overthrowing the domain or the family employing them, and a deadly instrument for cutting off the (cultivating common) people. How can such be tolerated?

5.—Henceforth no social intercourse is to be permitted outside of one's own domain, with the people (gentry and commoners) of another domain.

In general, the customs of the various domains are all different from one another, each having its own peculiarities. To divulge the secrets of one's own domain to people of another domain, or to report the secrets of another domain to people of one's own domain is a sure indication of an intent to curry favour.

6.—The residential castles in the domains may be repaired; but the matter must invariably be reported. Still more imperative is it that the planning of structural innovations of any kind must be absolutely avoided.

A castle with a parapet exceeding 100 *chi* is a bane to a domain. Crenelated walls and deep moats (of castles) are the causes of anarchy.

7.—If in a neighbouring domain innovations are being hatched or cliques being formed the fact is to be reported without delay.

Men are always forming groups; whilst, on the other hand, few ever come to anything. On this account they fail to follow their lords or fathers, and soon come into collision with those of neighbouring villages. If the ancient prohibitions are not maintained, somehow or other innovating schemes will be formed.

8.—Marriages must not be contracted at private convenience.

Now, the marriage union is a result of the harmonious blending of the *In* and *Yō* (*i.e.* the *Yin* and *Yang* of Chinese metaphysics, the female and male principles of nature). It is therefore not a matter to be lightly undertaken. . . . To form cliques (*i.e.* political parties) by means of matrimonial connections is a source of pernicious stratagems.

9.—As to the rule that the Daimyos shall come (to the Shōgun's Court at Yedo) to do service.

In the *Shoku Nihom ki* (*i.e.* The Continuation of the Chronicles of Japan) it is recorded amongst the enactments:—

"Except when entrusted with some official duty no one (dignitary) is allowed at his own pleasure to assemble his whole tribe within the limits of the capital, no one is to go about attended by more than twenty horsemen, etc." Hence it is not permissible to lead about a large force of soldiers. For Daimyos whose revenues range from 1,000,000 *koku* down to 200,000 *koku,* the number of twenty horsemen is not to be exceeded. For those whose revenues are 100,000 *koku* and under the number is to be in the same proportion.

On occasions of official service, however (*i.e.* in time of warfare), the number of followers is to be in proportion to the social standing of each Daimyo.

10.—There must be no confusion in respect of dress uniforms, as regards the materials thereof.

The distinction between lord and vassal, between superior and inferior, must be clearly marked by the apparel. Retainers may not, except in rare cases by special favour of their lords, indiscriminately wear silk stuffs. . . .

11.—Miscellaneous persons are not at their own pleasure to ride in palanquins.

There are families who for special reasons from of old have (inherited) the privilege of riding in palanquins without permission from the authorities; and there are others who by permission of the authorities exercise that privilege. But, latterly, even sub-vassals and henchmen of no rank have taken to so riding. This is a flagrant impertinence. Henceforward the Daimyo of the provinces, and such of their kinsfolk as are men of distinction subordinate to them, may ride without applying for government permission. Besides those the following are receiving permission, viz. vassals and retainers of high position about their lords; doctors and astrologers; persons of over sixty years of age; and sick persons and invalids. If ordinary or inferior henchmen (*sotsu*) are allowed to ride in palanquins it will be considered to be the fault of their lords.

This proviso, however, does not apply to Court Nobles, Abbots, or ecclesiastics in general.

12.—The samurai throughout the provinces are to practice frugality.

Those who are rich like to make a display, whilst those who are poor are ashamed of not being on a par with the others. There is no other influence so pernicious to social observances as this; and it must be strictly kept in check.

13.—The lords of the great domains (*kokushu,* lit. masters of provinces) must select men of capacity for office.

The way to govern a country is to get hold of the proper men. The merits and demerits (of retainers) should be closely scanned, and reward or reproof unflinchingly distributed accordingly. If there be capable men in the administration that domain is sure to flourish; if there be not capable men then the domain is sure to go to ruin. This is an admonition which the wise ones of antiquity all agree in giving forth.

The tenor of the foregoing rules must be obeyed.

Keichō, 20th year, 7th month (August 24th, September 23rd, 1615).

[3] Clan Behavior: The Military Discipline of the Kai Clan

1. No rebellion should ever be plotted against the *Yakata-Sama* (The August Residence)[1] forever in future.

   The *Lun-yü:*[2] "Do not forget [justice] even for a moment or in the slightest degree, but serve the lord soul and body at your own cost."

2. Never should cowardice be betrayed on the battle-field.

   The *Wu-tzū:* "Life craved for means death; death craved for means life."

3. Good manners should be observed scrupulously.

   The *Shih-chi:* "One who is well-behaved will be obeyed without issuing orders; one who is ill-behaved will not be obeyed even when orders are issued."

4. Military bravery should be devotedly relished.

   The *San-liao:* "No brave general has cowardly ranks."

5. No lie should be told for any purpose.

   The *Shên-t'o:* "Honesty may for a while be treated biasedly but the sun and the moon will have pity on it in the end." (Additional: But end may justify the means in tactics.)

6. One should never be undutiful towards one's father and mother.

   The *Lun-yü:* "One should exhaust himself in serving one's father and mother."

7. One should show no sign of neglect even to one's brother.

   The *Hou-han-shu:* "The brothers are like two arms."

Takeda Shingen (1521-73), *The Military Discipline of the Kai Clan.* From "The Memoirs of Takeda-Shingen and the *Kai-no-Gunritsu,*" *Cultural Nippon,* trans. Atsuharu Sakai, III, Pt. 3 (1940), 95-102.

[1] The lord.
[2] All the books quoted in the *Kai-no-Gunritsu* are Chinese.

8. One should not utter a single word unworthy of oneself.

The *Ying-k'ang:* "Every word one speaks betrays one's merit or demerit."

11. Learning should be acquired scrupulously.

The *Lun-yü:* "Learning without thought is insidious; thought without learning is dangerous."

12. The *Kadō* (the art of Japanese poetry) should be carefully studied.

Japanese ode (free rendering): "We ourselves shall be held responsible if a sin committed should be attributed to the uneducated mind." [3]

14. Taste should not be over-indulged.

The *Shih-chi:* "Extreme drinking is debauchery; extreme pleasure is sorrow."

The *Tso-chüan:* "The banquet-pleasure is a poison; do not think of it."

The *Lun-yü:* "The wise should be esteemed as such and preferred to beauty." [4]

17. The lord's orders, whether important or not, should be obeyed.

The *Old Saying:* "Water conforms to the shape of its vessel, whether round or square."

18. Neither stipend nor the lord's help should be demanded.

The *Tso-chüan:* "An unmerited reward, like ill-got wealth, is a medium of evil."

24. A divergent view should not be disregarded.

The *Old Saying:* "Good medicine tastes bitter to the mouth, but it tells on illness; good counsel sounds harsh to the ear, but it tells on conduct."

The *Shang-shu:* "The tree that obeys the rope[5] is corrected; a monarch who listens to remonstrance is saintly."

25. A retainer who falls in distress for no fault of his should be helped out.

The *Old Saying:* "The best plan for a year is to sow the five cereals; the best plan for ten years is to grow trees; and the best plan for a life is to train men."

29. Discretion should be exercised in talking even among intimate friends.

[3] The ode means in effect that the mind must be trained so as not to commit a sin.

[4] "Beauty" here means "beauties" or "girls."

[5] A rope is used to give a good shape to a tree in Japanese horticulture.

The *Old Saying:* "Think three times before a word is said; think nine times before a deed is done."

32. However suspicious the *Yakata-Sama* (The August Residence) may be of you, you should say nothing in your own explanation.

The *Old Saying:* "Even though the lord should not act as befits him, the retainer should act as a retainer." "The mountain is lost on the hunter who chases a deer." "The subordinate should not criticize the superiors."

33. A minor offence on the part of a servant should be reprimanded, for a major offence will cost him his life. A repeated reproof of a minor offence will bring about yielding.

T'ai-kung: "Nip the bud, or else an axe will be needed."

The *Ch'un-ch'iu:* "A severe command is not listened to; a repeated prohibition causes disobedience."

34. A reward granted for every deed, important or not, will encourage the recipient.

The *San-liao:* "A merit should be recognized in time."

36. A farmer should be forced to do no more work than regularly allotted to him.

The *Chün-shih:* "If the upper are submissive, the lower are severe and harsh; if the tax is heavy and the punishment is repeated, the people will revolt."

37. The people should not telltale anything wrong to those outside the clan.

The *Old Saying:* "Good is hard to leave the gate; evil travels for a thousand miles."

The *Pi-yen:* "The dark side of the family should not be told outside."

39. Weapons should be carefully taken care of.

The *Old Saying:* "A nine-stratum dais is built up on the basis of the ground."

44. When victorious, press on without hesitation. If, however, the enemy maintains his order, rearrange the position of the troops.

The *San-liao:* "Battle is like the wind that comes nobody knows whence."

47. Both officers and men should avoid speaking ill of the enemy.

The *Old Saying:* "A clamour stirs bees and wasps, but a plunder irritates a dragon."

48. Even though an intimate relative is appointed to an office, anything weak should not be betrayed to him.

The *San-liao:* "Unless you show courage, the soldier will not obey you."

49. Excess in advance or retreat should be avoided.

The *Old Saying:* "Too much is as bad as too little."

51. If one asks you about what you are not sure of, it will be all right to say in reply that you do not know it.

The *Old Saying:* "One is given to a hobby only when one is young."

53. Even though the father may be condemned to death for his misconduct, the son should be pardoned if he distinguishes himself devotedly.

The *Old Saying:* "The calf of a brindled bull, if red and horned, will be used by the deities of the mountains and rivers even if men make no use of them."

[4] Bushidō, or the "Way of the Warrior"

Introduction

One who is a samurai must before all things keep constantly in mind, by day and by night from the morning when he takes up his chop-sticks to eat his New Year Breakfast to Old Year's night when he pays his yearly bills, the fact that he has to die. That is his chief business. If he is always mindful of this he will be able to live in accordance with the paths of Loyalty and Filial Duty, will avoid myriads of evils and adversities, keep himself free from disease and calamity and moreover enjoy a long life. He will also be a fine personality with many admirable qualities. For existence is impermanent as the dew of evening and the hoar-frost of morning, and particularly uncertain is the life of the warrior, and if he thinks he can console himself with the idea of eternal service to his lord or unending devotion to his relatives, something may well happen to make him neglect his duty to his lord and forget what he owes to his family. But if he determines simply to live for today and take no thought for the morrow, so that when he stands before his lord to receive his commands he thinks of it as his last appearance and when he looks on the faces of his relatives he feels that he will never see them again, then will his duty and regard for both of them be

Daidoji Yuzan, *Budo Shoshinshu.* From A. L. Sadler, trans., *The Beginner's Book of Bushido, Being a Translation of Daidoji Yuzan's Budo Shoshinshu* (Tokyo: Kokusai Bunka Shinkokai, 1941), pp. 3-7, 9-12, 20-23, 32-33, 38-39, 43-44, 50-53. Reprinted by permission of Kokusai Bunka Shinkokai.

completely sincere and his mind be in accord with the path of loyalty and filial duty.

But if he does not keep death in mind he will be careless and liable to be indiscreet and say things that offend others and an argument ensues, and though, if no notice is taken, it may be settled, if there is a rebuke, it may end in a quarrel. Then if he goes strolling about pleasure resorts and seeing the sights in crowded places without any proper reserve he may come up against some big fool and get into a quarrel before he knows it, and may even be killed and his lord's name brought into it and his parents and relations exposed to reproach.

And all this misfortune springs from his not remembering to keep death always in his thoughts. But one who does this whether he is speaking himself or answering others will carefully consider, as befits a samurai, every word he says and never launch out into useless argument. Neither will he allow anyone to entice him into unsuitable places where he may be suddenly confronted with an awkward situation, and thus he avoids all evils and calamities. And both high and low, if they forget about death, are very apt to take to unhealthy excess in food and wine and women so that they die unexpectedly early from diseases of the kidneys and spleen, and even while they live their illness makes them of no use to anyone. But those who keep death always before their eyes are strong and healthy while young, and as they take care of their health and are moderate in eating and drinking and avoid the paths of women, being abstemious and moderate in all things, they remain free from disease and live a long and healthy life. . . .

Education

Since the samurai stands at the head of the three classes of society and has the duty of carrying on the administration, it is incumbent on him to be well educated and to have a wide knowledge of the reason of things. However, in the period of civil war, the young warrior went out to battle when he was fifteen or sixteen so that he had to start his military education at twelve or thirteen, so since he had no time to sit down with a book or take up a writing brush he was often quite illiterate. In fact in those days there were a lot of samurai who could not write a single Chinese character.[1] So whether through their own want of inclination or the faulty instruction of their parents, nothing was done about it, because their

[1] Early Japanese was often written in Chinese characters.

whole life was devoted exclusively to the Way of the Warrior. Now, however, the Empire is at peace, and though one cannot exactly say that those born in samurai families are indifferent to military training, yet there is no question of their being forced to enter a warlike career at the age of fifteen or sixteen like the warrior of former days. So that at the age of seven or eight when he is growing up, a boy should be introduced to the Four Books, the Five Classics and the Seven Texts and taught calligraphy so that he remembers how to write characters. Then when he is fifteen or sixteen he should be made to practise archery and horsemanship and all the other military arts, for that is the way that the samurai should bring up his sons in time of peace. There is no excuse for illiteracy in his case as there was in that of the warrior of the civil war period. And children are not to blame for lack of education either. It is entirely due to the neglect and incompetence of their parents who do not really know the way of affection for their children. . . .

Samurai Ordinances

In Bushidō there are two ordinances and four sections. The two ordinances are the ordinary and the extraordinary, and the ordinary is divided into the two sections of the officials and of the soldiers, while the extraordinary is similarly divided into those of army and of battle affairs. As to the section of the samurai officials, they must wash their hands and feet night and morning and take a hot bath and so keep themselves clean. A samurai must do his hair every morning and keep the hair properly shaved from his forehead. Then he must always wear the ceremonial dress proper to the occasion and of course wear his two swords as well as carry a fan in his girdle. When he receives a guest he must treat him with the etiquette due to his rank and must refrain from idle talk. Even in taking a bowl of rice or a cup of tea it must be done correctly without slovenliness and with no lack of vigilance. If he is serving in some capacity when he is off duty he must not lounge about doing nothing but should read and practise writing, storing his mind with the ancient history and precepts of the warrior houses and in short conducting himself at all times so that his manners are those proper to a samurai.

Next comes the section on soldiers. This concerns the exercise of fencing, spear practise, horsemanship and shooting with bow and matchlock together with all else that pertains to the military art which must be enthusiastically studied and practised so that all will be disciplined and resolute. And if these two codes of the samurai and the soldier are well understood, the ordinary ordinance may be considered complete, and this would appear to most people to be sufficient for the good warrior or official. But a samurai is an official for extraordinary conditions, and when the country is in a state of disorder he must lay aside the ordinary rule for samurai life and serve under his lord as commander, the greater and lesser retainers becoming officers and soldiers. Then all put away their dress of ceremony and don their armour and take arms in hand to advance into the enemy territory, and it is the various methods of arranging matters on such a campaign that are known as the rule of army affairs, and this is a thing that must be known. Then comes the rule of battle affairs which is the method of handling the army when it comes into contact with the enemy to give battle. And if things go according to plan there is victory, and if not, there is defeat. This too is a thing the secrets of which must be understood. And what is called a first-class samurai is one who is skilled in all four sections of these two ordinances. To be experienced only in the two sections of the ordinary one may be sufficient for the duties of the average cavalier, but no one who is ignorant of the extraordinary sections can become a commander or high officer. . . . It is therefore most important that all samurai should consider and realize that they cannot rise to the highest positions without profound study of the extraordinary ordinance.

Never Neglect the Offensive Spirit

It is most important that one who is a samurai should never neglect the offensive spirit at any time and in all matters. For our country is different from other lands in that even the least of the people, farmers, merchants and artisans, should all cherish some rusty blade, wherein is revealed the warrior spirit of this Empire of Nippon. These three classes are not, however, soldiers by profession, but it is the custom in the military families for even the very least of the servants of the samurai never to be without a short sword for a moment. Much more must the higher samurai always wear their girdle. And some very punctilious ones wear a blunt sword or a wooden one even when they go to the bath. And if this is so in the house how much more is it necessary when one leaves it to go somewhere else, since on the way you may well meet some drunkard or other fool who may suddenly start a quarrel. There is an old saying, 'When you leave your gate, act as though an enemy was in sight.' So since he is a samurai and wears a sword in his girdle he must never forget this spirit of the offensive. And when this is so the mind is firmly fixed on death. But the samurai who does not maintain this aggressive spirit, even though he does wear a sword at his side, is nothing but a farmer or a tradesman in a warrior's skin. . . .

Bravery

For Bushidō the three qualities of Loyalty, Right Conduct and Bravery are essential. We speak of the loyal warrior, the righteous warrior and the valiant warrior, and it is he who is endowed with all these three virtues who is a warrior of the highest class. But among the myriads of samurai it is rare to find one of this kind. Now the loyal warrior and the righteous one may not be difficult to be distinguished by their ordinary, everyday conduct but it may be doubted whether in times of peace and quiet like the present it will be so easy to single out the brave one. This, however, is not so, for bravery does not show itself first when a man puts on armour and takes spear and halberd in hand and goes out to battle. You can see whether he has it or not when he is sitting on the mats leading his ordinary life. For he who is born brave will be loyal and filial to his lord and parents, and whenever he has any leisure he will use it for study, neither will he be negligent in practising the military arts. He will be strictly on his guard against indolence and will be very careful how he spends every penny. If you think this shows detestable stinginess you will be mistaken since he spends freely where it is necessary. He does not do anything that is contrary to the ordinances of his lord or that is disliked by his parents however much he may wish. And so, ever obedient to his lord and his parents he preserves his life in the hope some day of doing a deed of outstanding merit, moderating his appetite for eating and drinking and avoiding over-indulgence in sex, which is the greatest delusion of mankind, so that he may preserve his body in health and strength. For in these as in all other things it is rigid self-control that is the beginning of valour. . . .

Respect

The two Ways of Loyalty and Filial Duty are not limited to the samurai. They are equally incumbent on the Farmer, Artisan and Merchant classes. But among these classes, for example, a child or servant while sitting with his parent or master may have his legs crossed or his hands anyhow or he may speak to them standing while they are sitting or may do various other unceremonious and impolite things and it does not matter. If he is really sincere in his filial feelings and truly cherishes his master or parent, that is all that is expected in the case of these three classes. But in Bushidō however loyal and filial a man may be in his heart, if he is lacking in the correct etiquette and manners by which respect is shown to lord or parent, he cannot be regarded as living in proper conformity with it. Any negligence of this kind not only towards his lord but also towards his parents is no conduct for anyone who sets up to be a samurai. And even when out of their sight and in private, there must be no relaxation and no light and shade in the loyalty and filial duty of a warrior. . . .

Thrift

Samurai who are in service, both great and small, must always practise thrift and have the discrimination to do it so that they do not have a deficit in their household expenditure. As to those with a large income if they do find they are living beyond their means they can quickly make a change in their affairs, and by taking care and making a saving here and cutting down something there, they can soon recover their solvency because they have a certain surplus. But if a small retainer tries to live like a great vassal and so incurs unnecessary expense and gets into difficulties he cannot recover himself because he has nothing to fall back on, and however much he tries to economize, he only becomes more involved till at last he comes to complete ruin. And as people's domestic affairs are a private matter, and one who is in service has to do as his colleagues do and must incur certain necessary expenses, he will be driven to every possible trick and device, even to saying what should not be said and doing what should not be done, for it is financial difficulty that induces even those with a high reputation to do dishonest things that are quite alien to them. So that one must make a firm resolve to live only according to one's means and be very careful not to indulge in any useless expenses, spending money only on what is necessary, for this is what is called the Way of Economy. . . .

Samurai

Since samurai are officials whose business it is to destroy rebels and disorderly elements and give peace and security to the three classes of the people, even the least of those who bear this title must never commit any violence or injustice against these three classes. That is to say, he must not demand any more revenue than is customary from the farmers or wear them out by forced service. He must not order articles from artizans and then neglect to pay them, neither must he send for things from townspeople and tradesmen and keep them waiting for their money, while it is most incorrect to lend them money and take usury on it as a mere sleeping partner. One should always be considerate to these people, sympathetic to the farmers on one's estates and careful that artizans are not ruined. And though you may not at once settle the debts, you may have incurred in transactions with townspeople and tradesmen, you certainly ought to pay something off them from time to time so as not to cause these classes loss and distress. Samurai who are officials to chastize robbers and thieves must not imitate the ways of these criminals. . . .

Reputation

One who is a samurai should continually read the ancient records so that he may strengthen his character. For those works that are famous everywhere, such as the *Kôyô Gunkan,* the *Nobunagaki* and the *Taikôki,* give accounts of battles with detailed descriptions and the names of those who did gallant deeds as well as the numbers of those who fell. And among these latter the greater vassals ought presumedly to have figured considerably, but actually they were not so conspicuous for their valour and so their names are not recorded. Even among the small retainers only those whose martial valour was preeminent have been selected, and their names inscribed for posterity. And both the fallen who have left no name behind and those whose exploits are famous through the ages felt only the same pain when their heads were cut off by the enemy. So consider this well. As he has to die, the aim of a samurai should be to fall performing some great deed of valour that will astonish both friend and foe alike and make his death regretted by his lord and commander and so leave behind a great name to the generations to come. Very different is the fate of the coward who is the last to charge and the first to retire, and who, in an attack on a stronghold, uses his comrades as a shield against the enemy missiles. Struck by a chance arrow he falls and dies a dog's death and may even be trampled under foot by his own side. This is the greatest disgrace for a samurai, and should never be forgotten but pondered over earnestly day and night. . . .

The Latter End

The samurai whether great or small, high or low, has to set before all other things the consideration of how to meet his inevitable end. However clever or capable or efficient he may have been, if he is upset and wanting in composure and so makes a poor showing when he comes to face it all, his previous good deeds will be like water and all decent people will despise him so that he will be covered with shame.

For when a samurai goes out to battle and does valiant and splendid exploits and makes a great name, it is only because he made up his mind to die. And if unfortunately he gets the worst of it and he and his head have to part company, when his opponent asks for his name he must declare it at once loudly and clearly and yield up his head with a smile on his lips and without the slightest sign of fear. Or should he be so badly wounded that no surgeon can do anything for him, if he is still conscious, the proper procedure for a samurai is to answer the enquiries of his superior officers and comrades and inform them of the manner of his being wounded and then to make an end without more ado.

Similarly in times of peace the steadfast samurai, particularly if he is old but no less if he is young and stricken with some serious disease, ought to show firmness and resolution and attach no importance to leaving this life. Naturally if he is in high office, but also however low his position may be, while he can speak he should request the presence of his official superior and inform him that as he has for long enjoyed his consideration and favour he has consequently wished fervently to do all in his power to carry out his duties, but unfortunately he has now been attacked by this serious disease from which it is difficult to recover, and consequently is unable to do so; and that as he is about to pass away, he wishes to express his gratitude for past kindness and trusts to be remembered respectfully to the Councillors of the clan. This done, he should say farewell to his family and friends and explain to them that it is not the business of a samurai to die of illness after being the recipient of the great favours of his lord for so many years, but unfortunately in his case it is unavoidable. But they who are young must carry on his loyal intentions and firmly resolve to do their duty to their lord, ever increasing this loyalty so as to serve with all the vigour they possess. Should they fail to do this or act in any disloyal or undutiful way, then even from the shadow of the grass his spirit will disown and disinherit them. Such is the leave-taking of a true samurai. . . .

15 / RELATIONS WITH CHINA

China's overwhelming grandeur, wealth, and power were fully appreciated in a Japan which owed so much of its own heritage to Chinese culture. The Japanese acknowledged the suzerainty of

Ming Shih, or History of the Ming Dynasty. From Ryūsaku Tsunoda, trans., and L. Carrington Goodrich, ed., Japan in the Chinese Dynastic Histories: Later

China and normally made no objection to accepting their place in the Chinese hierarchy of vassal states nor to sending tribute missions at specified times to the imperial court. At times when either China or Japan, or both, were beset by internal difficulties or other distractions, the regular acknowledgement of vassalage might have been withheld. The principle, however, of China's suzerainty and Japan's vassalage was tacitly accepted by both countries and can be considered generally descriptive of their fundamental relationship when the Europeans arrived in eastern Asia.

Between 1433 and 1549, eleven Japanese tributary missions visited China, while China dispatched just one mission to Japan in 1434. At first the Ashikaga shogunate and certain Buddhist temples cooperated to promote the exchange of goods and cultural articles. Following the Ōnin wars (1467-1477) the Hosokawa and Ouchi, major daimyo families of western Honshu and western Shikoku, became fierce rivals for the prize of controlling the legitimate trade with China. They carried over their hostilities to China, and their unruly behavior eventually drove the Chinese to limit to fifty the number of embassy personnel allowed to travel inland to the capital. Japanese embassies comprised several hundred persons as a rule, but in 1547 the four ships belonging to the Ouchi family brought no fewer than six hundred people to China. The suspension of official relations that occurred in 1549 can be blamed on Chinese opposition to an adverse trade balance, to the growing internal disorganization of Japan, and to the spread of piracy.

Standard tributary goods from Japan included horses, folding screens, inkslabs, sulphur, agate, and armaments—armor, lances, and swords of Japanese manufacture were at first much sought after. In return, the Emperor of China usually sent gifts of silver articles, several varieties of silk, fine paper, porcelain, and various other luxuries. In the supplementary category, to be sold to the Chinese government, the Japanese submitted finished and raw materials such as swords, lances and lacquer ware, rare woods, sulphur, and copper ore. Envoys were permitted to bring articles for personal trade, and in one of the last missions nearly three hundred members were classed as independent trading agents.

Throughout the period of Ming-Japanese official contacts, piracy menaced or actually interrupted amicable relations. The suspension of relations in 1549 invited further trouble. Early in the 1550's very large numbers (estimated at perhaps 100,000) of Japanese "dwarf

Han through Ming Dynasties (South Pasadena, Calif.: P. D. and Ione Perkins, 1951), 113-43 *passim.* Reprinted by permission of Ryūsaku Tsunoda, L. Carrington Goodrich, and Perkins Oriental Books, Kyoto, Japan.

robbers" (wako) *who often received aid, comfort, and active collaboration from Chinese seamen, smugglers, gentry, and officials, terrorized the coast and delta of the Yangtze. Portuguese, who had found their way eastward, sometimes joined in these raids. Called Fo-lang-ch'i ("Franks") by the Chinese, the Portuguese had at first no place in the tributary system, and had to satisfy their appetite for trade, like the Japanese, by extralegal means. Beginning in the 1550's daimyos of Kyushu welcomed Portuguese merchants and missionaries as intermediaries who had connections in India and China. This open season lasted until the 1590's when Japan began enforcing a system of licensed trade of her own devising.*

Toward the end of the sixteenth century, the growing strength of the central government in Japan made it possible to initiate the "Red Seal Ship" system which confined Japanese foreign trade to authorized merchants, Europeans, and daimyos and others who could obtain the official license. For a time Japanese commerce with Indochina, the Philippines, and China flourished. However, the skies began to darken in 1616 when the first of four shogunal decrees limiting trade confined European ships to two ports. Succeeding decrees choked off trade with the Spanish-held Philippines (1624-1625), tightened control over Red Seal Ships (1633-1634), and ultimately restricted foreign intercourse to the Chinese and Dutch, who were required to confine their activities to Nagasaki (1639).

In reading the following extracts, it is important to remember that the chroniclers are writing from the Chinese viewpoint and that they accept unquestioningly the basic premises of the tributary system. The Chinese dynastic histories, including the Ming shih *or* History of the Ming Dynasty, *were usually compiled by a board of editors in the early years of the next dynasty. Work on the* Ming shih *began in 1646, continued for ninety years, and was first published in its final form in 1739.*

Japan in the Ming History

When Ch'êng-tsu [temple name of the Yung-lo emperor] came to the throne, he took the occasion of his inauguration to extend an invitation [to Japan]. Again, in the first year of Yung-lo (1403), he sent [to Japan] the Senior Commissioner of the Office of Transmission, Chao Chü-jên, and a member of the Court of State Ceremonies, Chang Hung-chieh, as well as the monk, Tao-ch'êng. They were about to leave the country when the tribute envoy [from Japan] arrived at Ningpo.[1] The officer of the Department of Ceremony, Li

[1] Authorized port of entry for envoys from Japan.

Chih-kang, then submitted a report on precedents in connection with visits of alien envoys to China which said: "Such envoys are not to be permitted to bring weapons secretly for sale to the people. The local officials are to be notified to investigate ships, and any cases of offenders are to be reported to the capital." The Emperor, however, said: "When outlying barbarians bring tribute, they come from afar and in the face of great risk and dangers. Their expenditure is really enormous, so that it is only human that they should try to defray expenses with what they bring with them. Sweeping application of the prohibitive statute, therefore, is not proper. As to the weapons they bring, purchase them at market price. Do not alienate their goodwill toward us. . . ."

In the eleventh month of the following year (1404), an envoy arrived with congratulations for the inauguration of the heir-apparent. Just at that time, pirates from the islands of Tsushima and Iki plundered the people on the seacoast. Therefore instructions were sent to the King [of Japan] to capture them. The King dispatched an army and annihilated the pirates, holding, however, twenty ringleaders in bonds to be brought as an offering to the Court [of China], together with tribute, in the eleventh month of the third year (1405). The Emperor was even more satisfied with this, and sent the sub-director of the Court of State Ceremonial, P'an Tz'ǔ, with the eunuch Wang Chin, to bestow on the King a royal robe with nine markers, copper coins and paper money, brocade and silks, together with a promotion in Court rank. The captives offered to the Court were sent back to be punished in their own country; but when the envoy reached Ningpo, he had all the captives placed in jars and stifled to death. . . .

In the early part of Yung-lo, an edict decreed that Japan might send tribute every ten years, that the personnel be limited to two hundred, and ships to two, and that weapons should not be carried. In case of violation, [the Japanese] would be treated as offenders. Two ships were then given to them to be used in carrying the tribute. But later everything did not turn out as decreed.

In the early part of Hsüan-tê (1425-1435), a convenant was entered into that personnel should not exceed three hundred and that there should not be more than three ships. The Wa [Japanese], however, being greedy, brought merchandise in addition to the tribute, ten times as much, and asked that the regular price be paid. The officer of the Board of Ceremony said: "During the Hsüan-tê era, they brought as tribute such things as sulphur, sapan wood, swords, fans and lacquer ware, and payment was made either in paper currency at the market price or sometimes with cotton and silks. The articles were not large in number, but the profit on them was enormous. If we now pay at the former rate, it will be two hundred seventeen thousand coins of silver. Therefore the price should be drastically reduced and about thirty-four thousand seven hundred coins of silver be paid." This suggestion was followed to the dissatisfaction of the envoy. . . .

Early in T'ien-hsün (1457-1464), [King] Minamoto Yoshimasa was eager to dispatch an envoy to the Court with an apology because his former envoy had offended the Celestial Court. Not daring to establish contact, he wrote a message to the King of Korea asking him to make a request on his behalf. Korea was instructed to state explicitly [to the Japanese] that when they chose an envoy this time, they should appoint one who was mature in experience and well informed as to his status, and that reckless disorder such as occurred the last time would never be tolerated again. After that, the tribute envoy did not arrive for some time.

During the summer of the fourth year of Ch'êng-hua (1468), [Japan] sent an envoy with tribute of horses and with an apology. He was treated according to precedent. . . .

Again in the eleventh month, the envoy Seikei arrived with tribute. [His men] wounded people in the market and officials appealed [to the Court] to administer justice for this offense. The case was referred to Seikei, who addressed a memorial to the Throne saying that the offenders should be subjected to the law of their own country, and that therefore they should be permitted to return home, where they would be lawfully punished. As for himself, he would hold himself responsible for his inability to hold them in restraint. [Thereupon] the Emperor set free [both Seikei and the culprits]. Thereafter the envoys became more and more unscrupulous. . . .

In the spring of the fifth year (1510), King Minamoto Yoshizumi sent his envoy, Sō Sokyo [in Chinese, Sung Su-ch'ing],[2] with the tribute. It was at this time that Liu Chin [a powerful eunuch] had come into power through intrigue and he accepted one thousand *liang* of gold and bestowed [on the envoy] the robe with a flying fish—an unprecedented thing. Sokyo was the son of the Chu family of Yin-hsien and his given name was Kao. When still a child, he had practiced singing and the Japanese envoy had seen him and liked him. [Now] Kao's paternal uncle, Têng, had owed money [to the Japanese envoy] and gave him Kao in payment. Sokyo now ar-

[2] He represented the Hosokawa family.

rived at Soochow as the legitimate envoy and met Têng, so that the matter came to light. According to the statute, this meant death [for Têng]. However, Liu Chin took him under his protection and by saying that Têng had surrendered himself, obtained a reprieve [for him]. . . .

In the ninth year (1530), a certain Liu-chiu envoy, Ts'ai Han, came [to China] by way of Japan. King Minamoto Yoshiharu entrusted to him a memorial to the Court which read [as follows]: "Because our country is in turmoil and recurring warfare obstructs communications, the tally[3] of the Chêng-tê era[4] failed to reach the capital. That was the reason why Sokyo [in 1523] had to go with the tally of the Hung-chih era. For this we beg your forgiveness. It is hoped that a new tally will be granted, as well as a gold seal, so that the tribute can be resumed regularly. . . ."

In the seventh month of the eighteenth year (1539), Yoshiharu's tribute envoy arrived at Ningpo. The local official made a report to the Court accordingly. It was seventeen years since the tribute had come, and so a special order was given to the circuit censor to direct three local commissioners to ascertain the true state of affairs—whether or not the delegation was loyal, obedient and law-abiding. If so, they were to be treated according to precedent and sent home. Otherwise, they were to be told peremptorily to return home. At the same time, the ban against contact of the coast people with foreigners was to be stringently enforced. . . .

In the seventh month of the twenty-third year (1544), the tribute arrived again. It was not yet time for it, and it was without a memorial. The official of the Ministry [of Ceremony] recommended that it should not be accepted and accordingly it was rejected. The envoy, however, lingered about near the shore because the trade brought profit, and would not go home. The circuit censor, Kao Chieh, requested that [the Court] deal with the officials and officers, civil and military, of the seacoast for their offenses and strictly forbid the big clandestine traders from establishing contact [with foreigners] and carrying on transactions secretly. But the greedy Chinese dealers, because of the profit they realized from this trade, were willing accomplices. Thus it was impossible to put an end to [the trading]. . . . Wan therefore issued a proclamation saying

[3] These were numbered pieces of paper torn from stub books and were given to legitimate missions as passports so that the Chinese could tell private traders or pirates from authentic Japanese emissaries.

[4] The Chinese calendar was based on a succession of "eras," or imperial reign periods, rather than on impersonal annual cycles.

that the ban against intercourse [with the Wa] would be stringently enforced. Those who were caught in clandestine transactions would instantly be put to death without waiting for [an] order from the Court. Now influential families of Chekiang and Fukien, who had been the Chinese connivers with Japanese piracy, were thus deprived of their profit and were very much aggrieved against Wan. Wan also from time to time wrote appeals to the Court dignitaries advising of the connivance of the rich traders with the pirates. On that account, the people of Min [Fukien] and of Chê all hated him —the Min people being especially resentful. . . .

Rebel leaders such as Wang Chih, Hsü Hai, Ch'ên Tung, and Ma Yeh were originally of the same breed [as the illicit traders]. Because in their own country [of China] they were unable to obtain what they wanted, they had made their way over the sea to the islands to become gang leaders. The Wa listened to them and were persuaded by them to start raids. Then these buccaneer chiefs, donning Japanese robes with Japanese ornaments and insignia, came in various craft to loot their native land. As the profit was always enormous, trouble with these pirates became worse day by day. . . .

Thereupon [1556] Tsung-hsien requested the Court that an envoy be dispatched to Japan, in order, first, to advise the King of Japan to ban or subdue the island raiders, and also at the same time to summon home those rebellious Chinese traders who had been conniving with foreigners. . . .

On his return [to China], K'o-yüan [the Chinese envoy] said that upon reaching Gotō [in Kyūshū], he had met with Wang Chih and Mao Hai-fêng, who had told him that during internal warfare in Japan both the King and the premier had died, so that the various islands were no longer unified and were out of control. It had become necessary to give specific instructions to each locality to put an end to depredations. He also said that there was a certain province of Satsuma from whence raiders already had set sail [for China]; but that these people of Satsuma said that raiding was not their real object. The resumption of the tribute and of trade was what they desired, and they had expressed willingness to kill the pirates in order to make clear their own sincerity. So he had left Chou [the other Chinese envoy] there to carry instructions to the various islands and he, K'o-yüan, had been escorted home. Tsung-hsien made a report accordingly. The Board of War recommended as follows: "As Chih and the others are duly registered subjects and say they are loyal and obedient, it is only proper that they should disband their forces; but without [sic] a word about that, they have asked for resumption of trade and of the tribute. Their actions resemble those of outlanders from across the sea. Moreover, their treachery is unpredictable. It behooves the government to issue commands to the officials concerned to uphold the national prestige by strict attention to military preparedness and defense, and at the same time to send notice to Chih and all the others to clean up the pirates' nest in Chou-shan [islands off the Chekiang coast] as an act of vindication. In case the seacoast is entirely cleaned up, gifts and favors might be in order." This recommendation was acted upon. . . .

From times of old, Japan has had a king. Below him, the title of *kwampaku* is the one most respected. At this time, Nobunaga, head of the province of Yamashiro, was *kwampaku*. One day while out hunting, he came upon a man lying beneath a tree, who, when suddenly awakened, jumped to his feet and ran into him. When this man was caught and reprimanded, he said he was Taira Hideyoshi, the servant of a man of Satsuma. Hale, strong, agile, and alert—he was clever too in speech. Very much pleased, Nobunaga put him in charge of his steed, calling him Kinoshita—"man beneath the tree." He was gradually given more responsibility and developed a plan on behalf of Nobunaga to capture more than twenty provinces. . . . But all of a sudden, Nobunaga was assassinated by the lieutenant, Akechi. Hideyoshi at that time had already defeated Akechi. When he was informed of the incident, he turned back with his lieutenant, Yukinaga, and, carried on by the momentum of victory, fought [with Akechi] and killed him. His prestige was thereby firmly established. [Then] he went on to dispose of the three sons of Nobunaga. Arbitrarily calling himself *kwampaku,* he took over their forces as his own. This was the fourteenth year of Wan-li (1586).

Carrying his arms farther and farther, he conquered sixty-six provinces. By means of threats, also, he compelled Liu-chiu, Luzon, Portugal, and Siam to send envoys with tribute. Then he rebuilt the mountain castle where the King used to live and made it into an enormous Court. He erected large castles and stockades, built mansions and pavilions—some nine storeys high—and filled them with beautiful women and rare treasures. He was stern in justice and in his military operations there were only advances—never retreats. All who did otherwise, even his own son and son-in-law, were put to death. Thus wherever he went, he was unconquerable.

When the era changed to Bunroku (1592-95), he thought he would attack China and [also] subjugate Korea and make it his own. . . .

In the fourth month of the twientieth year (1592), his [Hideyoshi's] generals, Kiyomasa, Yukinaga, and Yoshitomo, and the monks Ganso and Shuetsu, were dispatched at the head of a fleet many hundred ships strong. Going across the sea by way of Tsushima, they captured Kim-san in Korea, and taking advantage of this initial victory, drove forward rapidly. In the fifth month, they crossed the bay, harassed Kaesŏng, and made various prefectures of P'ungdok surrender. Korea was entirely swept off her feet. Kiyomasa and his men pressed on vigorously toward the capital. The King of Korea, Yi Yŏn, left his castle and hastened to Pyŏngyang and then to Uiju. Emissaries arrived [at the Court] one after the other with reports of imminent danger. The Japanese finally entered the capital and made the Queen and Prince prisoners. After a hot pursuit [of the King], the Japanese reached Pyŏngyang. There the soldiers were let loose to rape and pillage. . . .

The invasion [of Korea] by the *kwampaku* lasted nearly seven years. Casualties in the war exceeded many hundred thousand; wasted supplies amounted to many millions. Though China and Korea fought hand in hand, they had no chance of victory. Only the death of the *kwampaku* brought the calamities of warfare to an end and sent the Japanese forces back to their insular retreat. Then the east and the south began to enjoy a period of undisturbed peace.

Hideyoshi's line came to an end in the second generation. To the end of the Ming dynasty, however, the regulation forbidding intercourse with the Japanese was strictly enforced. At the very mention of Japanese, the people in the street became so excited that women and children held their breath in alarm.

16 / POPULAR BUDDHISM: THE PURE LAND AND TRUE LAND SECTS

In its pilgrimage across continental Asia to insular Japan, Mahayana or Northern Buddhism absorbed many of the religious and social practices of the peoples it conquered into its doctrines and practices. In exhibiting great tolerance for other beliefs, Mahayana added in its progress eastward a myriad of gods to its pantheon and evolved a vast literature directed to metaphysical speculation. The-

Rennyo Shōnin, *The Gobunsho*. From James Troup, trans., "The Gobunsho or Ofumi of Rennyo Shōnin," *Transactions of the Asiatic Society of Japan*, XVII (1889), 108-16, 123-25, 135-36. Reprinted by permission of the Asiatic Society of Japan.

ologically, the emphasis in Mahayana Buddhism shifted away from a doctrine of enlightenment through personal effort to a doctrine of salvation with the help of intermediaries. Faith became the first and only prerequisite to enlightenment, and the gods were pictured as being merciful, compassionate, and comforting. Northern Buddhism, thus stresses, particularly in the teachings of its popular sects, a simple and unquestioning faith that is coupled with works of charity to help others and to aid in one's own salvation.

Buddhism, which was known in China as early as the first century A.D., *came to full flower there between the middle of the fourth and the end of the eighth century. One of Buddhism's greatest achievements of this period was its conquest of Japan, beginning in the mid-sixth century. Officially adopted by the court, Buddhism soon replaced the native creed of Shinto as the dominant belief of the aristocrats. True to the tendencies it had exhibited elsewhere, Buddhism soon filtered down to the Japanese lower classes, and absorbed elements from Shinto into its own tolerant creed. However, even in periods when Buddhism was at peak strength, Shinto retained a separate identification as Japan's unique national cult.*

Buddhism was to feudal Japan what Christianity was to medieval Europe. All classes of society, especially the warriors, became ardent and fervent followers of the Buddha. A religious revival of the twelfth century led to the creation of a number of popular Buddhist sects as part of a reaction against the aristocratic, hierarchic, and orthodox rigidity of the older sects. The leaders of the new sects were men of common background who preached and wrote in the simple Japanese of the day. They translated the Buddhist texts from classical Chinese, the language preferred by the older sects, into a Japanese easily understandable to all. They sought, as they carried their message to the people, to avoid metaphysical speculation and to simplify the teachings of the Buddha. The equality of all social classes—laymen and clergy, men and women, and adults and children—under Buddhist law became a focus of their preaching and a key to their appeal.

The Jōdo or Pure Land sect of Buddhism was founded in the late twelfth century by a popular preacher who is usually known as Saint Honen. He taught that salvation could be won simply by repeating the name of the Buddha Amida. Amida (meaning "Infinite Light") is one of the many bodhisattvas in the Mahayana pantheon. Bodhisattvas are deities who, having attained enlightenment themselves, temporarily eschew Nirvana (annihilation of suffering), to guide others to salvation or freedom from the unrelenting rounds of birth and death to which the unredeemed are doomed. Amida, according to tradition, had vowed that all creatures of this earth might enter the Pure Land simply by having faith and calling on his name. Amida's promise reads:

> I will not obtain perfect understanding if one of the living beings . . . who believe in me with the true thought and desire of being born in my country, and repeat my name ten times in thought, was not born again in my Pure Land.[1]

The teachings of Saint Hōnen were further simplified and popularized by his disciple Shinran (1173-1262). Merely calling sincerely on the Buddha's name once was thought to be enough for salvation, and Shinran roundly condemned vain and unwarranted repetitions. In elevating Amida to primacy, Shinran all but forgot about the historic Buddha, the traditional ecclesiastical organization, and most of the Buddhist scriptures. Virtue, learning, ascetic practices, celibacy, monasticism could avail nothing, because salvation for all, irrespective of sex, was foreordained by Amida's original vow. Shinran's teaching were eventually institutionalized and the sect devoted to them was called Shinshū, or True Land.

Their simple doctrines and devotion to the equality of all true believers won immense popularity for the new sects. In the beginning these faithful possessed almost no ecclesiastical organization or hierarchy. Somehow, in the tumultuous times of the late fifteenth century, the loosely organized Shinshū believers began to establish religious communities in and around the imperial city of Kyoto. The congregations of Shinshū, as well as those of other popular Buddhist sects, then became rich, militant, and politically powerful. Under the leadership of Shōnin Rennyo (1415-1499), the Shinshū congregations were built into an effective political and military movement which contested for local power on equal terms with feudal lords and other armed sects. Militant Shinshū was one of the most powerful political forces of central Japan in the early sixteenth century, and it withstood for a full decade (1570-1580) the determined efforts made by Nobunaga to crush its temporal power. The sects of the Pure Land and the True Land are still numerically the strongest of Japan's Buddhist congregations.

Of the Desire to Quit the Family

The principle of Shinran Shōnin was not to insist on making a desire to quit the family an essential. He did not set up the form of leaving the family and putting away desire. When, by following the

[1] As translated by E. Steinilber-Oberlin, *The Buddhist Sects of Japan*. . . . (London, 1938), p. 200.

behest [of Amida] in once calling [the Name] to remembrance, faith by the power of Another is confirmed, there is no distinction between male and female, between the old and the young.

And so, the condition of having attained this faith is explained in the Sûtra as being 'to attain salvation and to remain in the state of not returning[1] to revolve' [in the cycle of birth and death]. It is [further] explained as 'to conceive once the remembrance [of the Name of Buddha] and to enter the company of the steadfast.' This is, in a word, what is meant by there being 'no coming [of Buddha] to meet' one [at the end of life][2], and 'Karman being completed in one's ordinary lifetime.' [3]

It is said in the hymn [by Shinran Shōnin]:—'The outward conditions of those who desire Amida's Land-of-reward differ from each other; they who receive with faith the Name of Him who uttered the Prayer forget it not, sleeping or waking.' By 'outward condition' is meant that there is no distinction of laity and priesthood, of male and female. What is termed 'receiving with faith the Name of Him who uttered the Prayer, and not forgetting it, sleeping or waking,' is said of the person,—whatever may be his condition, and notwithstanding that his sins may have been those of them who commit any of the ten evil deeds[4] of the five classes of reprobates, of the revilers of the [Buddhist] Law, or the unbelievers, if he has changed the heart and repented, and profoundly believes that the Great Prayer of Amida the Tathâgata [Buddha] is that which affords deliverance to such vile classes of beings,—who, with singleness of mind, has the heart habitually relying on the Tathâgata, and, whether sleeping or waking, is constantly in the frame of mind of repeating, millions of times, the remembrance of Buddha,—who follows the practice of the faith which is the attainment of unforgetting, confirmed reliance on the Great Prayer.

Thenceforward, indeed, when those of the company who follow

[1] That is, entering directly into Nirvâna.

[2] That is, that salvation is present, and there is no waiting for the end of life to be received by Buddha.

[3] Karman (Karma) is defined as "(the law of) moral action," and "the recompense attending on moral action." It may be termed the power of good or evil in the character to affect the state of the individual in a future existence.
In the Shinshū system, belief in the power of the Prayer of Amida, becoming portion of the chain of causation, secures to the believer, from the moment of his attaining this faith, his attainment of Nirvâna at the end of his present life. His salvation, thus, is no more contingent on the goodness of his acts in this life; the chain of causation leading to this "recompense" is completed in his ordinary time,—secured to him at every moment of his present life.

[4] The ten evil deeds are: taking away life, stealing, lewdness, lying, ornate language, slander, double tongue (hypocrisy), covetousness, anger, heresy.

this practice, whether sitting up or lying down, chant the Name, it is to be understood that this is repeating the Name of Buddha as an expression of gratitude for His Mercy. These are they whose salvation is settled through their having attained true faith.

With much respect.

My sweat pours down in the heat of day, like tears; after I have laid down my pen, this appears as foolishness.

Bummei, 3rd year, 7th month, 18 day.

(4th August, 1471.)

Of the Determining of the Name of the Sect

It is asked:—Our sect (system) is vulgarly called, by everybody, the "Ikko-shyu," (the only sect,)—how about this? We wish to be informed.

I reply:—That our sect (system) should bear the name of the "Ikko-shyu," was never specially appointed by the Founder. It is so termed by everybody on account of the fact that we place our reliance on Amida Buddha *"only."* However, seeing that it is set forth in the Sûtra:—*"Only* concentrate the mind on the Buddha of Immeasurable Life (Amitâyus),"—when the intention is to express the injunction:—"Call to remembrance *only* the Buddha of Immeasurable life,"—there is no objection to our being called the "Ikko-shyu."

Nevertheless, the Founder settled that the sect was to be termed the "Jōdo-Shinshyu;" so that, it is to be understood that the name "Ikko-shyu" is not one which is used by us ourselves of our sect.

Now, the other Jōdo sects allow the practice of all sorts of austerities, while Shōnin eliminated the practice of austerities. In this way is attained the salvation of the True Land-of-Reward, and for this reason the term "Shin" ("True") is specially inserted [in the name of the sect.]

Further, it is said:—We understand clearly that our sect is denominated the Jōdo-Shinshyu; but, although the sin of living in the family is a thing characterized as being of profound wickedness and reprobation, yet, according to the system (form) of our sect,[5] by leaning on the power of the Prayer of Amida, the attainment of salvation in the Land of Bliss is an easy matter;—on this point we should like to be fully enlightened.

To this I reply:—According to our doctrine (system), they who

[5] Where living in the family is the rule with the priesthood.

have got settled faith of a surety will attain the salvation of the True Land-of-Reward. If you ask, what sort of a thing is this faith? It is this:—relying, without any anxiety, only on Amida the Tathâgata, and, not concerning oneself about other Buddhas or Bodhisattvas, to believe only, in singleness of mind, on Amida. This is what is termed attaining settled faith. The two characters "Shin-jin" are to be read "True mind." The "true" (or "believing") "mind" is not that which depends on the depraved self-power of the practice of austerities; its dependence is on the excellent other-power of the Tathâgata; and therefore it is called the "true mind" (= "believing mind," = "faith").

Again, it is not by merely chanting the Name, without any understanding, that assistance will come. And so it is expressed in the Sûtra:—'To hear the Name, and rejoice in believing.' This hearing of the Name is not a hearing of the name composed of the six characters, "Na-mu-A-mi-da-Butsu," in a reasonless (lit: nameless) and unreal manner. The rationale of the thing is that, on a man coming into contact with the good and wise, receiving their teaching, and, in saying "Namu," placing reliance on the Name, Namu Amida Buddha,—then will, of a certainty, Amida Buddha afford his aid to him who does this. And his condition is what is expressed in the Sûtra as "rejoicing in believing." And thus you are to understand that the formula 'Namu Amida Buddha' expresses the condition of the rendering of assistance to us. After you have understood this, whether while in motion or at rest, whether while sitting up or lying down, the chanting of the Name, with the mouth, you are to consider simply as the calling of Buddha to remembrance in rendering thanks to Him, Amida the Tathâgata, for His Mercy in having vouchsafed us assistance. And they who thus have settled faith are they who are to be called practisers of the remembrance of Buddha by the strength of Another, whereby we are born into the Land of Bliss.

With much respect.

The collection and writing down of the above was completed at the baths of Yamanaka, in Kaga, at four o'clock on the 2nd day of the latter third (22nd day) of the 9th month of the 5th year of Bummei. (Ten o'clock, of the 13th October, 1473.)

Of the Sleeve of the Tathâgata

For those who wish exactly to understand the meaning of what we term peace of mind, it is not essential to have also knowledge, ability and learning. Realizing merely that their personalities are things of deep sinfulness and vileness, and knowing that Amida the Tathâgata only is the Buddha who aids even such as they, they simply, with the whole heart, cling firmly to the sleeve of this Amida Buddha, and while they, in this frame of mind, place their reliance on Him for the next life, this Amida the Tathâgata, rejoicing exceedingly and throwing out from His person Eighty-four thousand (innumerable) great radiances, will receive and lay up such within His radiance. This it is what you are to understand by that which is set forth in the Sûtra:— "[His] radiance, pervading the worlds of the ten regions, embraces and rejects not the sentient beings who call Buddha to remembrance."

About the fact of our personalities becoming Buddhas there is no difficulty. Oh! it is by the Great Prayer, preeminent above (surpassing) the world! It is by the gracious radiance of Amida the Tathâgata! Without the influence of this radiance, no recovery whatsoever from the dreadful malady of darkness (ignorance and evil passions), and of the obstruction of [evil] Karman, from when there was no beginning, until now, has been possible. But they who, by the means of the operation of the influence of this radiance, have a store of merit from a previous life, have already attained that which is called faith by the power of Another. But this, it is at once plainly understood, is the faith which is bestowed on the part of Amida the Tathâgata. And thus it is not a faith which is excited by the observance of religious austerities. So you can now clearly understand what is meant by the great faith by the power of that Other,— Amida the Tathâgata. And thus, also, they who have by grace once attained this faith by the power of Another should all think upon the mercy of Amida the Tathâgata, and, in thankfulness for the mercy of Buddha, habitually chant the Name in remembrance of Him.

With much respect.

17 / THEATER AND THE DRAMA

The civil wars and political anarchy that tore Japan intermittently throughout the fifteenth and sixteenth centuries did not stifle

A Kyōgen ("Mad Words") entitled *Busu*, trans. Donald Keene. From *Anthology of Japanese Literature: From the Earliest Era to the Mid-Nineteenth Century*, compiled and edited by Donald Keene. Copyright 1955 by Grove Press. Reprinted by permission of Grove Press.

the growth of culture. The Ashikaga shoguns, who centered their activities at Kyoto, sought to preserve the traditional court culture and to blend it with new popular movements and with the influences coming into the country from China. The chief transmitters of Chinese culture were the Zen monks, the most influential Buddhists at the court, and the arbiters of taste and scholarship in the Ashikaga period. The most distinctive of the arts cultivated under Zen tutelage were the tea ceremony, landscape painting, and gardening, and the Nō drama.

In its origins the Nō drama evolved from symbolic dances performed to music at the imperial court. These stately dances were transformed into dramas during the fourteenth and fifteenth centuries. Nō theater in its most traditional form combines strictly defined drama and conventionalized dance patterns with prose and poetry chanted by a chorus to musical accompaniment. Ordinarily, the cast consists of a principal actor (shite or protagonist) and an assistant (waki) with, perhaps, several attendants. In the one hour normally allotted to a performance, the Nō players are required, through restrained and stylized words and movements, to inspire emotional feelings about a serious or tragic historical event. Nō's high priest was Seami Motokiyo (1363-1443) who, while enjoying the favor of the shogunate, formulated the aesthetic principles still governing the medium. Suffused with symbolism and played in gorgeous costume before a cultivated and critical audience well-versed in the recondite, allusive expressions associated with its Zen heritage, the Nō drama long remained a favorite pastime of the aristocracy.

Once Nō had reached maturity and attained a high degree of perfection in the fifteenth century, more attention was paid to the kyōgen or interludes, a form of comic relief. Kyōgen literally means "mad words," and the artistic rule governing the performance was: "On no account may vulgar words or gestures be introduced, however funny they may be." Themes for these brief diversions were drawn mainly from social situations, folklore, romances, or religious homilies; kyōgen are classified as "daimyo pieces," "retainer pieces," "priest pieces," "wooing pieces," "dance pieces" (parodies of Nō), and the like. More often than not kyōgen satirized the foibles of lords, and yet many of these very personages, from Hideyoshi and his successors onward, delighted in witnessing and performing in the kyōgen pieces.

Busu

Persons

MASTER
TARŌ KAJA
JIRŌ KAJA

(The Master, Tarō kaja, and Jirō kaja enter the stage along the Bridge. Tarō kaja and Jirō kaja seat themselves by the Name-Saying Seat. The Master as he introduces himself goes to the Waki's Pillar.)

MASTER: I am a gentleman of this vicinity. I plan to go away to the mountains for a few days, and now I shall summon my servants to give them instructions about what to do during my absence. Tarō kaja, where are you?

TARŌ: Here, Master.

(He gets up and goes toward the Master, then bows.)

MASTER: Call Jirō kaja too.

TARŌ: Yes, Master. Jirō kaja, the master wants you.

JIRŌ: I obey.

(He also comes forward and bows.)

TOGETHER: We are before you, Master.

MASTER: I have called you because I am going to the mountains for a few days, and I want you both to take good care of the house while I am away.

TARŌ: Your orders will be obeyed, Master, but you have always taken one of us with you on your journeys, and today too.

TOGETHER: One of us would like to accompany you.

MASTER: No, that is out of the question. Today I have something important to leave in your care, and both of you must guard it. Wait here.

TOGETHER: Very good, Master.

(The Master goes to the Flute Pillar where he picks up a round lacquered cask about two feet high. He deposits it in the center of the stage, and returns to his former position.)

MASTER: This is what is known as *busu*, a deadly poison. If even a wind blowing from its direction should strike you, it will mean instant death. Be on your guard.

TARŌ: Yes, Master.

JIRŌ: Excuse me, Master, but I would like to ask you something.

MASTER: What is it?

JIRŌ: Why do you keep such a dreadful poison in the house?

MASTER: The *busu* loves its master, and as long as it is the master who handles it, there is not the slightest danger. But if either of you so much as approach it, you will suffer instant death. Beware even of being touched by the wind from its direction.

JIRŌ: Yes, Master.

MASTER: Now I shall be leaving.

TARŌ: May you have a pleasant journey,

TOGETHER: And come back soon.

MASTER: Thank you.

(*The Master goes to the Bridge, where he seats himself at the First Pine, indicating that he has disappeared. Tarō and Jirō see him off, then seat themselves at the back of the stage.*)

TARŌ: He always takes one of us with him. I wonder why today he left both of us to look after the house.

JIRŌ: I wonder why.

TARŌ: At any rate, it's always lonesome being left here by oneself, but since we are both here today, we can have a pleasant talk.— Oh!

JIRŌ: What is the matter?

TARŌ: There was a gust of wind from the *busu!*

JIRŌ: How frightening!

TARŌ: Let's move a little farther away.

JIRŌ: A good idea.

(*They hastily move toward the Bridge, then sit.*)

TARŌ: Just as you said before, why should the master keep in the house a thing so deadly that even a breath of wind from it will cause instant death?

JIRŌ: However much it may love its master, I still don't understand why he keeps it.

TARŌ: You know, I'd like to have a look at the *busu*. What do you think it can be?

JIRŌ: Have you gone mad? Don't you know that even the wind from its way means certain death?

TARŌ: Let's go up to it fanning from this side. In that way we won't get any wind from it.

JIRŌ: That's a good idea.

(*The two men stand, and fanning vigorously approach the cask.*)

TARŌ: Fan, fan hard.

JIRŌ: I am fanning.

TARŌ: I am going to untie the cord around it now, so fan hard.

JIRŌ: Right!

TARŌ: I've unfastened it. Now, I'll take off the cover.

Jirō: Do it quickly!

Tarō: Keep fanning!

Jirō: I am fanning.

Tarō: It's off! *(They flee to the Bridge.)* Oh, that's a relief!

Jirō: What's a relief?

Tarō: That thing—it's not an animal or it would jump out.

Jirō: Perhaps it is only playing dead.

Tarō: I'll have a look.

Jirō: That's a good idea.

(They approach the cask as before.)

Tarō: Fan, fan hard!

Jirō: I am fanning!

Tarō: Now I'm going to have a look, so fan hard!

Jirō: Right!

Tarō: I've seen it! I've seen it! *(They flee as before to the Bridge.)*

Jirō: What did you see?

Tarō: Something dark gray that looked good to eat. You know, I think I'd like a taste of that *busu.*

Jirō: How can you think of eating something which will kill you even if you only catch a whiff of it?

Tarō: I must be bewitched by the *busu.* I can't think of anything but eating it. I will have a taste.

Jirō: You mustn't.

(He takes Tarō's sleeve, and they struggle.)

Tarō: Let me go!

Jirō: I won't let you go!

Tarō: I tell you, let me go!

Jirō: I tell you, I won't let you go!

(Tarō frees himself and approaches the cask. He uses his fan to scoop out the contents.)

Tarō: *(singing):* Shaking off with sorrow the sleeves of parting, I come up to the side of the *busu.*

Jirō: Alas! Now he will meet his death.

Tarō: Oh, I am dying. I am dying *(He falls over.)*

Jirō: I knew it would happen. Tarō kaja! What is it? *(He rushes to him.)*

Tarō: It's so delicious, I'm dying. *(He gets up.)*

Jirō: What can it be?

Tarō: It's sugar!

Jirō: Let me have a taste.

Tarō: Go ahead.

Jirō: Thank you. It really is sugar!

(The two of them eat, using their fans to scoop out the busu. Tarō, seeing that Jirō is too busy to notice, carries off the cask to the Waki's Pillar. While he is eating, Jirō comes up and takes the cask to the Facing Pillar.)

TARŌ: You mustn't eat it all by yourself. Let me have it!

JIRŌ: No, you were eating before I did. Give me some more.

TARŌ: Let's both eat it.

JIRŌ: A good idea.

(They put the cask between them.)

TARŌ: Delicious, isn't it?

JIRŌ: Really delicious.

TARŌ: The master told us that it was *busu,* thinking we wouldn't eat it then. That was really most disagreeable of him. Eat up! Eat up!

JIRŌ: It was disagreeable of him to have told us that we would die instantly if we got so much as a whiff of it. Eat up! Eat up!

TARŌ: I can't stop eating.

JIRŌ: It feels as if our chins are sagging, doesn't it?

TARŌ: Eat up! Oh, it's all gone!

JIRŌ: Yes, all gone.

TARŌ: Well, you can be proud of yourself.

JIRŌ: *I* can be proud of myself? It was *you* who first looked at the *busu* and first ate it. I'll tell the master as soon as he gets back.

TARŌ: I was only joking. Now, tear up this *kakemono.*[1]

JIRŌ: Very well.

(He goes to the Waki's Pillar and makes motions of tearing a kakemono.)

Sarari. Sarari. Pattari.

TARŌ: Bravo! First you looked at the busu, then you ate it, and now you've torn up the master's *kakemono.* I'll inform him of that as soon as he returns.

JIRŌ: I only did it because you told me. And I shall inform the master of that.

TARŌ: I was joking again. Now smash this bowl.

JIRŌ: No, I've had enough.

TARŌ: Then let's smash it together.

JIRŌ: All right.

(They go to the Facing Pillar and make motions of picking up a large bowl and dashing it to the ground.)

TOGETHER: *Garari chin.*

TARŌ: Ah—it's in bits.

[1] A picture or writing on silk or paper.

JIRŌ: Now what excuse will we make?

TARŌ: When the master returns, the first thing to do is to burst into tears.

JIRŌ: Will tears do any good?

TARŌ: They will indeed. He'll be coming back soon. Come over here.

JIRŌ: Very well.

(They go to the back of the stage and sit there. The Master stands up and speaks at the First Pine.)

MASTER: I have completed my business now. I imagine that my servants must be waiting for my return. I shall hasten home. Ah, here I am already. Tarō kaja, Jirō kaja, I've returned!

(He goes to the Waki's Pillar.)

TARŌ: He's back! Now start weeping! *(They weep.)*

MASTER: Tarō kaja, Jirō kaja! Where are you? What is the matter here? Instead of being glad that I have returned they are both weeping. If something has happened, let me know at once.

TARŌ: Jirō kaja, you tell the master.

JIRŌ: Tarō kaja, you tell the master.

MASTER: Whichever of you it is, tell me quickly.

TARŌ: Well, then, this is what happened. I thought that it wouldn't do for me to sleep while on such important duty, but I got sleepier and sleepier. To keep me awake I had a wrestling match with Jirō kaja. He is so strong that he knocked me over, and to keep from falling, I clutched at that *kakemono*, and ripped it as you can see.

MASTER: What a dreadful thing to happen! *(He looks at the Waki's Pillar in amazement.)* How could you tear up a precious *kakemono* that way?

TARŌ: Then he threw me back and spun me over the stand with the bowl on it, and the bowl was smashed to bits.

MASTER: What a dreadful thing! *(He looks at the Facing Pillar in amazement.)* You even smashed my precious bowl. What I am going to do?

TARŌ: Knowing that you would soon return, we thought that we could not go on living, so we ate up the *busu*, hoping thus to die. Isn't that so, Jirō kaja?

JIRŌ: Exactly.

TARŌ *(singing):* One mouthful and still death did not come.

JIRŌ *(singing):* Two mouthfuls and still death did not come.

TARŌ *(singing):* Three mouthfuls, four mouthfuls

JIRŌ *(singing):* Five mouthfuls

TARŌ *(singing):* More than ten mouthfuls
(They get up and begin to dance.)
TOGETHER *(singing):* We ate until there wasn't any left,
But still death came not, strange to tell,
Ah, what a clever head!
(They approach the Master while fanning, then suddenly strike him on the head with their fans. They run off laughing.)
MASTER: What do you mean "clever head"? You brazen things! Where are you going? Catch them! You won't get away with it! *(He runs after them to the Bridge.)*
TOGETHER: Forgive us! Forgive us!

INTRODUCTION

In the eyes of sixteenth-century Europeans, Asia was seen at first as a strange, fascinating, and undifferentiated whole. It was only gradually that India, Southeast Asia, China, and Japan became known as definite and distinct parts of Asia, with independent and diverse traditions, customs, and beliefs. As the realization dawned that Asia was not of one piece, comparisons and contrasts of the various Asian countries became more common in European writings. Some inquisitive and daring souls even began as early as the sixteenth century to compare Asian to European civilization, and not always to the advantage of Europe!

18 / SOCIAL AND CULTURAL CONTRASTS: JAPAN AND EUROPE

Light from the Land of the Rising Sun was transmitted to Europe primarily by the letters and writings of the Jesuit missionaries. St. Francis Xavier, the first Jesuit to visit the Japanese, esteemed them to be "the best [people] who have yet been discovered." His successors quickly converted large numbers of Japanese to Christianity,

Translated from Luis Fróis, S.J., *Kulturgegensätze Europa-Japan* (*1585*); *Tratado em que se contem muito susinta e abreviadamente algumas contradições e diferenças de custumes antre a gente de Europa e esta provincia de Japão. Erstmalige, kritische Ausgabe des eigenhändigen portugiesischen Fróis-Textes in der Biblioteca de la Acádemia de la História in Madrid mit deutscher Übersetzung, Einleitung und Anmerkungen von Josef Franz Schütte, S.J.* (Tokyo: Sophia Universität, 1955) (Monumenta Nipponica, No. 15). Reprinted by permission of Monumenta Nipponica.

and the Jesuit mission to Japan became one of the Church's proudest accomplishments of the sixteenth century. As a testimonial to the prosperity of their enterprise in Japan, the Jesuits sent four young Japanese legates to Europe, who traveled widely in Portugal, Spain, and Italy from 1584 to 1586. Their triumphal tour, as described earlier (pp. 100ff.), inspired genuine interest, and in the last years of the sixteenth century the Jesuits helped to satisfy the growing taste in Europe for news of the island kingdom through their letters.

The best informed and most prolific letter writer in Japan was Luis Fróis, a Portuguese Jesuit. Fróis joined the Society of Jesus in 1548 and during the following fifty years he untiringly promoted missionary efforts in India, Malacca, and Japan. During the thirty-five years of his residence in Japan, Fróis dispatched to Europe more than one hundred long and informative letters. In the extant letters he discusses Japanese religious beliefs, describes shrines, temples, palaces, and castles in minute detail, comments on leading political personalities whom he knew personally (such as Nobunaga and Hideyoshi), and delights in depicting the culture and customs of town and countryside. His command of the Japanese language and his frank admiration of Japanese civilization enabled him to get inside the life of Japan to a degree that has rarely been equaled by foreign observers. Only recently a short manuscript of 1585 by Fróis has been discovered and published. In the following distichs he compares aspects of daily life in Japan and Europe, the two societies he knew best.

Chapter I: Of the Men, Their Personal Appearance and Clothing

With us it would be considered frivolity and buffoonery to wear gay-colored clothes; with the Japanese it is customary to wear all colored clothes except in the case of Buddhist monks and old people who have withdrawn from the world.

With us articles of men's clothing cannot be useful to women; the *kimono* and *katabira* serve equally well for men and women in Japan.

We wear leather shoes and cavaliers [have] shoes of velvet; the Japanese, high and low, use sandals fashioned out of rice straw.

In Europe it would be considered effeminate if a man carried a fan and fanned himself with it; in Japan it is a sign of lowliness and poverty not always to carry a fan in the waistband and to use it.

The courtliness we show by kneeling on one knee the Japanese show by throwing themselves down with feet, hands and head close upon the floor.

Chapter II: Of the Women, Their Personal Appearance and Their Customs

European women seldom add strange hair to their own; Japanese women buy many wigs which are imported commercially from China.

In Europe property is held jointly by married couples; in Japan each possesses his separately, and sometimes a woman collects usurious interest from her husband.

With us it is not very commonplace for women to write; among Japanese noblewomen it is considered degrading if one does not understand how.

In Europe the women ordinarily prepare the meals; in Japan the men do it, and even the nobles consider it smart to go into the kitchen and prepare food.

Chapter III: Of the Children and Their Customs

With us a child of four years can not yet eat by himself; Japanese children of three eat unassisted with *hashi* [chopsticks].

With us one learns reading and writing from secular teachers; in Japan all children study in Buddhist monasteries.

With us twenty-year-olds almost never as yet wear swords; Japanese boys of twelve and thirteen wear both *katana* [sword] and *wakizashi* [dagger].

European children are reared with much caressing, tenderness, good food and clothing; Japanese [grow up] half naked and almost entirely without demonstrations of solicitude and tender treatment.

With us children frequently visit relatives and are intimate with them; in Japan they seldom go to their [relatives'] houses and they treat them like strangers.

Chapter IV: Of the Monks and Their Practices

People of our orders do not indulge in singing of secular drama or comedy or in the playing of musical instruments; the Buddhist monks are thoroughly accustomed to doing so, and thereby get their relaxation.

We believe in future glory and punishment and in the immortality of the soul; the Zen monks deny all that and [believe] there is nothing more than to be born and to die.

When members of our orders understand medicine, they heal for nothing but love of God; most Japanese doctors are monks who live on their income.

We preach standing and make gestures by moving our hands; *bonzes* [Buddhist priests] preach sitting and make gestures with the head without moving their hands.

Chapter V: Of the Temples and Pictures and Things Pertaining to Worship and Religion

Our books are made up of folded sheets [of paper] and closed with clasps; those of the *bonzes* are rolled and tied with a ribbon.

Our pictures are mostly painted altar pieces; in the temples of the *bonzes* all representations are sculptures.

Chapter VI: Of the Offensive and Defensive Weapons of the Japanese and of War

If our swords, although quite new, are very good, they are of great value; the Japanese ones [swords], even if new and good, are not costly and the quite old ones are precious.

Our kings and captains pay soldiers wages; in Japan each person, while he is at war, must provide at his own cost, his food, drink and clothing.

Chapter VIII: Of Horses

All our horses are shod with iron and nails; none of the Japanese [horses] are, on the contrary they wear straw shoes which last them half a mile.

Chapter IX: Of Diseases, Doctors, and Medicines

With us, scrofula, stones, podagra, and plague are common; all these diseases are uncommon in Japan.

We suture wounds; the Japanese lay a bit of adhesive paper upon them. [Editor's note: This Japanese practice seems to approximate the treatments devised only very recently which are considered preferable to taking stitches.]

Chapter X: On the Writing of the Japanese, of Their Books, Paper, Ink, and Letters

We write with goose feathers or with feathers of other birds; they [write] with paint brushes made out of rabbit hair with a handle of bamboo.

Our paper is of only four or five kinds; theirs is of more than fifty varieties.

Our letters reproduce concepts only through detailed descriptions; the Japanese [letters] are quite brief and very full of meaning.

Chapter XI: Of Houses, Buildings, Gardens, and Fruits

Our [houses] are built out of stone and mortar; theirs out of wood, bamboo, straw and mud.

Our room dividers are made of stone and mortar or out of brick; the Japanese out of panels of paper.

In Europe one makes square, neat, walled ponds; in Japan they make little lakes or pools with tiny corners and inlets, with boulders and small islands in the middle, and, of course, dug out of the ground.

Chapter XIII: Of the Drama, Comedies, Dances, Song, and Musical Instruments of Japan

Our dramas are spoken in performance; theirs are almost always sung or danced.

With us music for several voices in sonorous and mild; although they all sing together in a single voice in falsetto, Japanese [singing] is the most horrifying that can exist.

Our spinets have four strings which are played through a keyboard; the Japanese have twelve strings and are played with a kind of wooden claw expressly made for that.

Chapter XIV: Of Various Extraordinary Things Not Fitting Well into the Foregoing Chapters

In Europe one seeks clarity of expression and avoids ambiguity; in Japan expressions with double meanings are the best speech and are prized most of all.

19 / ASIA IN THE EYES OF SIXTEENTH-CENTURY EUROPE

The composite picture presented below of what Europe knew about Asia in the sixteenth century is based on a comprehensive survey of extant, published materials: chronicles, travel books, Jesuit letters, and maps. The data in these publications came to Europe from sailors, merchants, colonial administrators, and missionaries who recorded their experiences in and reactions to the East. In Europe, the new information so acquired was blended with the

From *Asia in the Making of Europe* (Chicago: University of Chicago Press, 1965), by Donald F. Lach. Epilogue from Volume I: *The Century of Discovery*, Book II, 825-35. Copyright © 1965 by The University of Chicago. Reprinted by permission of the University of Chicago Press.

view inherited from the prediscovery era to produce a more realistic and complicated image of Asia.

The physical landscape of Asia, except for Australia and eastern New Guinea, had been uncovered by 1600 from western India to eastern Japan as far south as Java and as far north as the Hokkaido and the Liaotung peninsula. Even the approaches from the Pacific ocean to insular and eastern Asia are described in books and depicted on maps. The revelation is by no means total, because the Europeans were naturally far better informed on the coasts than about the interiors. With the passage of time the Europeans improve their knowledge of interior areas and acquire steadily a more exact knowledge of spatial relationships. They continue to over-emphasize the regions and physical features which they know most intimately: the Ghats and the deltas of the Irrawaddy, Ganges, Mekong, and Yangtze. They remain relatively ignorant of the Indus and Yellow River valleys and the internal geography of northern India and Japan. Nonetheless, before the century ends, they know a few details about the peoples of the Himalayas (Tibetans), the steppe north of the Great Wall, and the topographical outlines of Korea and Hokkaido. . . .

The human masses of continental Asia and Japan leave the Europeans aghast, and the densely populated and extensive cities of the East astound them. They give rough estimates of the numbers living in Vijayanagar, Kyoto, Pegu, and Canton. From these statistics it appears that Kyoto, and possibly Canton, were estimated to be larger than any European city of the sixteenth century. They describe in vivid detail a number of great Asian cities which have since disappeared: Dabhul, Gaur, Vijayanagar, Golconda, Pegu, and Ayuthia. Frequently they compare the Asian capitals or lesser centers to European cities: Sakai and Pegu to Venice, Champener to Evora, Canton to Lisbon, and Kyoto to Rome. The Europeans were not similarly impressed with the agricultural and village centers of Asia, and in many instances find rural conditions shocking and inexcusable. They are impressed, however, particularly in China and Japan, by the great productivity possible in a crowded countryside. . . .

The peoples of Asia are divided roughly into several types by color: black, shades of brown, and white. The black people are the Africans, natives of south India, and the East Indians. The indigenous people of north India and continental Southeast Asia are often described as being tawny or swarthy. The Japanese and Chinese are white both to the merchants and the missionaries. . . . The black peoples are generally conceived of as being inferior, incapable of improvement, and hopelessly sunk in superstition. The whitest peoples generally meet European standards, may even be superior in certain regards, and are certainly good prospects for conversion. The males of Asia are generally divided into those who are fighters and those who are timid; the only truly warlike groups are the Muslims of the Mughul empire, the Japanese, the Nāyars of Malabar, and the Malays. Asian women are universally attractive; respectable women are closely watched and not permitted to go about freely except in Japan; the Japanese women are also exceptional inasmuch as upperclass ladies can usually read and write. Concubinage, polygamy, and prostitution are to be found in all the Asian lands.

The Europeans are mainly interested in those countries where effective unity and central authority help to provide stable conditions for trade and a favorable climate for evangelizing. China, Siam, and Pegu seem to meet these conditions best, though the missionaries certainly managed to reap a bountiful harvest in Japan despite divided and uncertain political conditions. Nonetheless, both the religious and secular commentators concentrate their attention on the kingship, the aristocracy, the bureaucracy, and the governing techniques employed in the most effectively unified states of Asia. Burma, Siam, and Cambodia are deemed to have the most absolute rulers, the land being entirely the royal domain and the tillers of the soil being royal chattels. Most of the Asiatic rulers have religious and ceremonial as well as political functions; the ruler of Japan, they realize, has had his political functions usurped by the shōgun and the daimyō. While the ruler of China is the greatest and most influential of Asian kings, his domestic power is shared with an elaborate bureaucracy recruited and advanced through a merit system based on examinations. In China there is no hereditary aristocracy of the type know in Europe; in Siam, similarly, grants of land are never given in perpetuity and so a landed aristocracy cannot become an entrenched establishment standing between the king and his people. In Japan and the Deccan, where aristocracies exist, the custom is for the powerful lords to live away from their jurisdictions and to be at the royal court under the watchful eye of the king at appointed times or for stated periods. The Europeans also observe and comment upon the intermediary political role played by the eunuchs at the courts of Bengal, China, Pegu and in the Mughul empire. The problem of succession in an absolute state is also examined and remarks are made upon the system of primogeniture obtaining in China and Japan, of assassination in Sumatra and Bengal, and of self-immolation in Malabar. Royal monopolies of key economic activities are likewise highlighted: horses in Vijayanagar, land in Siam and Cambodia, the ruby commerce of Pegu, the clove trade of Ternate, and the mining of precious metals in China. While exercising control over religion, the rulers of Siam, China, and the Mughul empire are willing to let their subjects make their choices in faith and do not seek to impose religious uniformity on their realms.

In a vast, well-organized country like China the royal administration has its hand in every phase of human activity. While a system of mutual surveillance (*pao-chia*) manages justice at the local level, its members are individually responsible to the administrative hierarchy which culminates in Peking. The Chinese emperor not only controls; he also uses the power of the state to encourage his subjects. The national system of civil service examinations is supported by a national system of state-supported schools. The state even provides hospitals and homes for the blind, the indigent, and the orphans within its elaborate public welfare program. A bureaucratic state like China naturally has many official posts, and the Europeans provide the titles held by many of these officials and describe their functions. Many of the Europeans note with considerable approval that a governor may never rule in the province of which he is a native. China's encompassing bureaucratic organization wins great admiration, and the Middle Kingdom is placed in a class entirely by itself for achievements in government.

The Asiatic system of international relations based on the tribute system of China, does not win sympathetic understanding or approval from the Europeans. The relationship between trade and tribute is never clearly understood, even though the Europeans are quick to realize that most of the Asiatic states involved in international commerce have a vassal relationship to China. They also seem to comprehend the double vassalage of the Liu-ch'ius to China and Japan, and clearly indicate that Malacca in its pre-European days was in vassalage to Siam, itself a vassal of China. They also bring out clearly how Malacca by-passed Siam to achieve greater independence by appealing directly for help to China. A number of the commentators describe the customs followed in re-

ceiving embassies at the courts of Pegu, Siam, and China, and out-
line the conditions under which trade may be carried on in their
capital cities. . . .

In negotiating trade agreements with the Chinese, Japanese, and
Siamese, the Europeans, possibly because they had no alternative,
apparently accept written assurances and guarantees at their face
value. Elsewhere, the Portuguese take pains to make certain that
native oaths and guarantees are binding in heathen terms. For example, to testify to their sincerity the Deccanese in Goa are asked
to swear to their own gods and to put ashes on their bare heads.
In the Philippines the Europeans often follow local customs by
engaging in blood compacts. The initial commercial agreement
between Portugal and Pegu is ratified only after the Buddhists and
Christians, each following their own rites, have sworn by their own
deities to honor their obligations. The Christians . . . often question
whether their own sworn oaths are binding when given to a pagan.

The social beliefs and attitudes held in some parts of pagan Asia
appear intolerable to the Europeans. The caste system of India
(particularly of Malabar) is especially repugnant, particularly the
beliefs in untouchability and distance pollution. The missionaries
react very strongly against the idea that Christians may pollute the
higher castes. The matrilineal customs of the *nāyars,* and the strange
sexual practices which they follow, fascinate and repel the Europeans almost as much as do *sati* [widow-burning] and concrema-
tion. Even the otherwise admirable Japanese shock the missionaries
by their callousness toward human life, particularly in their indif-
ference to infanticide and their addiction to suicide. Such short-
comings in the civilized Japanese seem to them far more abhorrent
than the cannibalism which they hear about among the primitive
peoples of Sumatra, Borneo, the Philippines, the Spice Islands, and
the northern border region of Siam. While mildly interested in the
tattooed tribesmen of northern Celebes and northern Siam, the
Europeans generally react with hostility to strange customs and
seem always to fear that they are the work of the devil. The missionaries are absolutely horrified at the universality of sodomy,
even among the Buddhist priests, and by the widespread existence of
concubinage, polygamy, and prostitution.

The social institutions of China and Japan, especially the family,
arouse admiration and even stimulate suggestions for emulation. In
China the social tone is set by the court and the mandarins. While
Chinese officialdom is far from faultless, it sets a high standard.
Class lines are far sharper in Japan, where interclass marriages are

rare and different languages are used when speaking to women, inferiors, and superiors. Among the secular classes, the warrior occupies a much higher station in Japan than in China. Even the Buddhist monks of Japan have no hesitation in organizing themselves into military bands to fight against secular authorities. The nations of East Asia, however, have been spared from the caste system of Hinduism and are therefore much less strange and repugnant. Slavery is common, even in Japan, but it is clearly an institution different from European slavery. In Asia, slaves are not mere property: they intermarry with free persons, possess property of their own, and may regain their freedom by several relatively easy routes.

Freemen of all social levels may obtain an education in China at state expense. Centers of learning exist in every provincial capital and in smaller cities as well where students may prepare themselves to take civil service examinations. Printed books of all sorts are available in China, and the state of literacy is high by sixteenth-century standards. Both China and Japan are reported to have universities, but India has no major centers of learning. In Siam and Burma the Buddhist priests teach religious and secular subjects, and are credited with maintaining the cultural traditions of their lands. Pali, Sanskrit, Chinese, and Malay are all international languages through which the peoples of the area communicate with one another about religion and trade. In all of the great continental countries and Japan, the architectural monuments and sculptural masterpieces overawe the Westerners. From local informants much of the traditional oral history and mythology passed into the European learned tradition. Although not intimately involved themselves in the cultures of Asia, the Europeans were interested enough to gather significant materials on early Asian history, language and literature, arts, crafts, and sciences.

Most of the social, moral, and intellectual deficiencies of the Asians can be traced to the nefarious teachings of the Muslims and to the stubborn devotion of the pagans to their native faiths. . . . The only international religion native to Asia is Buddhism. Its priests and monks dominate the spiritual life of Ceylon, Burma, Siam, Cambodia, and Japan. While Buddhism flourishes in China, its clergy is not so powerful there and its teachings face strong competition from other native creeds. The Jesuits get their first real understanding of Buddhist teachings in Japan. There they learn Buddhism originated in India from whence it was carried into China, Korea, and finally Japan. Possibly because the Jesuits were never active themselves in continental Southeast Asia, no clear understanding emerges of the relationships between Japanese and Southeast Asian Buddhism, or of the differences between the Mahayana and Hinayana dispensations. The monastic system of Buddhism, often compared to its Christian counterpart, particularly attracts the attention of both secular and religious observers. The hierarchical organization of Buddhism, its relations to the ruler, its temples, idols, and stupas are described for all the Buddhist lands. Information on Buddhism's cosmography and doctrines emerges mainly from the missionary accounts of "pagan errors." The Buddhists are acknowleged as being the group mainly responsible for education in Burma, Siam, and Japan.

Hinduism is the greatest of the pagan faiths of India, though it is vaguely understood that certain of its dogmas and practices had emigrated in the past as far east as Cambodia. Brahmans and Gurus act as the secular clergy of Hinduism; the Yogis are cast in the role of ascetics or mendicant friars. The Hindus revere many idols reminiscent of Christian saints, and the Christians persist in seeking in Hinduism the vestiges of a primitive Christianity. Yogis are far more saintly, informed, and tractable than other Hindu teachers since they live abstemiously and will listen to Christian arguments. The Brahmans are particularly recalcitrant in their devotion to caste, and are hard to deal with because of their great political and social influence with the other castes. They also persist in living pristinely as vegetarians while making heavy exactions from other social groups and desecrating their own temples by supporting them from the earnings of prostitutes. Believing in the transmigration of souls, Hindus will not take life; but they persist in maintaining caste and slave systems which relegate some souls to an earthly perdition. The Jains and Parsees likewise come in for comment as other superstitious sects with incomprehensible social practices. The holy places of India, especially the Ganges, are shrines revered by people all over the sub-continent for reasons which generally escape or puzzle the Christians.

Far greater is Christian understanding for the practices of Shinto and Taoism. These are simple, animistic religions which are popular with the commoners of Japan and China. The Japanese faith is founded on the belief that the people of Japan are the children of the *kami* and the emperor is descended from the Sun-Goddess. Neither Shinto nor Taoism has a highly complex or powerful ecclesiastical organization. Both faiths, like the animistic beliefs of the East Indians and the Filipinos, are unsophisticated, unsystematized, and replete with obvious superstitions. Confucianism, mentioned only at the very end of the sixteenth century, is described primarily as a moral philosophy held by the ruler of China and his mandarins. Very little is known about its intellectual content, and it is mainly thought of in connection with the spring-ploughing ceremony presided over by the emperor. Practically nothing is known about the precepts of either Confucius or Lao-Tze. It is clear, however, that none of the Asian countries, except perhaps Burma, Siam, and Cambodia, is religiously united. And none of the pagan religions is militant, except for Buddhism in Japan, or bent upon proselytizing.

While religious warfare is not an Asian problem, it does not follow that Asians are devoted solely to the arts of peace. Warfare and militarism are chronic evils, witness the *nāyars* and *samurai* as professional warrior classes. Indeed, warfare involves greater masses of people than anything conceived of in Europe. In India, Burma, and Siam huge armies, constituting almost the entire population of the state, supplemented by numerous mercenaries, move into battle against each other. Such mass military movements leave in their wake badly ravaged land, totally devastated cities, and permanently dislocated multitudes. While most Asian states are only rarely mobilized totally, most of them keep permanent military establishments. Vijayanagar, for example, regularly recruits, enlists, trains, and maintains large corps of mercenaries, including Christians, Muslims, and Africans. Siam likewise hires mercenaries and requires military service of its own people. A few Indian rulers employ Amazons as palace guards and as warriors. Rivers, mountains, and ports are fortified permanently; sluices, walls, and moats protect capital cities like Champaner and Kyoto. China keeps fleets of war junks constantly in its coastal waters and garrisons its northern frontier with a Great Wall and permanent military settlements. The latest in firearms and artillery are quickly incorporated into the arsenals of these armies. Native arms and elephant cavalry are used in conjunction with more modern equipment.

In the sixteenth century the Europeans witness and participate in a number of major Asian wars. They record details about the wars between the Deccan states and Vijayanagar, between the Mughuls and Cambay and Bengal, between the Siamese and the Burmese, between the Burmese and Arakanese, between the Siamese and the Cambodians, between the rival contestants for power in Japan, and between Japan and China in Korea. On the seas pirates are a constant menace, and the Europeans participate in a number of sea-sweeping operations as well as in the defense of their outposts at Diu, Goa, and Malacca against maritime and overland attacks. Despite all their experiences, however, the Europeans persist in believing in the superiority of their own arms and martial valor. Siam, Cambodia, China, and Japan are designated by many in the field, as being easy and worthwhile conquests. It may be presumed that what they had in mind were limited acquisitions of territory in strategically-located areas through which broader regions could be controlled. In their prospectuses sent to Europe the men in the field document these optimistic hopes by reference to the timidity and unaggressiveness of the peoples of continental East Asia; the weakness of their large but slow, disorganized, and ineffective armies; the superiority of European vessels in size, maneuverability, and firepower; and the readiness of the East Asian populations to revolt against their arbitrary and despotic rulers.

While the Europeans in the field bemused themselves with hopes of conquest, their fellows collected weird bits of fact and fiction about Asian customs and traditions. Some of these stories are reportorial and true; others are myths, some of which are still current in Asia; and still others are probably distorted or imaginary. The dog-headed Indians and the gold-digging ants of antiquity have disappeared, but Asia has not lost any of its exoticism. For example, Javans and Malabars run amuck as a form of protest or revenge. Self-torture or destruction is a proof of sincerity. In Malacca nobody may wear yellow colors without royal permission. The Burmans have a temple guarded by tame fish which can be called to the surface by a particular spoken word. Neither a Javan nor a Malay will permit anything to be above his shoulders or head. The king of Arakan selects his harem by submitting his prospective brides to a smell test. Strangers are called upon in Tenasserim to deflower a virgin before her marriage. In Pegu merchants may legally contract temporary alliances with native women. Burmese and Cantonese will eat anything no matter how distasteful it appears to others. A vast lake stands high in the mountains of central Asia from which all of the continental rivers descend. Eclipses are traditionally believed in Siam to be caused by a huge snake which has swallowed the moon. Horses are unable to reproduce in India, hence the scarcity of them there. Hogs are ceremonially killed in the Bisayan islands and their flesh is reserved for old women to eat. White elephants are sacred in Siam and Burma, and wars begin over their possession. In Siam the nobles of the land delight in washing in the urine of the white elephant. Malabars worship for the day the first thing they meet each morning. Foot-binding was introduced into China by the men to keep their women at home and at work. These and a multitude of other curious stories added immeasurably to the repertory of the imaginative, and soon became a part of the stockpile of exotic items from which artists and poets still draw examples.

European characterizations of the national or regional qualities of various Asian people are likewise a mixture of the factual and fanciful, and, not surprisingly, resemble many of the beliefs still popular in the West. All of the islanders are fantastic swimmers and divers. The Sinhalese are effeminate and weak. Natives of Tana are brutish and self-centered. Malabars are dirty, superstitious, belligerent, and unperceptive. Bengalis are wary and treacherous but clever. Peguans are industrious, honest, peaceful, and timid. Provincialism, temperance, and peace are the fundamental qualities of the Siamese. Malays are frivolous poetasters who are more afraid of work than war. Moluccans are stupid and lazy. Cebuans love peace, ease, and quiet. The proud Japanese are overly sensitive, intellectually curious, formal, self-controlled, and warlike. The wise Chinese exhibit rational, just, and frivolous sides to their nature, are clever and industrious in the peaceful arts, and timid about fighting. Notice from the above how inferior the "blacks" of Asia are held to be in contrast to the "whites."

This stark picture of Asia with its shortage of grays and other shadings was transmitted to Europe over the entire sixteenth century through various channels. Pieced together from pamphlets, books, maps, and marketplace gossip, such an adumbration was reinforced and given reality in Europe by the influx in a steady stream of Asian products, works of art and craftsmanship, and peoples. More than two hundred different spices and drugs from all parts of the East filled the shops of Europe. Ship-builders in Portugal soon learned to use coir from India and tung oil from China to caulk and varnish their ships. Persons interested in sailing heard about keeled and unkeeled vessels without nails, Javan ships with four masts, Chinese junks with ingenious pumps, sailing chariots for use on land. The nautically minded also added new types of ships and their name to their vocabularies: *cuttar* (from which our word "cutter" may be possibly derive), sampans, houseboats, barangays, and praus. Those interested in the arts could find fancy textiles and embroideries, oriental rugs, finely wrought jewelry, swords inlaid with precious stones, lacquered screens and beds, printed books published in China, manuscript books written in Gujarati, and

Jesuit-printed books in Tamil, Chinese, and Japanese. Curiosa collectors might cherish plumages of the Bird of Paradise, poisoned arrows and darts, cowrie shells, bamboo furniture, costumes, carnelians, strange sexual devices, new plants, seeds, and fruits as well as live and stuffed animals from the East. Others interested in language could find sample words and terms from Malayalam, Kanarese, Konkani, Marathi, Tamil, Sanskrit, Pali, Mon, Talaing, Tai Cambodian, Malay, Tagalog, Bisayan, Chinese, and Japanese. Sample characters from Chinese and Japanese were available in printed and manuscript writings. Of Asian persons in Europe we have references and sometimes considerable detail on the activities of Arab and Malay pilots, Malabar students, Chinese merchants, Gujarati translators, Japanese emissaries, and a Filipino convert.

While concrete samples from Asia's life and cultures certainly testified to its existence as a civilized, rich, and variegated part of an expanding world, what were the products, institutions, and ideas which stimulated the Europeans most and which one most caused them to speculate about their own? On a realistic level they were especially fascinated by the mere existence of new places, by exotic varieties of flora and fauna, and by the crafts of silk production, rice cultivation, book-making, weaponry, and ship-building. Of the innumerable artistic products of Asia the Europeans are rapturous in their admiration for monuments, sculptures, porcelains, lacquers, and embroideries. They also evince profound interest in statistics on Asian populations, products, armies, exports, and imports. On a more abstract plane the Europeans were impressed by mass warfare techniques, the widespread existence of the lunar calendar, and the use of Malay as the *lingua franca* of Asian commerce. While merchants and missionaries used various Asian languages in their work, a few speculative minds began to concern themselves with the relationship of the Asian tongues to one another and of the possible relationships between the ideographic languages of the Far East and the hieroglyphics of Egypt and the Indian languages of America. Considerable scholarly interest also appeared with respect to the pre-European history of Asia, the oral and written sources for Asian history, the relative reliability of European and Asian chronologies and methods of dating, and the correlation or disparity between Europe's pre-discovery and post-discovery knowledge of Asia.

The nations of Asia were also billed as exemplars. China, the model state, was quickly recognized to be the possessor of unique and effective governmental and educational institutions: examinations for public office; state-supported schools; social services; and courier systems; and the law of avoidance or the requirement that provincial governors should never be natives of their jurisdictions. The West also had lessons to learn from Japan, particularly in physical and mental discipline. But perhaps what is most significant of all is the dawning realization in the West that not all truth and virtue were contained within its own cultural and religious traditions. The century of the great discoveries, viewed from the perspective of the present, can be taken as the date from which Westerners began self-consciously to question their own cultural premises, to weigh them in a balance against the presuppositions and accomplishments of other high cultures, and to initiate fundamental revisions in their own views of the world, man, and the future.

CHRONOLOGY

1245-1353	Medieval European travelers to Cathay include five Franciscan priest-legates and companions and the Venetian merchant family, the Polos
late 13th century	Islam reaches northern Sumatra
1293-*ca.* 1520	Indonesian empire of Majapahit
1336	Kemmu code (*Kemmu shikimoku*) issued by founder of Ashikaga shogunate
1338-1573	Ashikaga shogunate of Japan; an age of Zen culture
1368-1644	Ming dynasty of China
1392-1910	Yi dynasty of Korea
15th century	Italian, Portuguese, and Russian overland travelers visit India and points to the east
1403-1424	Yung-lo period, third of the Ming reigns
1403-1511	Malay rulers of Malacca
1403-1424	Parameswara (Muslim name, Megat Iskander Shah), first ruler of Malacca
1405-1433	Chinese maritime expeditions to the West under the command of the Muslim eunuch, Cheng Ho
1415-1499	Rennyo Shōnin, High Abbot of the True Pure Land sect (*Shin-shū*) of Buddhism in Japan
1421	Ming capital moved to Peking, leaving Nanking as the subsidiary capital
1433-1549	Eleven Japanese tributary missions visit Ming China
1446-1459	Reign of Sultan Muzaffar Shah; fourth ruler of Malacca, first of the (Muslim) Malay Sultanate

1448-1488	Reign of Boromo Trailokanat of Siam
ca. 1450-1498	Tun Perak, Paduka Raja and Bendahara of Malay Sultanate, in power
1472-1529	Wang Shou-jên, known as Wang Yang-ming, Chinese Neo-Confucian philosopher
1488-1511	Reign of Sultan Mahmud, seventh and last ruler of the Malay Sultanate; died in exile in Kampar, Sumatra, in 1528
1491-1529	Reign of Rama Tibodi II of Siam, who gave trading privileges to Europeans at his capital, Ayut'ia, and elsewhere
1495-1521	Reign of Manuel the Fortunate, King of Portugal
1498 (May 27)	Vasco da Gama reaches Calicut
ca. 1498	Moluccas become Muslim
1505-1541 or 42	Tuluva dynasty of Vijayanagar
1506-1521	Chêng-tê reign period, eleventh of the Ming, during which Europeans arrived on the China coast
1509-1515	Afonso de Albuquerque, Governor of Portuguese India
1509-1529?	Reign of Krishnādēvarāya, second of the Tuluva dynasty of Vijayanagar
1510-1534	Reign of Ismā'il 'Ādil Shăh, second sultan of Bijapur
1510-1961	Goa, seized from Bijapur, in Portuguese hands
1511-1641	Malacca in Portuguese hands
1511-12	Portuguese reach Spice Islands
1513	Jorge Alvares makes first recorded visit to China by a Portuguese
1517-1521	Tomé Pires acts as first Portuguese ambassador to China
1520-22?	Domingo Paes visits Vijayanagar and writes a description of it
1521	Philippines discovered by Magellan, a Portuguese in Spanish service, in the course of the first circumnavigation of the globe, 1519-1522
1521-1573	Takeda Shingen, Japanese warlord
1524	Babur's first invasion of north India; he became first Mughul emperor, dying in 1530

1530	Goa named the seat of the administration and headquarters of the armed forces of the Portuguese East
1531-1550	Reign of Tabinshwehti of the Toungoo dynasty, who endeavored to reunite the whole of Burma
1532-1623	Tulasī Dās, author of the Hindi classic, the *Rāmacaritamānasa*
1532-1597	Father Luis Fróis, S.J., missionary and commentator on Indian, Southeast Asian, and Japanese civilization for nearly fifty years
1534-1582	Oda Nobunaga, first of the three *daimyo* who unified Japan; ended Ashikaga shogunate in 1573
1536-1598	Toyotomi Hideyoshi; *kampaku* (old post of regent for an adult emperor), 1585-1591, and *taiko* (title used by retired *kampaku*), 1591-1598, of Japan
1542	First missionaries of new Society of Jesus, led by Francis Xavier, reach India; from there they spread throughout the East; their observations frequently published in Europe
1542-1605	Akbar, the "Great Mogor"; reigned after 1556.
1542-1616	Tokugawa Ieyasu, founder of the Tokugawa shogunate; shogun, 1603-1605, retiring in favor of his son, Hidetada
1556	Second battle of Panipat decides the Afghan-Mughul contest for supremacy in north India in favor of the Mughuls
1557-present	Portuguene colony at Macao on the south China coast
1565	Four sultanates of the Deccan band together to defeat the Hindu empire of Vijayanagar at the battle of Talikota
1577-1580	Second circumnavigation of the world: by Francis Drake
1573-1620	Wan-li reign period, longest of Ming; dynasty shows definite signs of decline
1592-1593, 1597-1598	Japanese invasions of Korea with armies numbering about 160,000 and 140,000 men
1600	Battle of Sekigahara establishes the supremacy of the Tokugawa shogunate over Japan
1603-1867	Tokugawa shogunate

1610	*The Golden Lotus,* author uncertain, first published after having circulated in manuscript
1615	Promulgation of the Laws for the Military Houses (*Buke shohatto*) by the Tokugawa and expanded from time to time
1616-1639	Tokugawa shogunate limits foreign trade and influence by a series of four decrees
1624-1627	"Gangster regime" of palace eunuch, Wei Chung-hsien (1568-1627)
1628-1643	Ch'ung-chên reign period, seventeenth and last of the Ming

BIBLIOGRAPHY

Aston, W. G. *A History of Japanese Literature*. London, 1933.

Bagchi, P. C. *India and China: a Thousand Years of Cultural Relations*. 2d ed.; New York, 1951.

Boxer, C. R. *The Christian Century in Japan, 1549-1650*. Berkeley and London, 1951.

Boxer, C. R. (ed.) *South China in the Sixteenth Century*. London, Works issued by the Hakluyt Society, Second Series, No. CVI, 1953.

Cady, J. F. *Southeast Asia, Its Historical Development*. New York, 1964.

Ch'en Shou-yi. *Chinese Literature, A Historical Introduction*. New York, 1961.

Cressey, G. B. *Asia's Lands and Peoples*. 2d ed.; New York, 1951.

De Bary, W. T. (ed.) *Approaches to Asian Civilizations*. New York, 1964.

De Bary, W. T. (ed.) *Sources of Chinese Tradition*. 2 v.; New York, Columbia University Press paperbacks, 1965.

De Bary, W. T. (ed.) *Sources of Indian Tradition*. 2 v.; New York, Columbia University Press paperbacks, 1965.

De Bary, W. T. (ed.) *Sources of Japanese Tradition*. 2 v.; New York, Columbia University Press paperbacks, 1965.

Fergusson, James. *History of Indian and Eastern Architecture*. New York, 1899.

Fisher, C. A. *South East Asia, A Social, Economic and Political Geography*. London and New York, 1964.

Forbes, W. C. *The Philippine Islands*. Rev. ed.; Cambridge, Mass., 1945.

Fung Yu-lan. *A Short History of Chinese Philosophy*. Ed. by Derk Bodde. New York, Macmillan paperback, 1960.

Ginsburg, Norton (ed.) *The Pattern of Asia*. Englewood Cliffs, N. J., 1958.

Hall, D. G. E. *A History of South-east Asia*. 2d ed.; London and New York, 1964.

212

Ho Ping-ti. *The Ladder of Success in Imperial China; Aspects of Social Mobility, 1368-1911.* New York, Science Editions paperback, 1964.

Hsu, F. L. K. *Under the Ancestors' Shadow: Chinese Culture and Personality.* New York, 1948.

Hucker, C. O. *The Traditional Chinese State in Ming Times, 1368-1644.* Tucson, 1961.

Lach, D. F. *Asia in the Making of Europe.* Vol. I: *The Century of Discovery.* Chicago, 1965.

Latourette, K. S. *The Chinese, Their History and Culture.* 3d rev. ed.; New York, 1957.

Major, R. H. (ed.) *India in the Fifteenth Century.* London, Works issued by the Hakluyt Society, Old Series, No. XXII, 1857.

Majumdar, R. C., and others. *An Advanced History of India.* 2d ed. with corrections; London and New York, 1961.

Nakamura, H. *The Ways of Thinking of Eastern Peoples: India, China, Tibet, Japan,* revised English trans. (Honolulu, Hawaii, 1964).

Nilakanta Sastri, K. A. A. *A History of South India from Prehistoric Times to the Fall of Vijayanagar.* Madras, 1958.

Paine, R. T., and Soper, A. *The Art and Architecture of Japan.* Baltimore, Penguin Books, 1955.

Parry, J. H. *The Age of Reconnaissance.* New York, Mentor Books, 1964.

Patterson, M. L. P., and Inden, R. B. (eds.) *Introduction to the Civilization of India* . . . Chicago, 1962.

Reischauer, E. O., and Fairbank, J. K. *East Asia* . . . 2 v.; Boston, 1958-65.

Saletore, B. A. *Social and Political Life in the Vijayanagara Empire, 1346-1646.* 2 v.; Madras, 1934.

Sansom, Sir G. B. *A History of Japan.* 3 v.; Stanford, Calif., 1958-1964.

Sickman, L., and Soper, A. *The Art and Architecture of China.* Baltimore, Penguin Books, 1956.

Srivastava, A. L. *The Mughul Empire, 1526-1830 A.D.* 2d ed.; Agra, 1956.

Vlekke, B. H. M. *Nusantara, A History of the East Indian Archipelago.* Rev. ed.; Chicago, 1960.

Waley, Arthur (tr.) *Monkey.* New York, Evergreen Books, 1958.

Wickizer, V. D., and Bennett, M. K. *The Rice Economy of Monsoon Asia.* Stanford, Calif., 1941.

Winstedt, Sir R. O. *The Malays, A Cultural History.* Rev. ed.; London, 1950.

Wood, W. A. R. *A History of Siam from the Earliest Times to the Year 1781.* Rev. ed.; Bangkok, 1933.

THE GLOBAL HISTORY SERIES